Village Society

Readings on the Economy, Polity and Society

This series is being published as part of a University Grants Commission project to promote teaching and research in the social sciences in India. The project (2010–12) has been jointly executed by the Tata Institute of Social Sciences, Mumbai, and the *Economic and Political Weekly*. The series is meant to introduce university students and research scholars to important research that has been published in *EPW* in specific areas. The journal has, over the decades, published a large number of research papers in all the social sciences. The readers draw on this archive of *EPW*'s published articles. The titles—in economics, politics, sociology and the environment—reflect *EPW*'s strengths as well as the interests of the academic community. Each set of readings is compiled by a senior academic who has also written an introductory essay for the volume. TISS and *EPW* are grateful to the authors of the articles included here for permission to reprint them.

Village Society

Edited by

Surinder S. Jodhka

EPW

Orient BlackSwan

TATA INSTITUTE OF SOCIAL SCIENCES

VILLAGE SOCIETY

ORIENT BLACKSWAN PRIVATE LIMITED

Registered Office
3-6-752 Himayatnagar, Hyderabad 500 029, Telangana, India
e-mail: centraloffice@orientblackswan.com

Other Offices
Bengaluru, Chennai, Guwahati, Hyderabad, Kolkata,
Mumbai, New Delhi, Noida, Patna, Visakhapatnam

First Published 2012
Reprinted 2013, 2014, 2015, 2022

ISBN 978-81-250-4603-5

034997

Typeset by
Le Studio Graphique, Gurgaon 122 001
in Adobe Garamond Pro 10.5/12.5

Printed at
B. B. Press, Noida

Published by
Orient Blackswan Private Limited
3-6-752 Himayatnagar, Hyderabad 500 029, Telangana, India
e-mail: info@orientblackswan.com

Contents

Tables and Figures

Tables

Figure

Introduction

Surinder S. Jodhka

I

The two-fold classification of human settlements into 'rural' and 'urban' has been fundamental to the ways in which we have made sense of social, cultural and economic life in modern times, the world over. The two categories do not merely describe 'rural' and 'urban' as two different types of settlements; they also represent them as two different types of social formations. While the 'rural' is often seen as an epitome of 'tradition', the 'urban' symbolises modernity. A rural settlement, or a village, is not simply smaller in size; it presumably also has a simpler mode of social and economic organisation. The city, on the other hand, is not only demographically much larger than the village but is also organised around a fundamentally different type of economy, culture and normative order. The modern city is symbolised by complexity of life, where a diverse variety of populations, belonging to different ethnic groups and cultures, live together, but without a strong sense of identification with one another.

Rural economic life is always seen as being organised around agriculture. Apart from being a source of livelihood, cultural life of the cultivating peasants is almost completely woven around the land. In other worlds, for a typical peasant, agriculture is a way of life. The plot of land that a peasant cultivates along with members of his family gives the peasant a source of livelihood and a sense of identity and belonging. It also connects him to the community and past generations of his kin group. The smaller size of the settlement makes it possible for rural residents to know each other intimately and remember past histories of every household. Even when not belonging to the same kin group they relate to each other as a community with a feeling of oneness and a shared identity. Rural settlements presumably also have a different type of household system where several families live jointly under one roof and extended kinship plays an active role in shaping personal lives of individuals.

In contrast, urban economic and cultural life is very different. Though industry and commerce are seen as main sources of livelihood in the city, urban residents practice a much larger range or variety of occupations. Compared to the village, the city is much more differentiated and unequal. Historically speaking, it is in the city that the modern individual is born and where the ties of community life become significantly weak, or simply non-existent. Urban identities are thus formed around occupations, social class and consumption patterns.

Interestingly, this binary construction of rural and the urban social life is not confined to the popular imagination about the village and city. It has also been quite fundamental to the classical theorisations of human societies by sociologists and other social scientists.

II

Study of Rural Society in the Modern West

The discipline of sociology emerged in the West European societies in the wake of the changes and challenges brought about by two great revolutions of modern times, namely, the French and the Industrial Revolutions. While the former introduced a new set of values—equality, freedom and fraternity—the latter initiated far-reaching changes in modes of organising economic and social life. Introduction of modern industry attracted labour for productive work, which resulted in the growth of new industrial cities. It was in the wake of these changes that the discipline of sociology was born. Sociology is often defined as 'the study of human groups and societies, *giving particular emphasis to the analysis of the industrialized world*' (Giddens 1989: 732 emphasis added).

In its most fundamental self-image, the Western capitalist world defined itself as a 'world without peasants'. The division of societies into 'modern' and 'backward' in the evolutionist schema of early social theory also meant that conceptually the rural populations were reduced to an unspecified part of the mixed bag of 'remainders of the past' (Shanin 1987: 468).

However, notwithstanding this significant shift in the ideological self-image and its reduced role in the economic life, the 'rural' did not disappear from the social and demographic landscape of Western societies. Until around the middle of the twentieth century a good proportion of population continued to live in the countryside even in the industrialised countries, and this population continued to exercise political influence. Growing rural-urban disparities and the prospects of exodus of rural population to urban centres also alarmed policymakers and political elite. In other words, the ruling establishment could not ignore what was happening in the rural areas of these rapidly developing industrial societies of the West (Galeski 1972: 1). It was in this context that a specialised sub-discipline of rural sociology was born in the United States (US).

Among other things, the long Civil War in the US during the late nineteenth century created a serious 'farm crisis' in the countryside. The farmers' organisations demanded federal aid to solve the problems of rural areas afflicted by severe depression. Rural sociology, as an applied discipline, came into existence essentially in response to this crisis (Newby 1980: 10). Appointment of the Country Life Commission by the US President Theodore Roosevelt in 1908 provided a big boost to the sub-discipline. As an applied area of study, the main concern of 'rural sociology' came to be the understanding and diagnosing of social and economic problems of the American farmers, with a greater focus on questions such as the internal structure of 'community life' and the changing composition of rural populations (Schwarzweller 1984: xi). In the European context also rural sociology grew with a similar perspective after the Second World War (Galeski 1972: 2).

Though rural sociology emerged in the context of a social and political crisis that inflicted the American farmers and the problems they encountered emanating from national-level political processes, the sub-discipline saw itself as a science of rural society and approached its subject matter as a *sui-generis* reality, as if it existed in isolation. In other words, it did not view the rural society as being integrated into the political and economic life of the rest of the country or just a segment of the larger society. As A. R. Desai writes:

> All rural sociologists recognise that the social life of the community is divided into two distinct segments, rural and urban. Though these segments interact among themselves, each is sufficiently distinct from the other.
>
> All of them hold the view that social life in rural setting exhibits characteristics and tendencies which are peculiar to it ... and ... therefore sharply distinguish it from life in urban setting.
>
> ... the prime objective of rural sociology should be to make a scientific, systematic and comprehensive study of the rural social organisation, of its structure, functions and objective tendencies of development, and, on the basis of such a study, to discover the law of its development. (Desai 1969: 9)

Another textbook of rural sociology similarly emphasises on the distinctive nature of rural social life. The 'distinctive characteristics of rural life', the author argues, could be 'easily discerned by comparing them with those of the city life':

> ... The culture of city is one thing, the culture of the country is quite another. Cities are by comparison large, impersonal, and complex in social structure; country communities are small, intimate, and simple in organisation. (Nelson 1948: 14)

Though some scholars criticised such a view of seeing rural and urban as distinct types of society and pointed to the continuum between the two (Redfield 1947), theoretically rural sociology remained caught up in the bi-polar notions of social change where 'rural' was defined as the opposite of 'urban' and 'rurality' was conceptualised as an autonomous or a *sui-generis* reality (Bonnano 1989), which could be understood and analysed in isolation of the larger social, historical and political context (ibid.: ix).

Scholars have also pointed to other problems. Human civilisations have had a large variety of settlements. As there are big, medium and small size cities, there are similarly a wide range of 'rural' settlements. This sociological distinction between 'rural' and 'urban' has become even more difficult to sustain in the rapidly globalising world where telecommunication and mass media have nearly erased the old differences of the city and the countryside. The sub-discipline or rural sociology has also been experiencing a crisis identity in the Western countries because of the rapidly declining numbers of people living in rural areas (Friedland 1982: 590).

III

Rural Society in India

The idea of the village has occupied an important place in the history of contemporary India. It was one of the core categories through which India was imagined and imaged by the British colonial rulers and the nationalist leadership during the nineteenth and twentieth centuries. So much attention was paid to it that the Indian village came to be seen as a signifier of the 'native life', a place where the local level patterns of economic life, social organisation and cultural belief could be observed. As Beteille has pointed out,

> ... the village was not merely a place where people lived; it had a design in which were reflected the basic values of Indian civilisation. (Beteille 1980: 108)

Even though one could find many detailed references to village life in pre-colonial history of the South Asian region, it was only during the British colonial rule that the village acquired centrality in the popular imaginations about the traditional Indian civilisation. Notwithstanding the diverse nature of writings produced by different people during the colonial rule, a stereotypical image of India as 'a land of village republics' did acquire wide acceptance. Along with the earlier writings of James Mill, Charles Metcalfe's notion of the 'Indian village community' set the tone for much of the later writings on rural India. Metcalfe, in his celebrated remark, stated that:

> ... the Indian village communities were little republics, having nearly everything they wanted within themselves, and almost independent of foreign relations. They seemed to last where nothing else lasted. Dynasty after dynasty tumbled down; revolution succeeded revolution but the village community remained the same. (Cohn 1987: 213)

Though not all the colonial administrators shared Metcalfe's assessment of the Indian village, it nevertheless became the most popular and influential representation. In the colonial discourse it was a self-sufficient community, with communal ownership of land, and was marked by a functional integration of diverse occupational groups. As Inden observes:

> Each village was an inner world, a traditional community, self-sufficient in its economy, patriarchal in its governance, surrounded by an outer one of other hostile villages and despotic governments. (Inden 1990: 133)

From Sir Henry Maine to Karl Marx, almost everyone uncritically accepted this stereotype of unchanging communal settlement. When Marx and Engels wrote in *The New York Daily Tribune* on the possible effects of British rule on 'stagnant India', they too viewed the Indian village in similar terms. It was in this context that they thought that British rule could create conditions for a social revolution in India. The social organisation of the Indian village thus came to be viewed as a classic example of a pre-modern/traditional society by a wide range of social theorists.

In many ways, even in the nationalist discourse, the idea of village as a representative of authentic native life was derived from the same kind of imagination.

Despite disagreements and differences in their ideological orientations or political agenda, the idea of the 'village' remained a core category though which they made sense of the 'traditional' Indian social life. However, unlike the British administrators, village, for the leaders of Indian nationalist movement, was not simply a given cultural artifact. Instead it was a site of politics. 'Village', for them, represented 'the real India', the nation that needed to be recovered, liberated and transformed. Given their political concerns, they used diverse perspectives to talk about village. While Gandhi saw it as a site of 'authenticity', for Nehru the village was the source and site of India's 'backwardness'. For Ambedkar village was a site of oppression where the institution of caste presented itself in its most brutal and inhuman form.[1]

After independence from colonial rule, the village has continued to be an important arena of engagement for different kinds of actors. It was in the rural setting that programmes for development were initiated by the Indian state. The Indian village also appears quite prominently in the popular media, cinema and television. It has also been a favourite site for social scientists to study Indian society, a methodological entry point, for undertaking investigations of different sets of subjects and questions.

IV

Studying Rural India

India's independence from colonial rule in 1947 and initiation of developmental processes provided a completely new context for the study of rural society. The village and its economy were among the most important targets for the development policy of the new state. Though the discourse on development was mainly led by economists in India, it was the sociologists and social anthropologists who provided leadership in the studies of rural India.

Basing their accounts, in general, on first-hand field-work carried out in most cases in a single village, working through the method of 'participant observation', social anthropologists wrote on the structures of social relationships, institutional patterns, beliefs and value systems of rural people. A good number of research articles, books and monographs were produced by them during the 1950s and 1960s.[2]

The Indian village studies were a direct offshoot of the newly emerged interest in the study of the peasantry in Western academia. The emergence of the 'new states' following de-colonisation during the post-War period had an important influence on research priorities in the social sciences. The most significant feature of the newly emerged 'Third World' countries was the dependence of large proportions of their populations on a stagnant agrarian sector. The struggle for freedom from colonial rule had also developed new aspirations among the 'masses' and the 'elites' of these societies. In some of these struggles, the peasantry had played a crucial role. Thus, the primary agenda for the new political regimes was the transformation of their 'backward' and stagnant economies. Though the strategies and priorities differed, 'modernisation' and 'development' became common programmes in most Third World countries.

It was in this historical context that development studies emerged as one of the most important areas of academic interest throughout the world, since it was expected to provide relevant data and prescriptive knowledge for socio-economic transformations. The Western powers also had a great deal of political interest in the 'paths' of development being pursued by different countries in the Third World. Much of this anxiety was about the possible choice of a socialistic pattern of development and a consequent tilt towards the then existing 'Soviet bloc'.

Since so many people in Third World countries were directly dependent on agriculture, understanding the prevailing structures of agrarian relations and working out ways and means of transforming them were recognised as being important priorities within development studies. Western political interest in the rural inhabitants of the Third World and the growing influence of modernisation and development theories also brought with them a great deal of funding for the study of peasant economies and societies (Silverman 1987: 11). The concept of 'peasantry' found currency in the discipline of social anthropology. At a time when primitive tribes were either in the process of disappearing, or had already disappeared, the 'discovery' of the peasantry also provided a new lease of life to the discipline of social anthropology (Beteille 1974b).

Robert Redfield, a well-know social anthropologist, argued that peasantry should be seen as a distinct type of social formation. 'Peasant society and culture had something generic about it. It is a kind of arrangement of humanity with some similarity all over the world' (Redfield 1965: 17). Elaborating this further, he writes:

> ... a peasant is a man who is in effective control of a piece of land to which he has long been attached by ties of tradition and sentiment. The land and he are parts of one thing, one old established body of relationships. (Ibid.: 19)

However, unlike the primitive tribal communities, peasant societies also produced surplus that was generally transferred to a dominant group of rulers in the city (Wolf 1966: 4). Thus peasant societies emerge with the development of civilisations and it is the surplus produced by the peasantry that sustains the ruling elite in the city. Writing in a similar tenor, Theodor Shanin developed an 'ideal type' of a typical peasant society with four core features, present in different degrees in all parts of the world. First and foremost, for the peasant, the family was the basic unit of production and consumption in a multi-dimensional social organisation. Second, land husbandry was the major means of livelihood. Third, there was a distinct traditional culture linked to the way of life of the peasant communities. Fourth, an elite living outside the community dominated the peasantry (Shanin 1987: 3–5).

The notion of peasant society being developed by the post Second World War social science and development studies in the West compared well with the notion of Indian village community constructed by the colonial discourses. As Breman points out, the 'village community' was identified as the social foundation of the peasant economy in Asia (Breman 1987: 1). In fact the influence of Robert Redfield on the Indian 'village studies' is quite evident. The single most popular concept used in studying the Indian village was the Redfieldian notion of the 'little community'.

Having found a relevant subject matter in the village, anthropologists (many of whom were either from the West or were Indian scholars trained in Western universities) initiated field studies in the early 1950s. A number of short essays providing accounts of individual villages were published in the newly launched Indian journal *The Economic Weekly* (later came to be known as *The Economic and Political Weekly*) during October 1951 to May 1954. These essays were put together by M. N. Srinivas in the form of a book with the title *India's Villages* in 1955. In the same year Marriott published another collection by the name of *Village India* (Marriott 1955). Interestingly, the first volume of *Rural Profiles* by Majumdar also appeared in 1955 (Majumdar 1955). The first full-length study of a village near Hyderabad in the Telangana region, *Indian Village,* by Dube, was also published in the same year (Dube 1955a).

Along with the sociologists and social anthropologists, some political scientists, historians and economists also wrote extensively on the village life. An anthropologist typically selected a single 'middle' sized village for intensive fieldwork, generally by staying there for a fairly long period of time, ranging from one to two years, at the end of which the aim was to come out with a 'holistic' account of social and cultural life. The key feature which qualified these studies to be called anthropological was the fieldwork component and the use of 'participant-observation', a method of data collection that anthropologists in the West had developed for studies of tribal communities. Intensive field-work came to be seen as the defining characteristic of the discipline of social anthropology and there was a fairly standardised pattern that had to be followed by the practitioners.[3]

Social anthropologists pointed to the fact that along with horizontal links, the village also has a structure of vertical ties, such as the caste based system of hierarchy. Village and caste were often cited as two sources of identity for the common villager in much of India. Different scholars placed different emphasis on the two sources of identity. M. N. Srinivas, for example argued that in his village, the residents had so strong a sense of identification that an insult to the village had to be avenged like an insult to oneself, one's wife, or one's family (Srinivas 1976: 270). Similarly, Dube stressed that:

> Village communities all over the Indian sub-continent have a number of common features. The village settlement, as a unit of social organisation, represents a solidarity different from that of the kin, the caste, and the class.... Different castes and communities inhabiting the village are integrated in its economic, social, and ritual pattern by ties of mutual and reciprocal obligations sanctioned and sustained by generally accepted conventions. Notwithstanding the existence of groups and factions inside the settlement, people of the village can, and do, face the outside world as an organised, compact whole. (Dube 1955b: 202)

It was Wiser who initially conceptualised the social relationships among caste groups in the Indian village in the framework of 'reciprocity'. It appeared in his classic study of *The Hindu Jajmani System*, first published in 1936. The framework of reciprocity implied that though village social organisation was hierarchical, it was the 'interdependence' among different caste groups that characterised the underlying village spirit. There were differences, but interdependence united the village community.

Reciprocity implied, explicitly or implicitly, an exchange of equal services and non-exploitative relations. Mutual gratification was supposed to be the outcome of reciprocal exchange. As Wiser explained,

> Each serves the other. Each in turn is master. Each in turn is servant. (Wiser 1969: 10)

Though the later studies were much more elaborate and contained long descriptions of different forms of social inequalities and differences in rural society, many of them continued to use the framework of reciprocity, particularly while conceptualising 'unity' of the village social life. Even while recognising the existence of 'vertical ties' between 'landlord and tenants, between master and servants, and between creditor and debtor' (Srinivas 1955a) as characteristic features of village social organisation, Srinivas, for example, did not see these relations as being necessarily conflictual or exploitative in nature. On the contrary, it was the interdependence of the caste groups resulting from such ties that defined the village. (Srinivas 1976: 185)

However, not everyone emphasised unity in the manner of Srinivas, Dube or Wiser. Some anthropologists explicitly contested the unity thesis, while others qualified their arguments by recognising the conflicts within the village and the ties that villagers had with the outside world. For instance, Paul Hiebert in his study of a south Indian village argued that the caste system provided a source of stability to the village, but he also underlined the fact that 'deep seated cleavages underlie the apparent unity of the village and fragmented it into numerous social groups' (Hiebert 1971: 13). Similarly, Majumdar pointed out that the assumption about village being an 'integrated whole, a way of living, thinking and feeling has its limitations in the Indian conditions' (Majumdar 1958: 325).

Among those anthropologists who questioned the idea of the communitarian unity of the Indian village were Lewis and Bailey. Comparing the Indian 'village community' with the American 'neighbourhood', Lewis argued:

> ... the caste system divides the village and weakens the sense of village solidarity. The caste generally represents a distinct ethnic group with its own history, tradition, and identification, and each caste lives in more or less separate quarters of the village ... each caste forms a separate little community. (Lewis 1958: 314)

Similarly, F. G. Bailey provided a radical critique of the 'unity-reciprocity' thesis and underlined the coercive aspects of caste relations (Bailey 1960: 258). Some others offered alternative interpretations of the *jajmani* relations and the prevailing values of reciprocity and hierarchy. They argue that dominant landlords used the system of hereditary obligations and occupational duties to perpetuate and legitimise the local variety of pre-capitalist/feudalistic relations (Beidelman 1959: 6; Djurfeldt and Lindberg 1976: 42). However, such critical perspective largely remained peripheral and until the 1970s the functionalist perspective continued to dominate the sociological and social anthropological writings on rural India.

Notwithstanding the predominance of functionalist orientation, village studies of the 1950s and 1960s were an important landmark in the history of Indian social sciences. They helped in contesting the dominant stereotype of the Indian village made popular by the colonial administrators. The studies showed that villages had been well-integrated into the broader economy and society of the region even before the colonial rule introduced new agrarian legislation. They also pointed to the regional differences in the way village social life was organised in different parts of the country.

The idealised model of the *varna* system as theorised in Hindu scriptures, the 'book-view', did not match the concrete realities of village life. While caste was an important institution in the Indian village, and most studies gave precedence to caste differences over other differences, empirical studies showed that it was not a completely closed and rigidly defined system. Caste statuses were also not exclusively determined by one's position in the ritual hierarchy and there were many grey and contestable areas within the system. Above all, village studies proved the usefulness of fieldwork for a social scientific understanding of the Indian society. It was partly because of the success of the village studies that fieldwork came to acquire respectability in other social science disciplines in India as well.

Historical researches on agrarian relations and the village life in medieval India further reinforced some of these formulations by pointing to the diversity and differentiated nature of rural life in pre-colonial period. Historians questioned the underlying assumption about the communal nature of pre-colonial agrarian economy and absence of private property. They have shown through their work that though superficially land appeared to be communally controlled, in reality, rights over land were quite differentiated. Since land was in abundant supply, there was no sale and purchase of land in most parts of the Indian countryside. However, not everyone had equal rights of cultivation or claims over the land produce, which were based upon customs or upon the grants made by the king (Neale 1962: 21). Irfan Habib, writing on the Mughal period, points out that these rights could even be purchased and sold (Habib 1963: 154). 'The village did not hold its land in common. Common were its officials and servants' (Neale 1962: 21).

The pre-colonial village was also linked to the central authority through the revenue bureaucracy. Land revenue worked as the dominant mode of surplus appropriation during 'medieval' times. Mughal authorities differentiated among the classes of landowners while fixing the revenue demands. The larger landholders, such as *zamindars* or headmen or a favoured community were required to pay less per unit (Kumar 1992: 239–40).

Pre-colonial agrarian relations were also not free from conflicts and tensions. Whenever the revenue demands became unbearable, the typical response of the peasantry was to flee en mass to other territories where conditions were more conducive to land cultivation (Habib 1963; Moore 1966: 332). There were also instances of the peasantry revolting against the local rulers. Most of these revolts however, were unorganised, inspired by some religious ideology or a millenarian dream (Dhanagare 1983: 29).

V

Rural Social Change[4]

Independence from colonial rule in 1947 in many ways marked the beginning of a new phase in the history of rural Indian society and its agrarian economy. Having evolved out of a long drawn struggle against colonial rule with the participation of people from various social categories, the Indian state also took over the task of supervising the transformation of its stagnant and backward economy to make sure that the benefits of economic growth were not monopolised by a particular section of the society. It is with this background that 'development' emerged as a strategy of economic change and an ideology of the new regime.

However, even though the political system had changed in a very fundamental sense, at the micro level the structures evolved during colonial rule still continued to exist. The local interests that had emerged over a long period of time continued to be powerful in the Indian countryside even after the political climate had changed. The 'agrarian question' had also been an important topic of discussion for leaders of the Indian freedom movement, starting with Ranade and Dutt, who extensively wrote and debated on how Indian society and economy ought to be reorganised after its independence from colonial rule (see Joshi 1987).

The 'land question' had become one of the most hotly debated topics during the final years of the struggle for independence. Land reforms also became a question of considerable academic interest and debate in the discourse on planning and development. They were viewed as necessary for initiating modernisation in agriculture. The Indian state chose to reorganise the agrarian relations through redistribution of land, but not in a comprehensive and radical manner. Joshi described it as 'sectoral or sectional reforms' (Joshi 1987: 56). The Government of India directed its States to abolish intermediary tenures, regulate rent and tenancy rights, confer ownership rights on tenants, impose ceilings on holdings, distribute the surplus land among the rural poor, and facilitate consolidation of holdings. A large number of legislations were passed by the State governments over a short period of time. The number of these legislations was so large that, according to Thorner, they could be 'the largest body of agrarian legislations to have been passed in so brief a span of years in any country whose history has been recorded' (Thorner 1956: 14).

The actual implementation of these legislations and their impact on the agrarian structures is, however, an entirely different story. Most of the legislations had intentionally provided loopholes with the help of which the dominant landowners could tamper with land records by redistributing land on paper among relatives, evict their tenants, and use other means to escape the legislations. In the absence of a concerted 'political will' (Joshi 1976), land reforms could succeed only in regions where the peasantry was politically mobilised and could exert pressure from below (Radhakrishanan 1989).

Despite the overall failure, land reforms succeeded in weakening the hold of absentee landlords over the rural society and assisted in the emergence of a class of substantial peasants and petty landlords as the dominant political and economic group' (Bell 1974: 196). In a village of Rajasthan, for example, though the 'abolition of *jagirs*' (intermediary rights) was far from satisfactory, it made considerable difference to the overall land ownership patterns and to the local and the regional power structures. The Rajputs, the erstwhile landlords, possessed much lesser land after the land reforms than they did before. Most of the village land had moved into the hands of those who could be called small and medium landowners. In qualitative terms, most of the land began to be self-cultivated and incidence of tenancy declined considerably (Chakravarti 1975: 97–98). The fear of losing land induced many potential losers to sell or rearrange their lands in a manner that could escape the legislations (Byres 1974).

However, it was only in rare cases that landless labourers living in the countryside, many of whom belonged to the ex-untouchable' caste, received land. Similarly, land reforms were 'gender-blind'. Very few women were recognised as potentially independent cultivators and land titles in case of the beneficiaries were mostly granted to men. Thus the beneficiaries, by and large, were men from the middle level caste groups, who were traditionally identified with cultivation as a part of the callings of their caste. Land holding structure in India continues to be fairly iniquitous though the proportion of smaller and medium size landowners has been expanding, primarily because of the sub-division of holdings within families.

While land reforms were supposed to deal with the problem of landlordism, the hold of moneylenders over the peasantry was to be weakened by providing credit through institutional sources, initially by credit societies and later by the nationalised commercial banks. According to the findings of an official survey carried out immediately after independence from the colonial rule, up to around 91 per cent of the credit needs of the cultivators were being met by informal sources of credit (RBI 1969: 15). Much of this came from usurious moneylenders (69.7 per cent). It was in recognition of this fact that the Indian state planned to expand the network of cooperative credit societies. With the imposition of 'social control' and later their nationalisation, commercial banks were also asked to lend to the agricultural sector on priority basis. Over the years, the dependence of rural households on informal sources has come down significantly. While in 1961, on an average only 18.4 percent of the total credit needs were being fulfilled by institutional sources of credit, in 1981 it had gone up to 62.6 per cent (Gadgil 1986: 296).

However, this is not the entire story. The assessment studies on the cooperative credit societies showed that much of their credit went to the relatively better off sections of rural society, and the poor continued to depend on the more expensive informal sources (Thorner 1964; Oommen 1984). This was explained as a consequence of the prevailing structure of land tenures (Herring 1977). The state response was to bureaucratise the cooperative societies. Though in some regions this helped in releasing the credit societies from the hold of big landowners, bureaucratisation also led to rampant corruption and increasing apathy among those whom they were supposed to serve (Jodhka 1995a). Although banks were never controlled directly by the rural rich, the benefit of their credit too has largely gone to those who had substantial holdings (ibid.: 1995b). However, despite this inherent bias of institutional credit against the rural poor, its availability played an important role in making the green revolution a success, and it definitely helped in marginalising the professional moneylender in the rural power structure.

As a strategy of development, the Community Development Programme (CDP) was conceptually very different from both, the idea of land reforms and the idea of making cheap institutional credit available to the cultivators. While the earlier programmes reflected an 'institutionalist' perspective, the CDP had emanated from the 'productionist' approach to rural development. It had been inspired by the agricultural extension service in the US (Dube 1958: 8) and was based on a notion of harmonious village community without any significant internal differences and conflict of interests (Dhanagare 1984). There was hardly any mention of the unequal power relations in the village. Its objective was to provide for a substantial increase in agricultural production and improvement in the basic services, which would ultimately lead to a transformation in the social and economic life of the villages (Dube 1958). Its basic assumption was that 'the Indian peasant would of his own free will, and because of his 'felt needs', immediately adopt technical improvements the moment he was shown them' (Moore 1966: 401).

The programme was launched on 2 October 1952 in a few selected 'blocks' and soon it was extended to the entire country. However, the enthusiasm with which the programme was started could not be sustained for very long. A non-political approach to agrarian transformation resulted in helping only those who were already powerful in the village. Most of the benefits were cornered by a small section of the rural elite.

Though the initial programmes of rural development initiated by the government of India did not succeed as expected, they created conditions for social and economic change, which came in some parts of the country with the green revolution. Of all the developmental programmes introduced during the post-independence period, the green revolution is considered to be the most successful. It was celebrated the world over and has been studied and debated upon quite extensively in academia. The green revolution led to a substantial increase in agricultural output, to the extent that it almost solved India's food problem. It also produced significant social and political changes in the Indian village and, in a sense, did bring about an 'agricultural revolution' in India. In purely economic terms, the agricultural sector experienced growth at the rate of 3 to 5 per cent per annum (Byres 1972), which was many times more than what it had been during the colonial period (less than 1 per cent). It conceptualised agrarian change in purely technological terms and was based on the 'trickle down' theory of economic growth. The expression 'green revolution' was deliberately coined to contrast it with the phrase 'red revolution'. It carried the conviction that 'agriculture was being peacefully transformed through the quiet working of science and technology, reaping the economic gains of modernisation while avoiding the social costs of mass upheaval and disorder usually associated with rapid change (Frankel 1971: v). The US played an active role in its conception and implementation. Many have argued that this was because of the strategic, geopolitical interests that the US had at that time in the changing social and economic conditions in the countries of the Third World (Harriss 1987).

The term 'green revolution' had been first used during the late 1960s to refer to the effects of the introduction of higher yielding variety (HYV) seeds of wheat and rice in developing countries. However, the green revolution was not just the use of HYV seeds. It was a package. The new varieties of seeds required fertility enhancing inputs, i.e., chemical fertilizers, controlled irrigation conditions and plant protecting chemicals (the pesticides). The other components of the package consisted of providing cheap institutional credit, price incentives and marketing facilities. In order to back up the application of new technology on the local farms, a large number of agricultural universities were also opened in the regions selected for the new programme. It was under the direct supervision of the Ford Foundation that Intensive Agricultural Development Programme (IADP) was started in 1961 initially in 14 districts on an experimental basis and was later extended to 114 districts (out of a total of 325) under the name of Intensive Agriculture Areas Programme (IAAP) in 1965.

Its advocates argued that the new technology was 'scale neutral' and could be used with as much benefit by the small, as by the big landowners. However, in the actual implementation, small holdings were not found to be viable units for the technological change. Joan Mencher during her fieldwork in South India observed that the concerned agriculture officers were far from being neutral. 'What they thought was needed to further the green revolution was to forget about small farmers ... because they could not really contribute to increased production. To these officials, progressive farmers are those who have viable farms and who are fairly well-off' (Mencher 1978: 239–40). Interestingly though, a study from Punjab showed that not only were the smaller landowners as eager to adopt the new technology but that their income from land for an acre was also slightly higher than that of the bigger farmers (Bhalla and Chadha 1983: 78).

However, participating in the green revolution did not mean the same thing to the smaller farmers as it did to the bigger farmers. While the bigger farmers had enough surplus of their own to invest on the new capital intensive farming, for the smaller landowners it meant additional dependence on borrowing, generally from informal sources. Though theoretically the new technology was 'scale neutral', it was certainly not 'resource neutral' (Harriss 1987: 231). The new technology also made everyone compulsively get involved with the market. Unlike traditional agriculture, the cultivators in the post-green revolution agriculture had to buy all farm inputs from the market for which they often had to take credit from traders or institutional sources. In order to clear the debts, they had no choice but to sell the farm yield in the market even when they were needed to keep it for their own consumption. They sold their farm yield immediately after harvesting when prices were relatively low, and bought later in the year for consumption when the prices were higher. Thus, though the small farmers did take to the new technology, their resources being limited, it brought in new dependencies for them as well. On the other hand, it strengthened the economic and political position of the rich farmers.

VI

Rural India Today

Perhaps the most important achievement of the green revolution was its ability to solve the critical problem of food scarcity in the country. However, notwithstanding a significant increase in production of food grains, a large proportion of the Indian population continued to be poor and deprived. Its benefits were confined to some sections of the rural population. The realisation that the 'trickle-down' theory of economic growth had its limitation made development planners to initiate target-group oriented programmes for the poor. Integrated Rural Development Programme (IRDP) and more recently the Mahatma Gandhi National Rural Employment Guarantee Scheme (MGNREGS) are examples of such initiatives.

Another problem with the new technology was that it was introduced only in some selected pockets of the northern, western and southern states of India. Central and eastern India did not experience much agricultural growth. In other words, the green revolution increased regional disparities across states.

As a programme of rural development, the green revolution had a very limited vision of economic growth. Social, political and cultural implications of the economic change were hardly reflected upon. Hence its momentum did not last for very long. By the mid-1980s the Indian country-side began to show a new kind of restiveness. The surplus producing farmers of the green revolution pockets began to mobilise themselves for subsidies on farm inputs and for higher prices for their produce. Market economy, they argued, was inherently against the farm sector and favoured the urban industry and middle class consumers. Given the unequal power relations between the town and countryside, they argued, agricultural sector suffered from unequal terms of trade, the evidence of which could be seen in the growth of indebtedness among the cultivating/farming classes.

Farmers mobilised themselves in different parts of India quite successfully for over a decade. Though the movements had a local character in terms of leadership and strategies of mobilisation, they coordinated their activities across regions. In a sense they were quite successful in getting their agenda accepted at the level of the national politics. The farmers' movements of the 1980s also signaled the rise of a new social category of rural people who had prospered with green revolution and were connected closely to the market economy and saw their fate being conditioned by the market. But they also aspired to go beyond the village. The agrarian economy could not satisfy their aspirations for social and cultural mobility. They began to move out of the village, from their local seats of power to legislative assemblies in the state capitals. The surplus they generated from agriculture went into education, urban trade and other non-agricultural activities (Upadhya 1988; Rutten 1995; Omvedt 1992). By the early 1980s, the social profile of this class had begun to change. The following lines of Balagopal provide a lucid account of this process of growing diversification:

> … a typical family of this class has a landholding in its native village, cultivated by hired labour, *bataidar*, tenant or farm servants and supervised by the father or one son;

> business of various descriptions in town managed by other sons; and perhaps a young and bright child who is a doctor or engineer or a professor. It is this class that is most vocal about injustice done to the village. (Balagopal 1987: 1545)

At another level, this process of economic development and growing integration of the village into the larger political and market system also brought about a social and cultural transformation. The old patron-client relations began to fast disintegrate and were replaced by formalised and contractual ties mediated through a purely market-driven regime of wages and payments. The jajmani type systems of caste based economic ties have also disintegrated almost everywhere in the country. Even when the traditional systems of labour-tying are invoked, rarely do they reinforce the traditional ties of patronage and obligation (see Chapter 7 in this volume). The decline of the old ideology of caste also enabled Dalit groups to mobilise themselves for better wages and social dignity. In Punjab, for example, not only did many of the Dalit groups withdraw from their old caste-based occupations, they also distanced themselves from the rural/agrarian economy and stopped working on farms as tied labourers. The change also provided them a sense of autonomy and a new political agency to assert for their rights and articulate their distinct social and religious identities (see Jodhka 2002, 2009). Even when in some cases this growing political assertion of Dalits led to increased incidents of violence and atrocities, it also infused energy in the local level political institutions. The rural panchayats have over the years become more representative, and inclusive of different caste groups and interests than they used to be in past.

Transformation of the rural power structure was an important component of the development process initiated by the Indian state during the post-independence period. One of the objectives of introducing land reform legislations was to weaken the power of absentee landlords and landed elite. Further, on the recommendations of the Balwant Rai Mehta Committee the three-tier Panchayati Raj system was introduced during the early 1960s in order to democratise the local level power structure and decentralise governance. Since then there have been several reviews of the working of the system by committees and commissions appointed by the Government of India. On the recommendations of these committees, several changes and reforms have also been introduced to make the system more effective.

The empirical literature that came out during the first two or three decades after independence pointed to the continued power of the traditionally dominant groups in most of rural India. Scholars repeatedly underlined the manner in which the vested interests in prevailing structures of power hindered the implementation of programmes meant for the welfare of the poor and the weak. In caste terms, the rural power revolved around the landowning dominant castes (Srinivas 1955). Those who used the framework of class argued that it was the rich landowners and moneylenders who controlled the rural economy (Thorner 1956). Independent studies by scholars from different regions tended to suggest that panchayats had become yet another arena of influence and power for the already dominant groups in rural India.

However, it was only in the 1980s with growing disintegration of old structures of caste-based hierarchies that a loosening of the power structures at the local level began to be reported. On the basis of his work in Rajasthan, Oliver Mendelsohn showed that though Srinivas was right in talking about 'dominant caste' during the 1950s, such formulations made lesser sense in the contemporary rural India. The 'low caste and even untouchable villagers are now less beholden to their economic and ritual superiors than is suggested in olden accounts' (Mendelsohn 1993: 808). Similarly, 'land and authority have been de-linked in village India and this amounted to an historic, if non-revolutionary transformation' (ibid.: 807). Empirical studies even from the less developed regions of India have reported the disintegration of the Jajmani system (Sahay 2004).

Apart from the questions of economic disparities, caste relations and changing power structure, questions of gender and ecology have also attracted a significant amount of attention of scholars since the 1980s. At one level, the question of gender was a matter of recognition (see Chapter 10 in this volume). Much of the scholarship of rural social change had been 'gender-blind'. Women were often seen as part of the household where the agency laid almost always with male members. Women contributions to the economic and social life of the village was rarely given due recognition. At another level, the process of development had different kinds of implications for men and women in rural India. Even today women workers, in most cases, are paid lesser wages than their male counterparts. The process of migration and mobility of the rural populations also has different sets of outcomes for men and women (see Chapter 11 in this volume).

Questions of ecology and environment have also acquired a new meaning over the last three decades. The famous 'Chipko' movement by the local poor against the felling of trees for commercial use and the mobilisations against the displacement of tribals and peasants from their villages for the building of a dam on the Narmada river, both acquired national and global visibility during the 1980s. Some scholars also wrote on questions relating to common property resources (CPR) in rural India and how their depletion was affecting the rural poor (see Chapters 9 and 16 in this volume).

VII

The Emerging Ruralities

The onset of a new phase of globalisation, coupled with a shift in India's economic orientation, during the early years of the 1990s has had several implications for the village society and its agrarian economy. As is evident from the discussion above, virtually all shades of 'rural' and 'agrarian' studies from 1950s to 1980s were, directly or indirectly, linked to the project of 'development' and the 'developmental state'. The growing influence of 'neo-liberal' economic philosophy not only led to an erosion of the 'developmental state' but also changed the priorities of social science research. In this changing environment, India's rural society no longer attracts the kind of public attention it deserves. The agrarian question no longer generated excitement in university seminars, or in the popular media.

Over the last decade or so, the only mode in which agriculture has been talked about in India has been that of 'crisis'. The contexts, or evidence, of these crises are several, the most immediate and compelling being the sudden spurt in cases of suicides by small and marginal farmers since the mid-1990s. The fact that this happened simultaneously in different regions of India, from Kerala and Karnataka to Maharashtra and Punjab, certainly points to some larger processes at work.

Since the early 1990s India's urban economy has been growing at a much faster rate than ever before. On the other hand the agrarian economy has either been stagnant or has grown at a much slower rate. While this should normally be seen in positive terms, as resembling the classical patterns of economic transformation experienced by the Western world, the reality in India is unfortunately much more complex. Unlike the modern West where development of city was accompanied by desertion and disappearance of the village, more than two-third of India's total population continues to live in more than half a million of its villages. This figure is close to 75 to 80 per cent in the relatively less developed states of India. More importantly, even while cities are growing quite rapidly, so far in India there is no indication of the rural population declining in absolute numbers.

The growing rural-urban difference has become one of the most challenging questions for the Indian political system. Interestingly, it was in the context of serious social crises like the one that India is confronted with today that the sub-discipline of rural sociology had emerged in the Western context. In contrast, social science interest in rural India has been steadily declining over the last two decades. Though some scholars have been working on the subject of farmers' suicides,[5] it is not the only thing happening in rural India.

Thus, beyond the imperatives of economic or state policy, a serious social science engagement with the village is also necessary for a fair understanding of the varieties of its social life, its possible political futures and dynamics of its cultural orientations.

The Reader

The *Economic and Political Weekly* (*EPW*) and its earlier avatar the *Economic Weekly*, has been a pioneer in publishing research on rural India. It continues to publish socially relevant social science research on a wide range of subjects. Over the last nearly six decades the journal would have published more than 500 papers on different dimensions of 'rural', and 'agrarian' society of India. This volume presents a select set of readings focusing specifically on the social, political and cultural aspects of village society of India. Though some of the readings also touch upon questions of agrarian change and economy of 'rural' India, the readings are primarily sociological in nature. The select 'readings' presented here could be of use to the students of Indian society and in different dimensions of rural life in India. Apart from the students of social sciences, the volume would be valueable to policymakers and civil society activists who are looking for a ready access to serious and important literature on the subject.

Notes

1. See Chapter 2 in this volume.

2. For a broad overview of village studies by social anthropologists see Jodhka (1998)

3. See Chapters 1 (M. N. Srinivas) and 2 (André Béteille) in this volume.

4. For a detailed introduction to the literature on agrarian social structure and change in India see Jodhka (2003)

5. Scholars working on agrarian change have identified various factors responsible for the current state of affairs in Indian agriculture (see Suri 2006; Jodhka 2006; Vasavi 2009; Mishra 2006; Mohanty 2005). While the reports of farmers committing suicides remind us about the growing difficulties and desperation being confronted by the poor and marginal farmers, they are not the only things happening in rural India.

References

Alexander, K. C. (ed.). 2000. *Rural Development Studies in the Eighties*. New Delhi: ICSSR and Manak Publication Pvt. Ltd.

Bailey, F. G. 1960. *Tribe, Caste and Nation*. Bombay: Oxford University Press.

Balagopal, K. 1987. 'An Ideology of the Provincial Propertied Class'. *Economic and Political Weekly* 21 (36–37): 2177–78.

Beidelman, T. O. 1959. *A Comparative Analysis of the Jajmani System*. New York: Association for Asian Studies.

Bell, C. 1974. 'Ideology and Economic Interests in Indian Land Reform'. In *Agrarian Reform and Agrarian Reformism: Studies of Peru, Chile, China, and India*, ed. D. Lehmann. 190–220. London: Faber and Faber.

Beteille, A. 1980. 'The Indian Village: Past and Present'. In *Peasants in History: Essays in Honour of Daniel Thorner*, ed. E. J. Hobsbaum et al. 107–20. Delhi: Oxford University Press.

Beteille, A. 1996. *Caste, Class and Power: Changing Patterns of Stratification in a Tanjore Village*. Delhi: Oxford University Press.

Bhalla, G. S. and G. K. Chadha. 1983. *Green Revolution and Small Peasants: A Study of Income Distribution among Punjab Cultivators*. New Delhi: Concept Publishing House.

Bonnano, A. 1989. *Sociology of Agriculture*. New Delhi: Concept Publishing House.

Breman, J. (ed.). 1997. *The Villages in Asia Revisited*. Delhi: Oxford University Press.

Byres, T. J. 1972. 'The Dialectics of India's Green Revolution'. *South Asian Review* 5 (2): 99–106.

Byres, T. J. 1974. 'Land Reforms, Industrialisation and Marketed Surplus in India: An Essay on the Power of Rural Bais'. In *Agrarian Reform and Agrarian Reformism: Studies of Peru, Chile, China, and India*, ed. D. Lehmann. 221–61. London: Faber and Faber.

Chakravarti, A. 1975. *Contradiction and Change: Emerging Patterns of Authority in a Rajasthan Village*. Delhi: Oxford University Press.

Cohn, B. S. 1987. *An Anthropologist among the Historians and Other Essays*. Delhi: Oxford University Press.

Dhanagare, D. N. 1983. *Peasant Movements in India: 1920–1950*. Delhi: Oxford University Press.

Dhanagare, D. N. 1984. 'Agrarian Reforms and Rural Development in India: Some Observations'. *Research in Social Movements, Conflict and Change* 7 (1): 178–93.

Deasi, A. R. 1969. *Rural Sociology in India*. Bombay: Popular Prakashan.

Djurfeldt, G. and S. Lindberg. 1976. *Behind Poverty: The Social Formation of a Tamil Village*. New Delhi: Oxford and IBH.
Dube, S. C. 1955a. *Indian Village*. London: Routledge and Kegan Paul.
Dube, S. C. 1955b. 'A Deccan Village'. In *India's Village*, ed. M. N. Srinivas. London: Asia Publishing House.
Dube, S. C. 1958. *India's Changing Villages: Human Factors in Community Development*. New Delhi: Allied Publishers.
Frankel, F. R. 1971. *India's Green Revolution: Economic Gains and Political Costs*. Bombay: Oxford University Press.
Friedland, W. H. 1982. 'The End of Rural Society and the Future of Rural Sociology'. *Rural Sociology* 47 (4): 589–608.
Gadgil, M. V. 1986. 'Agricultural Credit in India: A Review of Performances and Policies'. *Indian Journal of Agricultural Economics* 14 (3): 282–309.
Galeski, Boguslaw. 1972. *Basic Concepts in Sociology*. Manchester: Manchester University Press.
Habib, I. 1963. *Agrarian Systems of Mughal India*. Bombay: Asia Publishers.
Harriss, J. 1987. 'Capitalism and Peasant Production: The Green Revolution in India'. In *Peasants and Peasant Societies*, ed. T. Shanin. 227–45. London: Blackwell.
Herring, R. J. 1977. 'Land Tenure and Credit-Capital Tenure in Contemporary India'. In *Land Tenure and Peasants in South Asia*, ed. R. E. Frynkenberg. 120–58. New Delhi: Manohar.
Hiebert, P. G. 1971. *Konduru: Structure and Integration in a South Indian Village*. Minneapolis: University of Minnesota Press.
Inden, R. 1990. *Imagining India*. Oxford: Basil Blackwell.
Jodhka, S. S. 1995a. 'Bureacratisation, Corruption and Depoliticisation: Changing Profile of Credit Co-operatives in Rural Haryana'. *Economic and Political Weekly* 30 (1): 53–56.
———. 1995b. *Debt, Dependence and Agrarian Change*. Jaipur: Rawat Publications.
———. 1998. 'From "Book-View" to "Field-View": Social Anthropological: Constructions of the Indian Village'. *Oxford Development Studies* 26 (3): 311–32.
———. 2002. 'Caste and Untouchability in Rural Punjab'. *Economic and Political Weekly* 37 (19): 1813–23, 11 May,
———. 2003. 'Agrarian Structures and their Transformations'. In *Oxford India Companion to Sociology and Social Anthropology*. Vol. II. Ed. Veena Das. Delhi: Oxford University Press.
———. 2006. 'Beyond Crises, Rethinking Contemporary Punjab Agriculture'. *Economic and political Weekly* 41 (16): 1530–37, 22 April.
———. 2009. 'The Ravi Dasis of Punjab: Global Contours of Caste and Religious Strife'. *Economic and Political Weekly* 44 (24): 79–85, 13 June.
Joshi, P. C. 1976. *Land Reforms in India: Trends and Perspectives*. New Delhi: Allied Publishers.
Joshi, P. C. 1987. *Institutional Aspects of Agricultural Development: India from Asian Perspective*. New Delhi: Allied Publishers.
Karanth, G. K. 1996. 'Caste in Contemporary Rural India'. In *Caste: Its Twentieth Century Avatar*, ed. M. N. Srinivas. New Delhi: Penguin.
Kumar, D. 1992. *Land and Caste in South India*. New Delhi: Manohar.
Lewis, O. 1958. *Village Life in Northern India: Studies in a Delhi Village*. Urbana: University of Illinois Press.

Majumdar, D. N. (ed.). 1955. *Rural Profiles*. Lucknow: Ethnographic and Folk Culture Society.

Majumdar, D. N. 1958. *Caste and Communication in an Indian Village*. Bombay: Asia Publishing House.

Marriott, M. (ed.). 1955. *Village India: Studies in the Little Community*. Chicago: University of Chicago Press.

Mencher, J. P. 1978. *Agriculture and Social Structure in Tamil Nadu: Past Origins, Present Transformations and Future Prospects*. New Delhi: Allied Publishers.

Mendelsohn, O. 1993. 'The Transformation of Authority in Rural India'. *Modern Asian Studies* 27 (4): 805–42.

Mishra, Srijit. 2006. 'Farmer Suicides in Maharashtra'. *Economic and Political Weekly* 41 (???): 1538–45, April.

Mohanty B. B. 2005. '"We are Like the Living Dead": Farmer suicides in Maharashtra, Western India'. *Journal of Peasant Studies* 32 (2): 243–76, April.

Moore, B. Jr. 1966. *Social Origins of Dictatorship and Democracy*. Middlesex: Penguin.

Neale, W. 1962. *Economic Change in Rural India: Land Tenure and Reform in Uttar Pradesh, 1800–1955*. New Haven: Yale University Press.

Nelson, Lowry. 1948. *Rural Sociology*. New York: American Book Company.

Newby, H. 1980. 'Trend Report: Rural Sociology'. *Current Sociology* 28 (Spring): 1–141.

Omvedt, Gail. 1992. 'Capitalist Agriculture and Rural Classes in India'. In *Class, State and Development in India*, ed. B. Berberogly. New Delhi: Sage Publications.

Radhakrishanan, P. 1989. *Peasant Struggles, Land Reforms and Social Change: Malabar 1836–1982*. New Delhi: Sage.

Redfiled, Robert. 1947. 'The Folk Society'. *American Journal of Sociology* 52: 292–308, January..

Redfield, R. 1965. *Peasant Society and Culture*. Chicago: University of Chicago Press.

Reserve Bank of India (RBI). 1969. *Report of the All India Rural Credit Review Committee*. Bombay: RBI.

Rutten, M. A. F. 1995. *Farms and Factories: Social Profile of Large Farmers and Rural Industrialists in West India*. New Delhi: Oxford University Press.

Sahay, Gaurang R. 2004. 'Hierarchy, Difference and the Caste System: A Study of Rural Bihar'. *Contributions to Indian Sociology* 38 (1 and 2): 113–36

Schwarzweller, H. K. (ed.). 1984. *Research in Rural Sociology and Development*. Vol. 1. Greenwich: Jai Press.

Shanin, T. (ed.). 1987. *Peasants and Peasant Societies*. London: Blackwell.

Silverman, S. 1987. 'The Concept of Peasant and the Concept of Culture'. In *Social Anthropology of Peasantry*, ed. J. Mencher. 7–31. Bombay: Somaiya Publications.

Srinivas, M. N. (ed.). 1955. *India's Villages*. London: Asia Publishing House.

———. 1976. *The Remembered Village*. Delhi, Oxford University Press.

Suri, K. C. 2006. 'Political Economy of Agrarian Distress'. *Economic and Political Weekly* 41 (16): 1523–29, 22 April.

Thorner, D. 1956. *The Agrarian Prospects of India*. Delhi: Oxford University Press.

———. 1964. *Agricultural Co-operatives in India*. Bombay: Asia Publishers.

Upadhya, Carol B. 1988. 'The Farmer-Capitalists of Coastal Andhra Pradesh'. *Economic and Political Weekly* 23 (27): 1376–82, and 23 (28): 1433–42.

Vasavi A. R. 2009. 'Suicides and the Making of India's Agrarian Distress'. *South African Review of Sociology* 40 (1).

Wiser, W. H. 1969. *The Hindu Jajmani System*. Luchnow, Lucknow Publishing House.

Section I

Village Society: Methods and Perspectives

Introduction

This section provides a broad introduction to the study of Indian village societies. The first two chapters tell us about the value of doing 'village studies' and constructing a 'field-view' of the Indian village. The essays are based on the personal fieldwork experience of two eminent sociologists of contemporary India. The method of 'participant observation', as developed by social anthropologists, requires the researcher to stay in the village over a long period of time, empathise with the community and its 'way of life'. It is on the basis of such first-hand experience of village life that they write ethnographic accounts of the local level institutional arrangements, their logic and patterns.

A 'field-view' of the village, M. N. Srinivas shows in the first chapter, helps us develop a critique of the popular view of the village, usually held by the urban elite. The urban middle-class elite tend to look at village life through stereotypes, where those living in the village are often viewed as being conservative, irrational and completely bound by tradition. While some of it may be true, he argues, it cannot be generalised. Peasants, for example, possess deep knowledge of cropping patterns and agricultural practices. Though to an outsider, their way of doing agriculture may sound conservative, it may have its own logic in terms minimising risks/ uncertainties. A 'field-view' would also help policymakers to go beyond abstract models of change, which are also invariably based on stereotypical notions about village society.

In the following chapter, André Béteille takes us a step further and tells us about his experience of doing fieldwork in a village of Tamil Nadu and the difficulties a social anthropologist could encounter while trying to use the method of 'participant observation'. The method was first developed by social anthropologists while studying the so-called tribal communities. Unlike the tribal communities, a typical Indian village is sharply divided on caste lines. Different caste communities also live in different residential areas. It is not always easy for a researcher to negotiate with such differences because the villagers living in different settlements have their own view on the village. The dominant section of the village also tries to impose its own view of the village on the researcher and they clearly disapprove of the researcher's interaction with those living in the periphery of the villager. Notwithstanding the professional training of the social anthropologist, his or her research cannot remain immune to such pressures.

The third chapter offers a historical perspective on the idea the Indian village and the way it was constructed by prominent Indians during the nationalist freedom movement. Focusing primarily on writings of Gandhi, Nehru and Ambedkar, the chapter shows that though the village was a central category in the nationalist imaginations and there was virtual agreement that it represented the core of the traditional social order of India, the attitudes of the three leaders towards the village society varied considerably. While for Gandhi the village was a site of authenticity, to be recovered through his method of *swaraj* (true self-rule or independence); for Nehru it was a site of backwardness and therefore needed to be developed through modern technology. Though Ambedkar agreed with Nehru on the 'backwardness' of the Indian village, he also developed a political critique of the caste-based social organisation of the traditional Indian village. For him the village was a site of oppression and its value could only be negative.

1

Village Studies, Participant Observation and Social Science Research in India*

M. N. Srinivas

I

I shall not attempt here to trace the history of village studies in India but rest content with mentioning that a few early British administrators did carry out, as part of their duties, village surveys in their respective areas. And during the first few decades of this century, a few foreign economists and anthropologists studied villages in different parts of the country, notable among them being Harold Mann, Gilbert Slater, and the Wisers. Mann and Slater were interested primarily in the village economy while the Wisers were more comprehensive. William H. Wiser, as is well known to anthropologists, is the author of a brief monograph on the *Hindu Jajmani System* (1936) and this was preceded by the better-known, little classic Behind Mud Walls (Wiser and Wiser 1930), which he wrote jointly with his wife, Charlotte. The method adopted by the Wisers in their study of Karimnagar was quite different from the economists'. They spent years in the village, talked to the local inhabitants in Hindi, participated in their activities, and did their utmost to help the needy and suffering.[1] The quality of the information gathered by the Wisers was superior to anything collected before, and when this was put into a holistic framework, which William Wiser's anthropological training enabled him to do, the result was a memorable picture not only of Karimnagar but of village life in the subcontinent, the microcosm reflecting the macrocosm.

It is only fair to add here that in the inter-war years Indian scholars such as D. R. Gadgil and R. K. Mukherjee also studied aspects of rural life, while C. N. Vakil

---

* This chapter has been extracted from a longer paper published by the author in the *Economic and Political Weekly* 10 (33–35): 1387–94, August 1975.

I would like to thank my colleagues, S. Seshaiah, J. P. Singh, M. N. Panini and Gurushri Swamy for criticisms of an earlier draft of this paper. But, needless to say, the responsibility for the views expressed here is solely mine.

and G. S. Ghurye encouraged their students to carry out field-studies of villages. In retrospect, it is clear that this was a milestone in the development of the social sciences in India as it symbolised the recognition of the need, on part of scholars, to find out the facts of rural life for themselves. No longer were they going to rest content with what contained in the censuses, and reports, and administrators' surveys. It signified a cognitive turnaround among the new elite cut off by class as well as caste from the rural poor. One wonders whether Gandhi's stressing of the importance of living in the villages to understand the conditions and problems of villagers had had any effect on the elite. (This is a subject for research.)

The situation with regard to village studies underwent a radical change after the end of Second World War when Indian social anthropologists, trained abroad, and their foreign counterparts, began making systematic studies of villages in different parts of the country. These studies were different from the earlier ones, excepting, as already mentioned, the Wisers', in that they relied almost exclusively on the method of participant observation, and the presentation of the data was usually around a well-defined theme of theoretical or comparative interest though the theme used only a part, usually a minuscule part, of the information collected. In other words, there was no hiatus between description and theory, and instead the two were fused into a whole.[…]

That facts are, of course, marshalled to support or controvert an argument, but what is insidious is the existence of bias in the perception and interpretation of facts. Training in research methodology ought to make students more sensitive and honest observers, and in this context, the importance of contrary instances cannot be overemphasised.[…]

In India, the fieldwork tradition is strongest in social anthropology and is only less marked in sociology, while it is relatively weak in the other social sciences.[…]

The lack of a fieldwork tradition in the social sciences (excluding social anthropology and sociology) has had adverse results on their growth and development. Most important, it has alienated them from grassroots reality and led to fanciful assumptions about the behaviour of ordinary people. It has resulted in woeful ignorance about the complex interaction of economic, political and social forces at local levels.

The educated Indian elite commonly regard the peasant as ignorant, tradition-bound, and resistant to progress. His actions and motivations appear anything but rational to the elite: His agriculture is a 'gamble on the monsoon', his plough just scratches the earth, his bullocks are bags of skin and bones, he indulges in wasteful expenditure at weddings and funerals, he is hopelessly indebted to the moneylender, his caste prejudices come in the way of changing his occupation, and he lacks the sense to take advantage of the many benefits offered by a benevolent government working through a plethora of institutions and specialists.

The above image is only a caricature of the peasant, all the more untrue because it contains a grain of truth. Anyone who has tried to understand it knows that peasant agriculture is a highly-skilled enterprise, representing a subtle and delicate adjustment to an environment achieved over the centuries and taking note of soil, weather, climate and other ecological conditions as well as the peasant's poor resources and cultural traditions. The cultural traditions cannot be regarded as irrational as they represent, among other things, the peasant's psychological and social insurance in an extremely hostile world. Rationality does not exist in a vacuum but in a cultural context, and human satisfactions are themselves frequently culturally determined. The elite are annoyed with the peasant for not making choices which they want him to make, but they seem to be ignorant of the fact that choices are linked to structural, economic and cultural factors. This applies with particular force in a highly stratified and culturally diverse society such as India.

As in every other country, the poor in India have been subjected to gross exploitation, and this has been both facilitated and compounded by caste, but this should not make us blind to the fact that over the millennia they have evolved an outlook and strategies which have enabled them to survive a variety of predators such as tax collectors, landowners, village headmen, accountants, moneylenders, marauders and the like. The moral and manners preached by the landowning high castes belong to a different world from that of the poor peasant.

Even the peasant's alleged stupidity, his inability to grasp and follow the instructions of a self-confident elite, is frequently a cloak for his scepticism towards new ideas and nostrums, a scepticism that stems from a deep faith in his tried and trusted ways. If a new variety of seed or mode of cultivation fails, the man who pays the price—price which occasionally may mean starvation—for it is not the extension officer. Sometimes, however, the peasant senses that the new boon, institution, invention or technique advocated by the official is likely to place more power in the hands of rich and powerful men, and increase his dependence on them. (On the other side, I have heard a powerful headman dismissing the idea of building a new school building on the ground that it would only teach the poor to be arrogant. The same man wanted electric power instead for the village as it would enable an industry to be started. And he would make sure that he would start the industry.)

Another consequence of the lack of a serious fieldwork tradition in the social sciences is the implicit and absurd view that people are like dough in the hands of the planners and the government. Phrases such as 'social engineering', 'planned change' and 'directed social change', further the illusion that the government is able to change the lives of citizens in any matter it wants to. That people have resources of their own, physical, intellectual and moral, and that they can use them to their advantage, is not recognised by those in power. Such blindness is all the more surprising since in most parts of the country the benefits of development programmes have been collared by the higher landowners from the locally dominant castes, leaving the weaker sections of the society more or less where they were before. The point which I wish to make is that the well-made plans of government do not go the way they are expected to, because people are not pawns which can be moved about but have intelligence, resources and aims of their own. They manage either to find loopholes in the rules, or bypass them altogether, in order to achieve their own ends, and in the process, defeat the planners. The tendency to study development programmes from the point of view of the degree of success achieved appears to me to be too simple-minded. It would be more fruitful and interesting to look at them as providing examples of the responses of human beings with certain resources, values and aims to the policies and programmes of a powerful government acting through its officials who not only wish to achieve certain targets but have a culture of their own, a culture that is mediated through their different personalities. It is a complex, interactional situation and constitutes an ideal area for research by social anthropologists.

The divorce between field research and theory has had another grave consequence for the development of the social sciences. Unlike the natural sciences, the social sciences have a deep and organic relation with the social (including the political and economic) environment which encompasses them and in which they function. In this sense, they are relativistic, and this has to be accepted wholeheartedly if they have to develop and become an integral part of the country's intellectual life. They cannot hope to do this if Indian scholars keep continually looking to models, concepts and even empirical experience from Europe, the US, USSR or China. To state this is not to be chauvinistic or support obscurantism but only to make the obvious point that knowledge regarding an alien society and culture becomes meaningful only when compared with another of which one has first-hand knowledge. Such comparison is more often than not implicit than explicit, and that is certainly true in social anthropology. Further, Indian social scientists ought to realise that by concentrating on the Indian situation they are really enhancing the range of the social sciences. At the present moment, social sciences are drawing too heavily on a small range of human experience, viz., the western-industrial, and equating it with the global. (Built into that equation is an ethno-centric assumption on the part of many westerners that all societies are travelling towards the ultimate goal of a western-industrial type of society.) Indian social scientists have a responsibility to resist such an equation, firstly, in order to better understand their society, and secondly, to contribute to the greater universalisation of their disciplines.

The division of labour between the theoretician-analyst and the fact-gatherer is so firmly rooted in our country that I doubt whether it can be eradicated. Apart from organisations which already exist in order to conduct all-India surveys, the tendency to undertake big surveys will increase as administrators and politicians, partly for political reasons, and partly to demonstrate their own sophistication, demand that facts be collected in a wide variety of areas for taking or implementing 'policy decisions'. (It would be instructive to discover in how many cases the information gathered has been used for formulation or implementation of policy.) And during the last 30 years a class of academic-entrepreneurs have emerged in response to the demand for data and studies. They are usually senior men, heads of departments or institutions, who enjoy directing projects, appointing staff, distributing patronage and flying to Delhi, and other places for meetings of committees and seminars. Their intellectual interests are continually shifting to new areas: for instance, Indian social scientists have discovered in poverty a profitable area for research. Research in slums and villages is also becoming fashionable.[...]

The fieldwork done by a social anthropologist offers a sharp contrast to the approach, methods and techniques used in macro-surveys. In the first place, a crucial characteristic of the anthropologist's study is the absence of any separation between the fieldworker and analyst. Intensive fieldwork is now so integral a part of social anthropology that one who has not had the experience of carrying out at least one such study is regarded as lacking a basic qualification. The total impact of such an experience is lasting in the sense of influencing for good his approach to the study of social institutions. Two basic concepts of social anthropology are social structure and culture, and they result in emphasising the need to view particular phenomena in their social and cultural context to ascertain properly their meaning and function. This to some extent underlines the annoyance if not despair at the manner in which questions are asked in macro-surveys: Social facts are treated as though they are pebbles which can be lifted from a heap, an assumption that is frequently unconscious but nonetheless disastrous inasmuch as social facts are interrelated.

The method of participant observation has evolved through the efforts of successive generations of anthropologists, though the first practitioner of the method was Malinowski.[2] Under this method, the fieldworker spends a period of 18–24 months in a society different from his own, the time being distributed in two visits, uses the local language in talking with the indigenes, participates in their daily, seasonal and other activities, and as far as possible, gathers his information in the course of such participation. Before setting out for the field, the anthropologist is expected to be familiar with the literature available on the region he has selected and study the language spoken there.

The lone anthropologist who goes out to a people to do fieldwork has a vital stake in collecting accurate information on the areas he considers relevant. He is aware that his professional future depends on the success of his first field effort. Even when he has a narrow and well-defined theme he collects a considerable amount of information on other matters as he realises only too well that the different aspects of social life are intermeshed in a small community with unsophisticated technology.

As a result of their efforts, anthropologists have built up, over generations, a vast corpus of systematic information about the culture and social life of a large number of diverse groups, primitive, and now peasant, and on the whole, the quantity and quality of the information is better than what is available for the historic periods of civilised societies. Some anthropologists regard the information that has been collected above the wide range of cultures as the crowning glory of their discipline. This pride is justified particularly when it is remembered that the spread of western civilisation over the globe has been destructive of cultural diversity.

As stated earlier, throughout the development of social anthropology, there has been an intimate linkage between fieldwork and theory. Richer data have given rise to new ideas and theory while theoretical developments have resulted in a demand for more and better data. As a result, (a) anthropologists are now willing than before to quantify information and use statistical techniques; and (b) the range as well as the depth of the data collected has increased in response to new theoretical orientations and interests. There is much more interest nowadays in ecology, in native perceptions and ideas, ethno-science, symbolism and ritual, and in social change, development and modernisation. Intensive case studies are used in the analysis of selected aspects of social life, and this method has the advantage of dramatising the interrelationships between diverse individuals and groups, the frequent clash between norms and practice, and the creative manner in which leaders use situations to achieve their ends and strike out new paths. Ideally, a monograph can be written about a single case study and this might scandalise those to whom 'methodology' means essentially the application of statistical techniques.

II

I shall now touch briefly on the consequence of participant observation which, I think, reveals a dimension of social understanding which is now widely known.

There are two sides to the anthropologist's fieldwork, one which is open and exeteric, and the other, subterranean and esoteric. The former comprises carrying out censuses and surveys, collecting genealogical data, getting questionnaires completed, recording events as they happen be the life cycle ritual, calendrical festivals, agricultural and other activities, disputes, partitions, transactions, jokes, abuse, folklore, etc. The esoteric part, however, is more a by-product of the method employed by the anthropologist than a set objective. The anthropologist's long residence among the indigenes, his knowledge of the local language, and his participation in their day-to-day activities, his dependence on local people for the basic essentials of life including company, all produce over a period of time a sea change in his out-look and attitudes. The sense of strangeness if not bewilderment with which the anthropologist begins his fieldwork gives way, at some point along the way, to understanding which may be real, or partly real and partly illusory. He suddenly perceives the sense and rationality underlying indigenous institutions and behaviour, a perception the obverse of which is the awareness that the culture into which he was born was one of a myriad available to mankind, and any assumptions which he may have made about its universality were absurd. Anthropologists are known frequently to become advocates if not evangelists for the cultures, they studied as against their natal cultures. Even when it is only a passing phenomenon, it is indicative of the effects of the use of the methods of participant observation.

This radical shift in the anthropologist's stance is not the result of cogitation but the change outcome of living among the indigenes and sharing their life and experience. The change in his position is similar to that which a regular user of an automobile undergoes when he becomes, even for a brief while, a pedestrian, or that of a doctor who has to suddenly change his role for that of a patient.

The anthropologist's transformation is facilitated by certain objective conditions which have been mentioned earlier and which are incidental to the method he uses. In addition, however, he must have the gift of empathy, the ability to place himself in the shoes of others and to look at the world from their point of view. This means that he should go much farther than the collection of accurate data. Ideally, he should have the sensitivity of a novelist.

The feeling that he understands the people he is studying is a heady one indeed but is not exactly the ideal condition in which to write about them. A certain amount of distance, emotional and intellectual, is essential to the anthropologist for translating his personal and subjective experience into universal terms. This is helped, if not made possible by the necessity to describe his experience in the language and concerns of his discipline at that moment. Seminars, informal discussions with colleagues, the need to compare, explicitly or implicitly, the institutions of the people he has studied with those of others, and above all, the fact that while writing up his data the anthropologist inhabits a different universe from that which he was in when doing fieldwork, all help to put some distance between him and the people he studied. Reflection on one's fieldwork makes it more meaningful in the sense that the implications of seemingly trivial words, actions and gestures, which one had missed in the field, are brought home vividly. That it also leads to feelings of deep regret at missed opportunities is the other side of the coin.

The anthropologist knows that the information he collects during the first few weeks of his stay—representing frequently more than the total time spent by other social scientists on their fieldwork—is not only fragmentary but erroneous. While this is inevitable, the introductory period can be put to good use for collecting information of a routine nature on non-sensitive areas such as material culture, agricultural practices and genealogical data. The serendipity effects of this activity are at least as important as the information gathered, for in the course of going about his work the anthropologist becomes acquainted with the villagers, and they come to accept his presence everywhere as a normal phenomenon. Time spent in establishing friendly relations with the people who are the object of investigation is never wasted. It is the only means to the later securing of reliable information on sensitive areas. I am ignoring the richness of the human experience.

It is less difficult to look at the world from the point of view of the indigenes when they are a homogeneous group than when they are heterogeneous. The matter is compounded when indigenous society is hierarchical as the interests and perspectives of different groups conflict. The structural position of an individual largely determines how he perceives situations, and social interaction between people from different castes and categories involves the clash as well as accommodation of diverse perspectives. Add to this personality differences, and one gets some idea of the kind and degree of intellectual and emotional flexibility and sensitivity that the anthropologist ought to have to be able to study interaction between individuals in a complex and hierarchical society. He must not only understand the meaning of the words spoken but be sensitive to the tone and pitch of the voice used, the accompanying gestures and facial expressions, and finally, view all this in the total situational context of the exchange. Two identical words or phrases can have different meanings depending upon the context and the manner in which they are uttered.

The fruit of successful fieldwork is a large body of notes the weight and complexity of which only increase with the years. Anthropologists who, for one reason or other, do not publish at least some of the results of their fieldwork soon after leaving the field, live to rue their failure. As they become more active in teaching—and this is particularly true of anthropologists in developing countries—they find that they do not have the time to write up their notes. After a while, the anthropologist discovers that he needs at least a few months even to become reasonably familiar with his notes, and writing them up is not something he can do in short spells of time but only as a sustained and whole-time activity. The burden of unwritten notes is one with which most anthropologists have to learn to live. They come in the way of pursuing new interests. The value of old notes only increases with time: They become historical material.

III

I shall now refer briefly to a few common errors and misconceptions about village studies. An obvious objection to the study of a single village is its inability to inform us about the country as a whole. In one sense, the truth of this statement is obvious but in another sense it is not true. It is of course absurd to try and generalise on rural India from the study of a single village but if it is remembered that, in spite of its bewildering diversity, there are certain broad regional and even national similarities in India, even that study can be productive of knowledge and insights which could be translated into hypotheses and leads in future research. It also gives some idea of the quality of village life.

The Indian village has never been an isolate, being always connected, however tenuously, with neighbouring villages and towns in a variety of ways. Since independence the linkage between a village and its vicinage has grown more intimate. The social anthropologist who studies a village today will have to take serious note of its linkage with wider society. While the village offers a convenient locus for fieldwork the anthropologist who studies it cannot stop at its boundaries. He has to follow his people to the other villages with which they have contact, to the tehsil and district headquarters, and even the state capital. Network analyses are likely to prove indispensable for analysing the nature of the relationship which a village has with neighbouring villages and towns. Even in a single village, this may differ for different areas of behaviour such as kinship, economies, politics and religion. It may also differ from group to group.

It is argued that the method of participant observation, apart from being time-consuming and productive of an unmanageable quantity of notes, is useful only for studying small communities. This becomes a serious limitation where there is a need for social anthropologists to address themselves to problems at regional and state if not national levels. A great asset thus becomes a crippling liability.

There is some substance in the above argument. I would like, however, to distinguish between the value of the method of participant observation as a system of apprenticeship and its importance as a source of accurate and copious data. As already mentioned his field experience influences his approach to the analysis of social institutions and the interpretation of social data, and finally, enables him to refer what he reads and hears to his field-study.

In other words, his field experience is crucial for his intellectual development irrespective of the data it generates. Only a small part of the data produced may be used by him and he may not be able to use the rest.

The method of participant observation need not be confined to the study of communities. It can be used in case studies at various levels, from the national to local. A strike, a communal riot, a development project gone awry, the problems of an MLA or MP, etc. Obviously, the purpose of a case study is to reveal in depth the play, interrelation and dynamics of various forces, and it makes no claim whatever to be representative. But even then case studies of a phenomenon (riot or strike) can reveal a good deal about it which, apart from their intellectual interest, have practical implications.

Yet another way of using the participant observation method is for the anthropologist to leave his academic and social milieu, and take on a few temporary roles.[3] This has been done by literary men, either deliberately or under economic necessity, and it not only enlarged their experience but widened their range of empathy. Orwell's Down and Out in Paris and London and Laurie Lee's As I Walked Out one Midsummer Morning provide good example of the kind of thing I mean. Many other writers have chosen a similar course.

Nothing that I have written so far about participant observation is inconsistent with the researcher's having a clear idea of what to look for in the field or formulating a hypothesis for testing. But such a course can only be taken when some reliable information is already available about the region. In the absence of such information, a general survey is unavoidable though a researcher who has a sound grasp of theory and is also a keen observer is able to write a monograph with theoretical implication on the basis of his field experience.

Clarity about the aims of the project is essential in undertaking research at the regional or even higher level. The danger of dissipating one's energies in the pursuit of a vague and ill-defined objective are much greater when the area is large and the facts are not only more numerous but relationships between them extremely complex. Such projects are also likely to be costlier.

In brief the village studies carried out by anthropologists in the 1950s were quite different from similar studies carried out by the other social scientists, and helped to make it clear to everyone that the former's interests were not confined to the tribal world. Since then they have further extended their interests to include pockets of the urban and industrial world. It appears only logical for them to move now to regional and even higher level studies. If this is to be done effectively there is need for recasting the syllabi in social anthropology (and sociology). Apart from giving students in these disciplines a good knowledge of statistics and research methodology, provision must be made for their studying at least one of the allied social sciences, economics, political science and history. This is perhaps best done at postgraduate levels. Without such groundwork, talk about interdisciplinary work—which is both fashionable and fund-attracting—is a waste of time

To return to macro- and micro-studies: With some thought and planning they can be made to support and strengthen each other. Correlations and generalisations derived from macro-studies may be examined in depth in micro-studies to find out if they are the outcome of real inter-relations or only the accidental juxtaposition of unrelated events. Similarly, hypotheses and leads suggested by micro-studies can be tested systematically over wider regions.

Indeed, it would be worthwhile considering whether a certain number of villages from different regions of India, selected on the basis of relevant criteria, ought to be studied by anthropologists, economists and political scientists on a continuing basis, and it would be illuminating to canvass in them questionnaires used in macro-surveys. The responses of people living in the selected villages can be compared against information obtained in other villages, and the divergences between the two, if any, should provide a check against the kind of information collected in the 'general' villages. The organisation of these micro-studies would present problems and they would have to be gone into with care. But one thing ought to be clear: they ought not to become part of the empires of the managers of micro-surveys.

Notes

1. The Wisers were missionaries but the point which I wish to stress is that they collected information through the use of the method of participant observation.

2. For a brief account of this method, and the nature of the task which the social anthropologist sets out for himself when he undertakes a field-study see Evans-Pritchard (1951).

3. I believe this is what Saberwal has urged in his essay (1975: 58).

References

Evans-Pritchard. E. E. 1951. *Social Anthropology*. London: Cohan & West.

Saberwal, Satish. 1975. 'Leaves from a Field Diary'. In *Encounter and Experience: Personal Account of Fieldwork*, ed. A. Beteille and T. N. Madan. Delhi: Vikas Publication House.

Wiser, William H. 1936. *Hindu Jajmani System: A Socio-Economic System Interrelating Members of a Hindu Village Community in Services*. Lucknow: Lucknow Publishing House.

Wiser, William H. and Charlotte V. Wiser. 1930. *Behind Mud Walls in India*. London: George Allan.

2

THE TRIBULATIONS OF FIELDWORK*

ANDRÉ BÉTEILLE

Some of our best insights into kinship, religion and local-level politics come from intensive studies made by social anthropologists using the method of participant-observation. Although this approach has so far been used mainly in the study of village communities, it can be applied to the investigation of practically any sector of contemporary society.[...]

In the following paragraphs I shall describe, mainly with two ends in view, some of my experiences as a fieldworker in a village in Tanjore district in Tamil Nadu where I lived for a little less than a year in 1961–62. I shall try first of all to show the kinds of constraints that most investigators doing fieldwork under similar conditions have to face. I shall try also to show how I gained some of my deepest insights into the society and culture that I was investigating in the very process of trying to cope with these constraints.[...]

When I went to Sripuram I did not have a definite preference for any particular aspect of its social life, and I certainly did not have a clearly formulated plan of investigation. In this I was not very different from the sociologist Whyte or the many social anthropologists whose work is described by Evans-Pritchard (1951). I did have an interest in the problem of social inequality, but this interest took shape only in the course of my stay in the village. Had I gone to a village in some other area or been placed in a different set of conditions, I might have developed an interest in family and kinship, or in religion and ritual. I am sure that my interest came to be fixed on stratification because in the village where I found myself the marks of stratification were present in virtually every sphere of life.

In what follows I shall describe only some of the problems which confronted me in the course of my fieldwork and discuss the lessons I learnt by trying to deal with them. I do not intend to give a general account of the way in which my fieldwork took shape as Whyte (1955) has done. What I propose to do is to concentrate on only those problems which arose from the fact that the village in which I lived was a highly stratified community. In other words, what I shall do is to show how in

* This chapter has been extracted from a longer paper published by the author in the *Economic and Political Weekly* 32 (31–33): 1509–16, August 1972.

adjusting oneself to a stratified community one learns much about the nature of stratification itself.

Every anthropologist knows how difficult it was for him to find a congenial village (or city ward or some other compact unit) to live in and study. Having found such a community and worked in it for a year or so, he easily forgets the travails he had to undergo in establishing himself in his chosen field of investigation.

The first problem I faced after finding myself a village was where I should live in it. Malinowski, the first and most celebrated modern fieldworker, discussed the problem of choosing a place to live in his classic work, Argonauts of the Western Pacific published in 1922 (Malinowski 1922). According to him, the anthropologist should live among the natives, in the centre of their social life and at a sufficient distance from the white men's area of residence. For Malinowski the basic choice was between living with natives, away from white men, and living with white men, away from the natives. For an Indian anthropologist going to study an Indian village, the choices are of a different kind. He has in any case to live with the natives, but he must decide which sorts of natives.

The village in which I worked is divided into three residential areas. There is at one end the agraharam where the brahmins live, and at the other the *cheri* where the harijans live; in between is the non-brahmin sector. Although I was aware that the different castes in a village live in different residential areas, I was not in fact prepared for the extent of physical separation that I encountered. The agraharam in my village was so positioned that one could go from the main road into the rest of the village without passing it. At the other end, the cheri had a life of its own, and its daily round of activities was largely unnoticed by the rest of the village.

Since I could not live in three places at the same time, I decided to stay in the agraharam. There were various practical considerations behind my choice. Firstly, those who introduced me to the village felt that I ought to live in the agraharam since it was here that I could get the minimum material comforts they thought I ought to have. Secondly, from the agraharam I could gain access to the rest of the village more easily than from either of the two other sectors. Thirdly, most of the written material about the village both about its past and its present, could be secured more easily from the agraharam than from elsewhere.

Had I lived in the cheri, my study would almost certainly have acquired a different perspective, although I like to think that it would be complementary rather than contradictory to the one it actually acquired. Almost from the very beginning of my work I remained conscious of this, and I tried at every step to provide what I thought was a 'balanced account'. Had I lived in a village having less sharply graded inequalities, I might have paid little attention to this problem of balancing alternative perspectives.

I have often been asked why, since I lived in the village for many months, I did not divide my stay between the agraharam and the cheri. I could live in the agraharam only on certain terms, by accepting some of the duties and obligations of a member of the community. If, after adjusting myself to the role which had been assigned to me, I tried to move into the cheri, I would almost certainly become suspect in the eyes of both brahmins and harijans. Whyte describes how, after living with the corner boys for some time, he decided one evening to swear like them in the slum dialect. The boys were shocked since they had assigned to him a role in which he was not expected to speak in that way (Whyte 1955: 301). The villagers of Sripuram had also assigned me a role, and they would consider it most unnatural if I decided suddenly to act in ways that were quite contrary to what was expected. Human beings are not guinea-pigs, and you cannot make them either behave in arbitrary ways or accept arbitrary behaviour from you.

Different Perspective

Living in the agraharam, I soon discovered that its residents had a perspective on the village which was different from the perspective I was seeking to achieve. This difference revealed itself in a number of ways of which some were gross and others subtle. Let me begin with an example of the first. It took me some time to take a proper census of the village. Before I did this I asked various villagers to give me a rough idea of the population of the village and the number of households in it. I found that the figures given by the different villagers varied greatly from each other and from the estimate 1 had formed from first observation.

My neighbours in the agraharam said that the village had about a hundred houses of which some were uninhabited, their occupants having gone to live elsewhere. Some brahmins I knew in Tanjore who were familiar with the village also said that Sripuram had about a hundred households. When I pointed out that by my reckoning there would be at least three hundred households, it turned out that they and I were using the term 'Sripuram' to signify different realities. For them Sripuram was primarily the agraharam which had about a hundred households; if the households in all the other streets were included, they agreed, the total would be over three hundred.

N. K. Bose once narrated a similar experience from a village in West Bengal. He had taken a visitor from Calcutta to see the village and the visitor asked one of the villagers who was taking them around what the size of the village was. The villager mentioned a figure which was contradicted by Bose who gave a much higher figure for the total number of households including those of the harijan and adivasi residents of the village. The informant accepted this figure, saying, 'Ah, it will be about that if you include the et cetera'. The point to be noted is that the process of exclusion operates not merely in the counting of heads, but also in other, more subtle ways which often go unnoticed by the fieldworker who stays for only a short while in the village.

Having established myself in the agraharam, I found that my physical movements were greatly restricted. I could not go and come as I pleased, but was bound by the rules and conventions prevalent in the community. I had told my hosts that I had come to learn about their customs and that the only way in which I could do this was by living in their midst as one of them. If I was to be given access to their homes and temples—to which access was not easily given to outsiders—I could not violate their sentiments at will. The agraharam was in many ways a closed community and many of its members made me feel that by allowing me to live in it they had conferred a privilege on me.

The most manifest reasons behind the restriction of my movements to and from the agraharam—and indeed within the agraharam itself—had to do with the traditional attitudes to purity and pollution. Brahmins are debarred by ritual considerations from entering the streets where harijans live. Anyone who enters these streets puts himself in a state of pollution and has, in principle, to purify himself by a bath in the river before returning to the agraharam and entering a brahmin house. In practice, few residents of the agraharam ever have reason to visit the cheris openlly, and those who go there do not now bother to take a purificatory bath on return. Such visits have, however, to be made with care and circumspection, particularly when the visitor is an outsider whose presence in the agraharam is itself tolerated as a concession.

My first visit to the harijan cheri taught me that such a visit was not only frowned on by the brahmins but also viewed by the harijans with suspicion. I went there in the company of a brahmin, and most harijans had, until the end, no way of knowing that I myself could be anything but a brahmin. The harijans regard a visit to their homes by brahmins as unnatural, and some believe that it brings them ill-luck. I was later told that it was customary in the past for them to break earthen pots to ward off the ill-luck that such a happening occasioned.

There were some places in the village, such as the harijan cheri, which I felt I could not easily enter because of the low or negative ritual value attached to them. There were others, such as the inner sanctum of the Vishnu temple, which I at first hesitated to enter because of the high or positive ritual value with which they were invested. As I began to tread warily across the spaces in which the villagers lived their lives, I learnt something about the role of ritual values in defining the distances between people.

Social distances in Sripuram are not regulated merely by considerations of purity and pollution. They are regulated also by conceptions of deference and respect, or what the villagers call mariyadai. Each society has its particular code of deference which is largely an unwritten code. It would be difficult to get to know this code merely by asking people abstract questions about the conditions under which they give or receive deference. One observes the actions of others and one learns by adjusting oneself, as a member of the community, to the demands made under various conditions by other members.

I think that the brahmin elders were extremely pleased when they learnt from my friend and chief informant at the time that I had given up smoking, 'out of respect for them', as he put it. One shows respect towards elders—or towards any category of people—not simply by not smoking in their presence but by giving them precedence in a hundred different ways. Because I had myself to learn these things so as to fit into the life of the community, it became easier for me to understand what the whole thing was about.

I found that several of the brahmin elders were very happy to talk to me on most aspects of their life once I had established the proper relations with them on the basis of deference. I patterned my behaviour towards them after the manner of my first principal informant who was roughly of my own age. Some of the brahmin elders enjoyed a reputation for learning in the traditional Sanskrit scriptures. The principal criteria by which deference was accorded within the agraharam were age, kinship status, wealth and learning. I think it pleased them to find that I, who was reputed to be learned in the western sense, was prepared to show respect for their traditional learning.

Receiving Deference

As I established myself as a member of the agraharam community, I learnt that I was expected not only to accord deference but also to receive it in the proper way. This was brought home to me by a number of incidents of which I will give one illustration. I had taken photographs of some non-brahmin farmhands who were naturally eager to see their pictures. As I passed by the fields where they worked, they asked me every day when the pictures, which were being developed and printed in Tanjore, would be ready. I gave them a date and then forgot all about it. On that date, while I was away, they came to the agraharam and climbed straight into the upstairs room where I was staying. My landlord and his wife, who lived downstairs and were present when they came, were very displeased.

The landlord did not convey his displeasure directly but through an educated mirasdar who had in the meantime become my friend and principal patron in the village. He told me with much tact and circumspection that I ought not to encourage menials and labourers to become familiar with me. There were certain proprieties which had to be maintained. My landlord, though poor, was from a much respected family. They had let me live with them not merely because I paid a rent of Rs 10 a month but because of their personal regard for me. The kinds of non-brahmins who came to my house could not appreciate my proper worth and were bound to be lacking in respect for me. If I were shown any lack of respect, it would be a reflection on the entire agraharam, for they were responsible not only for my food and comfort but also for my being treated with due respect.

Social interchange in the village is thus governed by considerations not only of purity but also of respect. I noticed that there were two types of general conditions under which brahmins had quite close relations with non-brahmins. The first type involved non-brahmin professionals from the town who occasionally visited some brahmins in the village and were treated more or less as equals; the same brahmin mirasdar who had talked to me about the non-brahmin boy who came to get his pictures, was sometimes visited by a non-brahmin lawyer from Tanjore and he showed no disapproval whatever when I became involved with him in arguments about politics. But brahmin landowners were also often close to their non-brahmin tenants or farm servants; in almost all such cases these were unequal relations which were tacitly acknowledged as such by both parties.

These various restrictions had the consequence of making my observations on the non-brahmins and Adi-Dravidas less rich and detailed than I would have desired. During my first spell of fieldwork which lasted for a little over three months, I felt free to visit their streets only with notebook and pencil in hand, in order to elicit information on specific subjects. Further, I found it easier to observe them at work in the fields, and there to ask them such diverse questions about their life as time and circumstances allowed. This had constraints of its own because when people are at work in a paddy field or banana garden they are not always inclined to engage in lengthy conversations on unspecified subjects.

On my second visit to the agraharam I found that my position in the community had become much more secure. But even then I did not wish to appear in a hurry to move about independently and on my own. It was only during the last three months that I felt free to go anywhere I wanted in the village at more or less any time of the day. By that time I had made most of the observations I needed to make in the agraharam, and I felt that I could risk my status in the community to some extent in order to complete the work for which I had come.

My stay with the brahmins taught me that there are other obstacles to understanding besides the more obvious ones which restrict one's physical movements. My neighbours volunteered to supply me with information which I did not always seek from them, and sometimes this information revealed their own perception of village life more than this life as it was actually lived. At first, I found this puzzling but soon I became fascinated with the exercise of separating the one from the other.

One encounters a fairly complex and differentiated ritual life in the village. The brahmins practice the most elaborate set of rituals, and they have a certain pride in their command over the body of ideas on which these practices are based. Some of them, as I have already indicated, have considerable scholastic abilities, and all of them are proud of being the custodians of an ancient religious and literary tradition.

There are many differences between the domestic rituals of the brahmins and the non-brahmins. The priests who perform these rituals are also different. The domestic rituals of the non-brahmins are performed by brahmins of a lower rank, known as panchangakkaran, of whom there were none in the village where I lived, the local non-brahmins being served by priests from adjoining places. The temple priests constitute yet another category of brahmins known collectively as archakar. Some of the lesser temple deities are served by a category of priests called pandaram who are actually non-brahmins.

The brahmins were generally helpful in allowing me to observe as many of their domestic ceremonies as I could and in providing me with information about those which I could not. When I told them that I wanted similar data on the rites of the non-brahmins, they said that they themselves would provide me with the necessary information; as to the Adi-Dravidas, they did not, in the view of the brahmins, have any rites worth recording.

RITES OF NON-BRAHMINS

Few brahmins in the village regard the rites of the non-brahmins as having an independent existence; these rites are, in their view, simplified, attenuated or distorted versions of their own rites. Further, whatever the nature of these rites, they feel that it is not the non-brahmins but they alone who can provide a full and coherent account of them. The non-brahmins perform their rites mechanically without understanding their full significance. In order to be able to record the rites in the proper way one must know their meanings, and the brahmins alone can tell you what these meanings are, no matter who performs the rites. By way of a final and conclusive argument they would ask me how the non-brahmins could be expected to understand their rites since they did not know any Sanskrit.

When even after hearing all this I insisted on going to the non-brahmins to make independent inquiries about their rites, my brahmins friends were puzzled. They felt that I either did not understand the true significance of their culture or was a peculiarly suspicious and mistrustful person. The strange thing is that when I asked the non-brahmins about their rites, they at first became sheepish. They had taken me to be a brahmin since I was permitted to live in the agraharam, and they felt that I would know better than they.

The brahmins felt that they had superior and more complete knowledge not only of ritual but of most important subjects. It was only while living in Sripuram that I came to understand what a tremendous value is placed in Indian culture on any kind of formal education. The brahmins constituted the educated stratum in the village. Almost all their men could read and write Tamil and several of them could read Sanskrit, while several others knew English, having been educated up to high school or above. It therefore appeared natural that they should regard themselves—and be regarded by others—as having authoritative knowledge of most important subjects.

However, much the anthropologist might admire the ritual expertise of the brahmins, he cannot take the same view of their knowledge of agriculture. Traditionally the brahmins of Tanjore had dedicated themselves to priestcraft, scriptural learning and the cultivation of the arts of life, leaving the actual work of village to their non-brahmin and Adi-Dravida tenants and farm servants. In the entire agraharam there was not a single person who had drawn a plough, and most of the men were acquainted with only the principles of agriculture and not its practice.

Educated, city-bred people are inclined to regard traditional agriculture as unskilled or, at best, semi-skilled work. The anthropologist who does fieldwork in a rich deltaic district like Tanjore realises not only how difficult but also how complex and elaborate are the techniques of agriculture. The cultivators of Sripuram grow two paddy crops in a year and in addition they grow bananas, betel vines and a variety of other crops. The cultivation of each crop requires a detailed knowledge of soil, water, seeds and manure.

I found it hard to convince my brahmin friends that I wanted to learn about agriculture not from them but from those who actually practised it. They said that there were knowledgeable brahmins in the village from whom I could learn all that was necessary. In fact, I learned later that much of the information on agricultural practices provided by such people was vague and inaccurate. It took me a little time to discover the true nature of things because I had been initially misled by my own ignorance of the complicated character of agricultural practices and by the confident manner in which my informants claimed full knowledge of them.

My brahmin informants readily conceded that the non-brahmin and Adi-Dravida cultivators were fully acquainted with the practice of agriculture, but in their view it is not enough to know the practice in order to be able to explain how something works to someone who is unfamiliar with it. I said to my hosts that what I wanted was to learn about agricultural practices not by hearing about them from either brahmins or non-brahmins but by observing them in operation. They did not try to prevent me from going to the fields to do this, but I think that most of them felt that I was devoting much time and energy to very little purpose.

The social anthropologist views agriculture as involving not merely a set of technological arrangements but also a set of social arrangements. The social organisation of production in Sripuram is complex. The brahmins own most of the land but have it cultivated by non-brahmins and Adi-Dravidas who are related to them as either tenants or wage labourers. There are ambiguities and strains inherent in the relations between landowners, tenants and wage labourers.

I was doing fieldwork in Sripuram as a time when major changes were taking place in the relations between classes. In regard to tenancy the changes related to both the sharing of the produce and the security of tenure. Landlords and tenants naturally saw the advantages and the disadvantages of the old and the new arrangements in a different light. These differences in their perception of tenurial arrangements led them to emphasise different features of these arrangements in their descriptions of them. Each party was keen to emphasise its own rights and the obligations of the other. One encountered similar problems in examining the relations between landowners and wage labourers.

In situations of this kind one has to listen to what each party has to say about the same set of arrangements. But to do this is not always easy in practice. If I asked the tenant questions about tenancy in the presence of the landlord, he did not always feel free to speak frankly. If I arranged to meet the tenant separately to ask these questions, the landlord felt suspicious and displeased. Thus, asking what might appear to be simple questions about common social arrangements might involve the risk of spoiling one's personal relations with either or both parties to these arrangements. It is only by facing such problems in practical terms that the fieldworker learns what each party has at stake in these common arrangements.[...]

While it is important to realise that fieldwork is a complex experience with many unforeseen turns, it would be wrong to think that the social anthropologist gets all his material from chance encounters with persons and situations. No systematic recorder of facts would put his sole faith on such encounters, however rewarding they might appear in retrospect. On the other hand, he must be mentally prepared for unforeseen events and, when they arise, do his best to turn them to advantage for deepening his understanding of the community he is investigating.

As a matter of fact the sociologist spends much of his time in the village in routine investigations which have over the years acquired an increasingly standardised character. He takes a census of the village and prepares maps showing the location of houses, temples, panchayat office and other places of importance. He collects genealogies and kinship terms; land records and records of tenancy; the annual cycle of agricultural and ceremonial activities; and a variety of other facts which provide the necessary background for an understanding of any particular aspect of village life. There are, in addition, procedures for collecting systematic data on specific institutional fields such as religion, economics and politics.

Intensive fieldwork is now combined increasingly with the use of questionnaires and the collection of material in quantitative terms. If I have not said anything about this side of fieldwork, it is because I wished to draw attention not to abstract rules of procedure but to the actual ways in which problems are handled in the field. I hope I will not be considered to be lacking in modesty if I conclude with the well known words of Malinowski,

> A brief outline of an ethnographer's tribulations, as lived through by myself, may throw more light on the question, then any long abstract discussion could do. (1922: 4)

References

Evans-Pritchard, E. E. 1951. *Social Anthropology*. London: Cohen & West.

Malinowski, Bronislaw. 1922. *Argonauts of the Western Pacific*. London: George Routledge.

Whyte, Willaim Foote. 1955. *Street Cornor Society: Social Structure of an Italian Slum*. Chicago: University of Chicago Press.

3

Nation and Village

*Images of Rural India in Gandhi, Nehru and Ambedkar**

Surinder S. Jodhka

The village has for long been viewed as a convenient entry point for understanding 'traditional' Indian society. It has been seen as a signifier of the authentic native life, a social and cultural unit uncorrupted by outside influence. For the professional sociologists and social anthropologists, village represented India in microcosm, 'an invaluable observation centre' where one could see and study the 'real' India, its social organisation and cultural life. By studying a village, the pioneering Indian sociologist M. N. Srinivas claimed, one could generalise about the 'social processes and problems to be found occurring in great parts of India' (Srinivas 1955: 99).[…]

The historians of modern India have repeatedly pointed to the continuities between the orientalist/colonial categories of knowledge and the nationalist thinking (Chakravarty 1989; Breckenridge and van der Veer 1993; Uberoi 1993; Dirks 2001; Upadhya 2002). Like many other categories, the idea of village too was accepted as given, characterising the Indian realities. Leaders of the nationalist movement, for example, invoked it in many different contexts. Despite disagreements and differences in their ideological orientations or political agenda, the 'village' remained a core category through which most of them conceptualised or thought of the 'traditional' Indian social life. However, unlike the colonial administrators, the nationalist leadership did not see village simply as the constituting 'basic unit' of Indian civilisation. For most of them, village represented 'the real' India, the nation that needed to be recovered, liberated and transformed. Even when they celebrated village life, they did not lose sight of the actual state of affairs marked by scarcity and ignorance.

Apart from having been educated about the Indian society through the colonial writings on the subcontinent, the middle class nationalist leaders were also

* This chapter has been extracted from a longer paper published by the author in the *Economic and Political Weekly* 37 (32): 3343–53, 10 August 2002.

confronted with the village during their struggle for freedom, trying to mobilise the 'common masses' of the subcontinent against colonial rule. It was during this interaction of the received frameworks acquired through the colonial education and concrete realities of life that their ideas about rural India were formed. Nehru was not the only one who set out on a mission to 'discover' and 'rediscover' India; others active in the independence movement also observed and wrote a great deal about the social, economic and cultural life of the Indian people.[...]

A good deal of social scientific literature is available on the colonial constructions of the Indian village and the validities of their assumptions regarding the social and economic structures of the rural communities of the subcontinent (see for example Cohn 1987; Breman 1987; Breman et al. 1997; Habib 1995). Similarly, there have also been some studies on the manner in which village was used as a primary methodological category for understanding the Indian society by sociologists and social anthropologists during the 1950s and 1960s (Srinivas 1994; Breman et al. 1997; Jodhka 1998). Though one can also find a good deal of references on the ways in which the nationalist leadership approached the Indian village or the 'agrarian question', there have not been many comparative studies of the internal disagreements and differences within the nationalist leadership on the subject.[...]

Focusing primarily on writings of these three leading activists and ideologues of the freedom movement, Gandhi, Nehru and Ambedkar, I hope to show in this paper that though village was a central category in the nationalist imaginations and there was a virtual agreement on the fact that it represented the core of the traditional social order of India, the attitudes of these leaders towards the village society varied considerably. They disagreed, both on the merits of traditional Indian village life, and also on the place it should have in the future India of their visions.

The Indian nationalist movement has mostly been seen as a subject that ought to concern the historians, and to a lesser extent the political scientists. Anthropologists and sociologists have only rarely ventured into it as something of their interest.[1] Since the village has been one of the most popular categories among sociologists and social anthropologists in India, a comparative study of the representations of rural life in the nationalist imagination could perhaps also help us build a sociology of the Indian nationalist movement.

Further, available literature on the history of Indian sociology and social anthropology tends to attach a good deal of importance to the influence that colonial writings and the western theoretical traditions have had on the way these disciplines are practised in India today. However, it would be safe to underline that the nationalist movement for independence, and later, the programmes and policies of planned development introduced by the post-independence Indian state also influenced the practice of social science research and teaching in India. Sociology and social anthropology were no exception. Some of the founding fathers of Indian sociology and social anthropology, for example, were deeply involved with the nationalist movement.[2][...]

NATION AND THE VILLAGE

Gandhi, Nehru and Ambedkar, the three most important leaders and ideologues of the freedom movement, all, in a sense, belonged to the city. Not only did they spend most of their lives in cities, much of their political action was also performed in urban centres. Of the three, Ambedkar was the only one who had a first-hand experience of village life during his childhood. Though in terms of the class status of their families, the three came from completely different strata, they all belonged to mobile families, in the sense that even their parents had been 'mobile'. Occupationally also, they were engaged in 'secular' occupations.[3] They all went to foreign lands for education or work and came back to India.

Thus, notwithstanding their attitudes or commitments to rural life, their writings on the subject were mostly reflective, and not experiential in nature. Yet their views on village life were not mere observations of what was happening on ground. They reflect their visions of India's pasts and futures. In fact none of them looked at village as a concrete reality with regional variations and historical specificities having internal dynamics of change. Irrespective of their attitude and the overall ideological orientation towards it, village for all of them was a civilisational entity. More importantly, they seemed to have assumed that the social structure of the village was similar everywhere in the subcontinent.

GANDHI AND THE VILLAGE

Gandhi has been rightly known as the ideologue of the village. He celebrated the Indian village life as no one else did. He also wrote and spoke a great deal on various aspects of village life. Though, as mentioned above, he was not born in a village and did not even have 'an ancestral village' to identify with, much of his social and political philosophy revolved around the idea of the village.

Gandhi became preoccupied with 'the Indian village' right from his days in South Africa and remained so until the end of his life. However, his ideas on village, as also his politics, evolved with time and underwent some important changes along with his political career.

There are at least three different stages or ways in which he used the idea of the Indian village. In the first, he invoked it to establish equivalence of the Indian civilisation with the west. In the second, he counterposed the village to the city and presented the village-life as a critique of, and an alternative to, the modern western culture and civilisation. In the third phase of his engagement, he was concerned with the actual existing villages of India and emphasised on the ways and means of reforming them. Though he continued to see village as an alternative way of living, he also found many faults with the existing lifestyle of the rural people in the Indian countryside.

It was perhaps in 1894 that Gandhi for the first time invoked the idea of the Indian village as a political symbol. This was in a petition to the White government, an 'open letter' written to the Members of Legislative Assembly in Durban to demand voting rights for the people of Indian origin living in South Africa at par with the ruling English people. Gandhi argued in his petition:

> In spite of the Premier's opinion to the contrary...I venture to point out that both the English and the Indians spring from a common stock, called the "Indo-Aryan". (Gandhi 1958: 149)

The idea of village was used to further corroborate his argument and establish equivalence of the Indians with the ruling English community. In another 'petition to the Natal Assembly' in the same year he made reference to Sir Henry Maine's works on the village communities who,

> ... most clearly pointed out that the Indian races have been familiar with representative institutions almost from the time immemorial....The word panchayat is a household word throughout the length and breadth of India, and it means ... a council of five elected by the class of the people whom the five belong, for the purpose of managing and controlling the social affairs of the particular caste. (Ibid.: 94–95)

Apart from his assertion about the traditional Indian village and its core social institution, the caste, as being compatible with the modern western ideas of democracy for their having been similarly organised on the principles of representative governance, the text also points to his sources of understanding the Indian village. It was not just to strengthen his argument being presented to the White rulers that Gandhi invoked the writings of a western commentator on India. The influence of Sir Henry Maine and that of other western/colonial writings on the Indian village is visible all through his career.

Perhaps another important point that emerges out of these letters written to the White rulers of South Africa is his attitude towards the native African tribes. Gandhi, for example, makes no reference to the exclusion of 'Blacks' from such rights. The Indians deserved the right to vote not because democracy required universal franchise but because of the nature and evolution of traditions in different communities. By invoking the idea of 'village republics' he obviously wished to argue that the Indians who have had a system of representation built into the caste panchayats were as advanced a community as the Whites were.

His more substantive and better-known writings on the village began when he came back to India and got involved with the nationalist freedom struggle. His move from South Africa to India changed both his location and his political concerns. Though in some crucial sense his notion of the Indian village remained the same, the uses he put it to in the second phase were however very different. After he returned back to India and engaged himself with the movement for independence, his politics underwent a complete change. The question of securing voting rights for the Indian people and establishing equivalence with the Whites was no longer his agenda. He was to assume the leadership of movement for independence from the British, which required driving the White rulers out of India.

In order to wage such a struggle, he needed a different set of ideas or an ideology that would delegitimise the British rule over India. Such an ideology required construction of a difference that would establish the sovereign identity of India and restore its cultural confidence. The idea of village came in very handy in this endeavour.

He did this by counterposing the Indian village with the modern cities that were set up by the British in India. While the village-life represented the essence of India, the development of modern cities in India symbolised western domination and colonial rule. Village was the site of authenticity, the 'real/pure India', a place that, at least in its design, had not yet been corrupted by the western influence. The city was its opposite, totally western.

Though political freedom could be achieved by overthrowing the colonial rule, the real swaraj or self-rule, as Gandhi imagined, could be achieved only by restoring the civilisational strength of India through revival of its village communities. 'The uplift of India depended solely on the uplift of the villages'. The growth of big cities, particularly those established by the British, was no sign of progress. They were signs of degeneration, 'the real plague spots of India' (Parel 1997: xlii). In a letter addressed to Lord Ampthill in 1909, he wrote:

> To me the rise of cities like Calcutta and Bombay is a matter for sorrow rather than congratulation. India has lost in having broken up a part of her village system. (Gandhi 1963: 509)

He elaborated it further in *Young India* in 1921:

> Our cities are not India. India lives in her seven and a half lakhs of villages, and the cities live upon the villages. They do not bring their wealth from other countries. The city people are brokers and commission agents for the big houses of Europe, America and Japan. The cities have cooperated with the latter in the bleeding process that has gone on for the past two hundred years. (Gandhi 1966: 288–89)

He reiterated his views on cities in exactly the same tenure some 25 years later, in 1946 at a workers' meeting, where he said:

> When the British first established themselves firmly in India their idea was to build cities where all rich people would gravitate and help them in exploiting the countryside. These cities were made partially beautiful; service of all kinds were made available to their inhabitants while the millions of villagers were left rotting in hopeless ignorance and misery. (Gandhi 1982: 232)

Perhaps more important for the argument being developed here is the manner in which he counterposed the city with the village.

> The village civilisation and the city civilisation are totally different things. One depends on machinery and industrialisation, the other rests on handicrafts. We have given preference to the latter. After all, this industrialisation and large-scale production are only of comparatively recent growth. We do not know how far it has contributed to our development and happiness, but we know this much that it has brought in its wake the recent world wars…
>
> Our country was never so unhappy and miserable as it is at present. In the cities people may be getting big profits and good wages, but all that has become possible by sucking the blood of villagers. (Gandhi 1977a: 369)

Not only were the big cities symbols of alien rule and exploitation, they also had a morally corrupting influence on the village people. In another piece in *Young India* published in 1927, he wrote:

> Some of the villages are deserted for six or eight months during the year. Villagers go to Bombay, work under unhealthy and often immoral conditions, then return to their villages during the rainy season bringing with them corruption, drunkenness and disease. (Gandhi 1969: 151)

Apart from the critique of western civilisation and colonial rule that he attempted through counterposing the village and the city, his politics was perhaps also a pointer to the shift that he brought about in the nationalist movement, from an elite-bourgeois activity directed at mobilising the newly emerging middle classes to a popular movement with growing participation of the peasantry from India's hinterlands. As Embree rightly points out, he, for the first time, gave the masses of India 'a sense of involvement in the nation's destiny' (Embree 1989: 165). As is well known, until Gandhi arrived on the scene, the nationalist movement had largely been an urban phenomenon. 'For the early nationalist generations, independence meant being free to emulate colonial city life' (Khilnani 1998: 125). Gandhi turned it upside down. The new nation was not to be found in the cities but in the villages where a large majority of the Indians lived.

What exactly was his notion of the Indian village and how did he visualise the actually existing rural India?

Village, for Gandhi was not merely a place where people lived in small settlements working on land. For him, it reflected the essence of Indian civilisation. The Indian village had a design, a way life, which had the potential of becoming an alternative to the city based and technology driven capitalist west. Empirically such villages did exist in the past and one might still find them in the interiors of India. Drawing support for his argument from Sir Henry Maine's writings, he argued in Harijan in 1939:

> ... Indian society was at one time unknowingly constituted on a non-violent basis. The home life, i.e., the village, was undisturbed by the periodical visitations from barbarous hordes. Maine has shown that India's villages were a congeries of republics. (Gandhi 1978: 4)

Similarly, responding to a question from a group of foreign visitors he advised them that if they wanted to 'see the heart of India', they should 'ignore big cities'. The big cities here were but poor editions of their big cities. They ought 'to go to the villages, and those too not close to cities or to railway line, but unspoilt by them'. He suggested them to:

> Go 30 miles from the railway line, and you will see that the people show a kind of culture which you miss in the west...you will find culture which is unmistakable but far different from that of the west. Then you will take away something that may be worth taking. (Gandhi 1976: 116–17)

He was very unhappy with the nature of changes that the Indian village life had gone through during the British colonial rule. In his views, these changes had impaired the villagers, made them less creative and more dependent on the outside world:

> … the villager of today is not even half so intelligent or resourceful as the villager of fifty years ago. For, whereas the former is reduced to a state of miserable dependence and idleness, the latter used his mind and body for all he needed and produced them at home. (Gandhi 1974: 409)

Gandhi emphasised that freedom from colonial rule could become meaningful only if it was able to grant this autonomy back to the village:

> The cry of "back to the village", some critics say, is putting back the hands of the clock of progress. But is it so? Is it going back to the village, or rendering back to it what belongs to it? I am not asking the city-dwellers to go to and live in the villages. But I am asking them to render unto the villagers what is due to them. (Ibid.: 409–10)

While he asked for revival of the spirit of traditional village life, he also found many flaws with the actually existing villages, and not all these ills were a consequence of the western/urban influence. Two things that he commented quite frequently upon were the practice of untouchability and a general lack of cleanliness. Compared to the cities, where people were 'educated and broad-minded to a little extent at least', untouchability was a more serious problem in the villages, which were 'the centres of orthodoxy'.

While he wanted the village society to abandon the practice of untouchability, he also wanted untouchables to change themselves. He, for example, wanted them to 'observe common cleanliness', 'refrain from eating meat of dead animals and from drink, send their children to schools, remove untouchability among themselves and generally carry on such reforms from within as is possible' (Gandhi 1972: 406).

The lack of hygiene and sanitation were the other things that all villagers needed to pay attention to. He was often disappointed by the disregard for cleanliness that he observed in most of the villages he visited in different parts of the subcontinent. He also wrote quite extensively on this subject. In one of these typical comments, he wrote:

> If we approach any village, the first thing we encounter is the dunghill and this is usually placed on raised ground. On entering the village, we find little difference between the approach and what is within the village. Here too there is dirt on the roads…If a traveller who is unfamiliar with these parts comes across this state of affairs, he will not be able to differentiate between the dunghill and the residential parts. As a matter of fact, there is not much of a difference between the two. (Gandhi 1970: 445)

In another piece, he praised the Europeans in Africa as being worth imitating in this regard:

> There is no gainsaying the fact that our villager betrays a woeful ignorance of even the rudiments of village sanitation. One could deplore the race prejudice amongst the South African Europeans, but their attempts to keep their towns healthy and sanitary were heroic and worthy of imitation. (Gandhi 1969: 76)

Though he repeatedly talks about reviving the village, particularly its 'defunct handicrafts' to save the peasant from ills of industrialisation and inevitability of moving to the cities (Gandhi 1977b: 228), a closer look at his writings tends to suggest that his vision of village was essentially 'a futuristic one', representing an alternative society that was different from the modern-industrial west. His villages would have had similarities with what Sir Henry Maine had written in his book about the past village society, but not everything that is believed to have existed in the past needed to be there in such a 'model village'. His writings reflect more of a reformist rather than a revivalist urge. His village had to be constructed through a concerted effort, often by outsiders—the village workers. He wanted to initiate a movement of village 're-construction' which would translate his ideal into practice.

Such a village would provide an alternative not only to the industrial west, but also to socialism. He was averse to socialism because it required the use of 'violence as a measure to achieve it'. Villageism, on the contrary, could achieve social welfare without using such measures (Gandhi 1980: 192).

And perhaps most importantly, a village-centric society was the most pragmatic choice for a country like India because its 'crores of people would never be able to live in peace with each other in towns and palaces'. In a letter addressed to Nehru in October 1945, he had argued that a society based on the principle of non-violence was possible to achieve only 'in the simplicity of village life'. However, by simplicity he did not mean that his 'dream-village' would completely exclude modern science. A certain amount of science and modern means of communication could be integrated into such a village (as in Parel 1977: 150–51).

His idea of an alternative India is perhaps best spelt-out in one of his pieces published in *Harijan* in 1942 where he wrote:

> My idea of village swaraj is that it is completely republic, independent of its neighbours for its own vital wants, and yet interdependent for many others in which dependence is a necessity. Thus every villager's first concern will be to grow its own food crops and cotton for its cloth.... Then if there is more land available, it will grow useful money crops, thus excluding ganja, tobacco, opium and the like.... Education will be compulsory upto the final basic course. As far as possible every activity will be conducted on the cooperative basis. There will be no castes such as we have today with their graded untouchability.... The government of the village will be conducted by a panchayat of five persons annually elected by the adult villagers, male and female, possessing minimum prescribed qualifications.
>
> ... To model such a village may be the work of a lifetime. Any lover of true democracy and village life can take up a village, treat it as his world and sole work, and he will find good results.... (Gandhi 1979a: 308–9)

What would happen to the already existing cities? He did not ask for their destruction. The cities, he appealed, should also participate in 'the village movement'. Those living in cities and those working for the movement will 'have to develop village mentality and learn the art of living after the manner of villagers'. Though they need not 'starve like the villagers', they must change their old style of life radically. 'While the standard of the villagers must be raised, the city standard has to undergo considerable revision' (Gandhi 1975: 319–20).

Gandhi was certainly not the only one in the freedom movement who saw village and its social structure as something that needed to be sustained and strengthened.

He influenced a large number of others and his ideas on the village as an alternative to the modern/industrial west continue to inspire many even today. However, there were also some in the freedom movement who disagreed with him, particularly on the subject of the place of village in future India. Even some of those who worked very closely with him did not completely share his enthusiasm for the village. Nehru was one of them.

NEHRU AND THE VILLAGE

After Gandhi, Nehru was perhaps the most important and influential leader of the Indian nationalist movement. Apart from being an important ideologue of the Indian National Congress, he also became the first prime minister of independent India. He was the catalyst of the approach India chose for its development after it achieved independence from colonial rule.

Though Nehru worked under the leadership of Gandhi and gave him a good deal of respect, his ideas on the nature of India's past and his vision of its future were not the same as those of Gandhi. These differences were also reflected in his views on the Indian village.

Unlike Gandhi, Nehru perhaps never identified himself with the village. He was also quite self-conscious about his urban and upper middle class upbringing. He admits in his Autobiography (first published in 1936) that until 1920 or so his 'political outlook' was that of his class, 'entirely bourgeois' (Nehru 1980: 49). It was only when he started his political career and came in direct contact with the common rural masses of India that he began to think differently. It was 'a new picture of India..., naked, starving, crushed, and utterly miserable' (ibid.: 52).

As was the case with Gandhi, Nehru's writings on village too have several different strands and could be classified into two or three categories. First of all, as in Gandhi, the idea of the Indian village communities is also quite central to his notion of traditional India. However, his approach to the 'realities' of rural classes as he saw them during his encounters with 'the actually existing rural India' was very different from Gandhi's. As mentioned above, Nehru's importance also lies in the fact that he was the first prime minister of independent India and played a crucial role in shaping its policies and programmes for development. His comments on how rural India ought to be developed also reflect his notion of Indian village life.

His ideas on the traditional Indian society are perhaps best spelt out in his well-known book, Discovery of India (first published in 1946). Though Nehru's approach to the understanding of Indian past was historical in nature, he apparently looked at the 'old' social structure of Indian society from an evolutionary perspective. This is particularly so in his discussion on village and caste. 'The autonomous village community, caste and the joint family', that he identified as the three basic concepts of the 'old Indian social structure', had something in common with traditional societies in general as the organising principles were the same everywhere:

> In all these three it is the group that counts; the individual has a secondary place. There is nothing very unique about all this separately, and it is easy to find something

> equivalent to any of these three in other countries, especially in medieval times. (Nehru 1946: 244)

He further elaborated his 'functionalist' notion of an integrated traditional village society in the following text:

> ... The functions of each group or caste were related to functions of the other castes, and the idea was that if each group functioned successfully within its own framework, then society as a whole worked harmoniously. Over and above this, a strong and fairly successful attempt was made to create a common national bond which would hold all these groups together – the sense of a common culture, common traditions, common heroes and saints, and common land to the four corners of which people went on pilgrimage. This national bond was of course very different from present-day nationalism; it was weak politically, but socially and culturally it was strong. (Ibid.: 248)

Though Nehru did not celebrate the old 'village republics' of India as Gandhi did, the sources of their understanding of India's past seem to be common. Nehru too seems to have read the writings of colonial administrators and western scholars on the 'traditional Indian society' quite uncritically. This is best reflected in his comments on the 'old' agrarian economy. He writes:

> Originally the agrarian system was based on a cooperative or collective village. Individuals and families had certain rights as well as certain obligations, both of which were determined and protected by customary law. (Ibid.: 246)

He produced, almost verbatim, what Metcalfe and later Marx had said about the Indian village communities.[4]

> Foreign conquests brought war and destruction, revolts and their ruthless suppression, and new ruling classes relying chiefly on armed force.... The self-governing community, however, continued. Its break up began only under the British rule. (Ibid.: 246)

Similarly, in relation to village panchayats and political spirit of the traditional Indian village, he reinforced the prevailing notion about the village society as having been economically stagnant and community-oriented but democratically organised. The traditional social structure emphasised 'the duties of the individual and the group' and not 'their rights'.

> The aim was social security: stability and continuance of the group; that is of society. Progress was not the aim, and progress therefore had to suffer. Within each group, whether it was the village community, the particular caste, or the large joint family, there was a communal life shared together, a sense of equality, and democratic methods. (Ibid.: 252)

However, he also emphasised that such a system of village republics had long degenerated into a society that was marked by various ills. There was a clear shift in Nehru's discussion on village life as he moved closer to contemporary times. He appears to have become more and more critical of the past structures, particularly of caste based hierarchies, which, in his scheme of things, should have no place in modern societies. Unlike Gandhi, Nehru saw no virtues in reviving the traditional social order. His modernist critique of the village and caste system is best presented in the following passage from Discovery of India:

> … the ultimate weakness and failing of the caste system and the Indian social structure were that they degraded a mass of human beings and gave them no opportunities to get out of that condition—educationally, culturally, or economically.… In the context of society today, the caste system and much that goes with it are wholly incompatible, reactionary, restrictive, and barriers to progress. There can be no equality in status and opportunity within its framework, nor can there be political democracy, and much less, economic democracy. (Nehru 1946: 254)

This shift becomes even more evident as we move to his comments/writings on Indian rural society of the colonial period. Not only did he become more critical of the traditional social order but he also began to increasingly talk about the existing social and economic structures of the village society in terms of 'social classes'. The peasants/kisans and landlords were the two classes that he frequently made reference to.

His writings clearly reflect a modernist attitude to the village class structure. He, for example referred to the landlords as a 'physically and intellectually degenerate' class, which had 'outlived their day' (Nehru 1980: 52). On the other end, the peasants or 'the kisans, in the villages' constituted the real masses of India (Gopal 1973: 82).

The shift perhaps was also a consequence of his growing first hand encounters with the rural masses after the 1920s. He described quite lucidly the prevailing structure of agrarian relations while describing one such encounter with peasants in the following passage:

> I listened to their innumerable tales of sorrow, their crushing and ever-growing burden of rent, illegal extraction, ejectments from land and mud hut, beatings; surrounded on all sides by vultures who preyed on them—zamindar's agents, moneylenders, police; toiling all day to find that what they produced was not theirs and their reward was kicks and curses and a hungry stomach. (Nehru 1980: 52)

Nehru also developed his critique of the colonial rule through such accounts of the existing state of affairs in rural India. What he describes in the passage quoted above was not merely what he observed in a particular village. He saw landlordism as being organically linked to British rule. It was the British rulers who had in the first place implanted the landlord system in India 'with disastrous results' (Nehru 1946: 246) and they (the landlords) could survive in India 'only so long as an external power like the British government props them up' (ibid.: 58).

He also blamed the British for disturbing the old economic equilibrium of the village. They implanted exploitative agrarian relations and destroyed the local industry, taking away non-agricultural sources of employment that were available to the local people. Elaborating his argument on India's deindustrialisation, he writes:

> The Indian farmer who used to supplement his income by plying the *charkha* in his spare time was also suddenly deprived of his extra income. Weavers, carders and dyers became unemployed. They were forced to fall back on the land for livelihood, by

> cultivating the land or by working as labourers, but there was already enough pressure on the land. The result was that the majority of the people were compelled to act as farm labourers, and somehow keep alive.... And this poverty began from the time the British came here because they started their own trade while destroying ours. (Gopal 1972: 365)

Though he attributed the peasants' misery to their exploitation by landlords and the colonial rulers, he shared with western writers the popular opinion on the political character of Indian peasantry as being politically docile and fatalistic.

> Indian peasant has an amazing capacity to bear famine, flood, disease, and continuous grinding poverty—and when he could endure it no longer; he would quietly and almost uncomplainingly lie down in his thousands or millions and die. That was his way of escape. (Nehru 1980: 306)

How did he visualise the future of Indian rural society? How far did he agree and/or disagree with Gandhi?

Though Nehru and Gandhi seem to agree on the nature of traditional Indian village society, Nehru's critique of village life, as also of the British rule, are very different from those of Gandhi. Perhaps the most critical difference between Gandhi and Nehru was their attitude towards the question of class and the class structure of the Indian agrarian society. While Gandhi almost always spoke about the village in a populist language, in terms of village as a unit with an underlying assumption about the unity of its interests, Nehru recognised and, in his later writings, foregrounded the internal differences in the rural society, the contradictions between landlords and the peasantry. Similarly, while Gandhi advocated the need for reviving the 'essential spirit' of village life, Nehru wanted to transform the village social and economic structure by using modern technology and changing agrarian relations. The landlords and landlordism, in his scheme of things, would have no place in independent India.

The kisans, on the other hand, were the real 'masses of India'. The colonial rulers were not the only enemies that the kisans had. The local landlords were as much a problem. Their difficulties 'in the main related to such questions as rent, ejectment and possession of lands'. 'Swaraj would be of little avail if it did not solve' the problems of the kisans (Gopal 1973: 82).

The policies of land reforms introduced after independence were a direct translation of such thinking. If agriculture was to develop, it was necessary that we put 'an end to zamindari and jagirdari systems. We must ... eliminate all intermediaries and fix a limit for the size of holdings (Nehru 1954: 94).

Similarly, Nehru also had very different views on the place that industry would have in the Indian economy. While Gandhi thought that villages could largely be self-sufficient and rejected the modern cities for their being a sign of colonial domination, Nehru saw industrialisation as being inevitable. Industrial development and urbanisation would help in reducing the burden on land and therefore would be good even for those who would be left in the village. Addressing the Associated Chamber of Commerce in Calcutta in December 1947, he had said:

> ... while we want to help the peasants and agriculturalists, industry also is of dominant importance in India. Agriculture can produce wealth but it will produce more wealth (if) more people are drawn from agriculture and put in industry. In fact, in order to improve agriculture we must improve industry (*sic*). The two are allied. (Gopal 1986: 566)

He also differed with Gandhi on the use of modern technology in agriculture. Instead of celebrating the traditionalist streak among the cultivators, he criticised them for 'using outdated methods', and for being 'content with whatever little they produced'. In contrast to Gandhi, he thought that modern technology was good for farmers. They could produce twice or thrice as much as they did if they learnt new techniques of farming (Gopal 1997: 86–90).

However, he did share with Gandhi the need for a revival of handicrafts and cottage industry. The modern industry could not absorb all the surplus population, whatever may be its pace of development. 'Hundreds of millions will remain who would have to be employed chiefly in agriculture'. While development of the industry was necessary if we were to remain free, 'the development of heavy industry would not by itself solve the problem of the millions in this country'. Thus India needed to revive 'the village and cottage industry in a big way' (Nehru 1954: 84).

Need of reviving the cottage and small-scale industry was not the only point where Nehru spoke the language of Gandhi. He also shared with Gandhi his broad philosophical approach to the village (also see above his notion of the traditional Indian village in the beginning of this section). Though, economically the village of future India could not be self-sufficient, socially and politically his ideas were pretty much the same as those of Gandhi. The following text is useful evidence of this:

> The village, which used to be an organic and vital unit, became progressively a derelict area, just a collection of mud huts and odd individuals. But still the village holds together by some invisible link, and old memories revive. It should be easily possible to take advantage of these age-long traditions and to build up communal and cooperative concerns in the land and in the small industry. The village can no longer be self-contained economic unit ... but it can very well be a governmental and electoral unit, each such unit functioning as a self-governing community within the larger political framework and looking after the essential needs of the village ... I feel sure that the village should be treated as a unit. This will give truer and more responsible representation. (Nehru 1946: 534–35)

Thus, though Nehru's approach to industry and technology and the place they ought to have in the future of India were very different from Gandhi, he was not untouched by the influence of Gandhi. More crucially, perhaps, their sources of understanding India's past were mostly common. They both read the writings of colonial/western scholars on India rather uncritically. This seems particularly so with their understandings of the 'old' Indian village. The western writers, after all, had presented the Indian past in good light and these leaders had learnt much of their concepts of history and politics from the western education system.

It was left to B. R. Ambedkar, who hardly had any stakes in the glorification of traditional India, to develop a radical critique of the Indian village. Being a Dalit and having spent a part of his childhood in a village of Maharashtra, he knew what living in a village meant for a Dalit. He obviously had no attraction for orientalist notions of India that celebrated its past.

Ambedkar and Indian Village

When compared with Gandhi and Nehru, the influence of B. R. Ambedkar was rather limited, particularly during the movement for Indian independence. However, over the years, he has grown in stature. As Eleanor Zelliot has rightly pointed out, he is perhaps the only pre-independence leader who has continued to grow in fame and influence throughout the contemporary period (Zelliot 2001).

The significance of Ambedkar lies in his social background. Over the years, he has come to represent the most downtrodden sections of the Indian society, the 'untouchables' and the Dalits. Though like Gandhi and Nehru he too was well educated and had spent a good part of his youth in the west, he identified, almost completely, with the Dalit cause. This was reflected in his thinking and politics. Like Gandhi and Nehru he too wrote a great deal on India.[5]

As mentioned above, of the three ideologues of the freedom movement being compared here, Ambedkar was the only one who had a first-hand experience of village-life and that too of looking at it from below, as a Dalit child. Apart from having been born in a village, his last name, Ambavadekar, as it was initially registered in school, was also derived from his 'native' village called Ambavade. It was only later that a teacher in his school changed it to Ambedkar, giving him his own name (Keer 1962: 14).

Though his father was a mobile Dalit and was employed in a 'secular' occupation, Ambedkar could not escape the difficulties of his caste and class background during his childhood. The economic hardships that his family experienced during his childhood are quite starkly reflected in the fact that of the 14 children born to his mother, only five survived. Though he grew up to be a barrister with a degree in law and Doctor of Science from western universities, he could never forget the experiences of his childhood and the humiliations of being a Dalit. It is this experience that was, to a significant extent, to shape his political outlook as also his perspective on the village life. Thus, in Ambedkar we find, what could be called, a Dalitist view of the village.

Like most of his contemporaries, Ambedkar too spoke about the Indian society and the village life in civilisational terms. Despite recognising the obvious cultural diversities, the social structure of the Indian village was, for all of them, the same everywhere. However, unlike others, Ambedkar saw the Indian civilisation as being a Hindu civilisation. More importantly, he saw Dalits as not being a part of this Hindu society. The structure of village settlements too reflected this basic tenet. Quite like the Hindu civilisation, village too was divided:

> The Hindu society insists on segregation of the untouchables. The Hindu will not live in the quarters of the untouchables and will not allow the untouchables to live inside Hindu quarters. ... It is not a case of social separation, a mere stoppage of social

> intercourse for a temporary period. It is a case of territorial segregation and of a cordon sanitaire putting the impure people inside the barbed wire into a sort of a cage. Every Hindu village has a ghetto. The Hindus live in the village and the untouchables live in the ghetto. (Ambedkar 1948: 21–22)

Thus for Ambedkar, village presented a model of the Hindu social organisation, a microcosm. It was 'the working plant of the Hindu social order, where one could see the Hindu social order in operation in full swing'. Though he often used the expression Indian village, the village, for him, did not include the untouchables, who lived outside, in the 'ghetto'.

The Indian village was not a single unit. It was divided into two sets of populations: 'touchables' and 'untouchables'. The 'touchables' formed, what he called, 'the major community' and the untouchables 'a minor community'. The 'touchables' lived inside the village and the untouchables lived outside the village in separate quarters.

The touchables were economically the dominant community and commanded power; the untouchables were a 'dependent community' and a 'subject race of hereditary bondsmen'. The untouchables lived according to the codes laid down for them by the dominant 'touchable' major community. These codes laid guidelines regarding their habitations; the distance they ought to maintain from the 'Hindus'; the dress they should wear; the houses they should live in; the language they should speak; the names they should keep. They could not build houses having tiled roofs; they could not wear silver or gold jewellery (Moon 1979, 1989).

Though Ambedkar did refer to the Indian village and its casteist social structure in his earlier writings, most of his ideas on the subject were perhaps crystallised in response to the debates in the constituent assembly where many 'Hindu members' of the assembly made 'angry speeches' in 'support of the contention that the Indian Constitution should recognise the village as its base of the constitutional pyramid of autonomous administrative units with its own legislature, executive and judiciary' (1989: 19). In his well-known response to those who wanted village to be treated as the basic unit of Indian civilisation, he had said:

> I hold that these village republics have been the ruination of India.... What is the village but a sink of localism, a den of ignorance, narrow-mindedness and communalism? (Moon 994: 62)

His concern obviously emanated from the standpoint of the 'untouchables', for whom recognition of the village as a unit of legal structure of India would have been 'a great calamity' (Moon 1989: 19).

Though, as mentioned above, Ambedkar too was educated in the west, he was perhaps much more sceptical of western and colonial writings on the Indian society. While Gandhi and Nehru accepted the notion of 'village community' as a natural fact of Indian civilisation, Ambedkar perhaps saw it more in historical terms, as having been derived from the colonial/western imaginations of India, specifically from the writings of Sir Charles Metcalfe. He also thought that such a notion of village came to be accepted by the upper caste Hindus and the leaders of the independence movement because it projected them in a positive light. 'The average Hindu was always in ecstasy whenever he spoke of the Indian village. He regarded it as an ideal form of social organisation to which he believed there was no parallel anywhere in the world' (ibid.: 19).

The 'realistic picture' of village life was very different. For Ambedkar, the governing normative structure of the village was no way close to democracy. The village life was marked by experiences of exclusion, exploitation and untouchability. Not only did the members of upper/dominant castes make the untouchables live outside the village, in the ghetto, the untouchables were also excluded from most of the village festivities. 'When the whole village community was engaged in celebrating a general festivity such as Holi or Dasara, the untouchables must perform all menial acts which were preliminary to the main observance. These duties had to be performed without remuneration' (ibid.: 22).

Apart from the experiences of near complete domination, the untouchables were also exploited and oppressed by the upper castes. They were not allowed to acquire wealth in form of land or cattle; they could not practice agriculture. Even as labourers they could not demand reasonable wages. They must submit to the rates fixed or suffer violence (ibid.: 23). They lived a life that was full of humiliating experiences and dependency. There was only one source of livelihood open to them. It was 'the right to beg food from the Hindu farmers of the village. A large majority of the untouchables in the village were either servants or landless labourers. As village servants, they depended upon the Hindus for their maintenance, and had to go from door to door every day and collect bread or cooked food from the Hindus in return for certain customary services rendered by them to the Hindus' (ibid.: 24).

In his typically polemical style he concluded:

> This is the village republic of which the Hindus are so proud. What is the position of the untouchables in this Republic? They are not merely the last but are also the least... in this Republic there is no place for democracy. There is no room for equality. There is no room for liberty and there is no room for fraternity. The Indian village is a very negation of Republic. The republic is an Empire of the Hindus over the untouchables. It is a kind of colonialism of the Hindus designed to exploit the untouchables. The untouchables have no rights...They have no rights because they are outside the village republic and because they are outside the so-called village republic, they are outside the Hindu fold. (Ibid.: 25–26)

The 'Hindu domination' was not confined to the village. The local power/social structure was reflected at the macro/national level as well.

> From the capital of India down to the village level the whole administration is rigged by the Hindus. The Hindus are like the omnipotent almighty pervading all over the administration in all its branches having its authority in all its nooks and corners. (Ibid.: 104)

Ambedkar also contested the popular anthropological thesis about the ideological unity of the Hindu society that claims that ideologically the untouchables also subscribed to ideas of pollution and purity. Against the idea of 'cultural consensus' and 'reciprocity' as characteristics of the caste system, he draws an analogy between caste and class and looks at caste exactly in the terms in which Marx had talked about classes.

> The four varnas were animated by nothing but a spirit of animosity towards one another. There would not be slightest exaggeration to say that the social history of the Hindus is not merely of class struggle but class war fought with such bitterness that even the Marxists will find it difficult to cite parallel cases to match...It seems that the first class-struggle took place between the brahmins, kshatriyas and vaishyas on the one hand and the shudras on the other. (Ibid.: 193)

There is a remarkable continuity in his writings on the village. His critique of the village and caste system resembles quite closely those anthropological writings that tried to consciously look at caste from below (see, for example, Mencher 1975).

CONCLUSION

Gandhi, Nehru and Ambedkar were the three most important leaders of the modern India... Their legacy is also imbibed in the perspectives they articulated on India, its pasts and its possible futures. Their writings continue to be sources of inspiration for all those engaged in further consolidating Indian democracy in many different ways. Their legacies also reflect many of the dilemmas being faced by Indian society today.

The reformist vision of Gandhi, who wanted to construct a harmonious and self-contained village, uncorrupted by the modern life of the city and western technology continues to find its echoes in present times. It was only through the reconstruction of the village that India, for Gandhi, could recover its lost self and attain true freedom. Though not very widespread in the present-day India, his appeal remains quite powerful amongst those looking for alternatives to the conflict ridden, polluted and unlivable big cities.[...]

Nehru's modernist vision of the village has been the source of much of the official policies and programmes of rural development initiated by the government of India after independence, particularly during the 1950s and 1960s. Though he shared with Gandhi the notions of traditional Indian village having been a 'community' in the past, for him class divisions, backwardness and ignorance marked the actual existing villages. The question, for him was not to revive the old 'community' but to develop the village and the agriculture through new technology and abolition of 'outdated' structures of agrarian relations.[...]

Unlike Gandhi and Nehru, Ambedkar was a 'rebel'. He had neither the moral authority of Gandhi, nor the institutional power of Nehru. His influence, however, cannot be underestimated. Over the years, he has grown in stature and has emerged as a symbol of a potent Dalit identity all-over India. His writings articulate a 'subaltern view' on the village. When looked at from below, from the standpoint of those who were made to live outside the village and were treated as untouchables, the so-called virtues of traditional living turn into oppressive structures. The hope for the Dalits, therefore, did not lie in its revival/reconstruction, or for that matter, even in its development.[...]

Notwithstanding their differences on the nature of Indian village, there are many ways in which the three seem to agree ... they all spoke about the village in civilisational terms. The Indian village had a pan-Indian structure. Irrespective of the differences of region, language or culture, villages were the same everywhere. Village, perhaps, was the only 'concrete' denominator of the Indian nationhood. However,... their substantive notions of the empirical reality were shaped by a multitude of factors and the effects of their uses of such categories varied significantly. In other words, though orientalist/colonial categories provided them with conceptual resources; these categories could not completely limit/determine their politics and world views.[...]

Notes

1. There have been only a few sociologists, such as Desai 1948; Moore 1966; Dhanagare 1982, who have worked on the Indian nationalist movement.

2. For example, the early Indian sociologists like G. S. Ghurye (see Pramanick 1994; Upadhya 2002) and anthropologists like N. K. Bose (Sinha 1972) were deeply influenced by or were closely associated with the nationalist movement for independence.

3. Gandhi was born in 1869 in Porbandar in Gujarat. His family had been in the town for a long time. His grandfather was the administrator of Porbandar. Nehru's parents too had been urbanites. He was born in 1889 in the north Indian town of Allahabad in a prosperous and distinguished family of Kashmiri brahmins. His father was successful lawyer and admirer of western culture. Bhimrao Ambedkar was born in a village of Maharashtra called Mhow in 1891. His family belonged to the untouchable caste of mahar and came from the village Ambavadekar, located in the Ratnagiri district. His father was employed in the British Army.

4. Marx's writings on the Indian village communities too reflected a similar understanding (see, for a critical exposition of Marx's views on the Indian village community Habib 1995).

5. Most of his ideas on the Indian village are available in the fifth volume of his writings and speeches published by Government of Maharashtra in 1989 (edited by V. Moon), which were not easily available earlier.

References

Ambedkar, B. R. 1948. *The Untouchables: Who Were They and Why They Became Untouchables?* New Delhi: Amrit Book Company.

Beteille, A. 1980. 'The Indian Village: Past and Present'. In *Peasants in History: Essays in Honour* of *Daniel Thorner*, ed. E. J. Hobsbawm et al. Calcutta: Oxford University Press.

Brecher, M. 1959. *Nehru: A Political Biography*. London: Oxford University Press.

Breckenridge, C. A. and Peter van der Veer (ed.). 1993. *Orientalism and the Postcolonial Predicament: Perspectives on South Asia*. Philadelphia: University of Pennsylvania Press.

Breman, J. 1987. *The Shattered Image: Construction and Deconstruction of the Village in Colonial Asia*. Amsterdam: Comparative Asian Studies.

Breman, J., P. Kloos and A. Saith (ed.). 1997. *The Village in Asia Revisited*. Delhi: Oxford University Press.

Brown, J. M. 1989. *Gandhi: Prisoner of Hope*. New Haven and London: Yale University Press.

____. 1999. *Nehru*. London and New York: Longman.

Chakravarti, U. 1989. 'Whatever Happened to the Vedic Dasi? Orientalism, Nationalism and a Script for the Past'. In *Recasting Women: Essays in Colonial History*, ed K. Sangari and S. Vaid. New Delhi: Kali for Women.

Cohn, B. S. 1987. *An Anthropologist among the Historians and Other Essays*. Delhi: Oxford University Press.

____. 1996. *Colonialism and its Forms of Knowledge: The British in India*. Princeton: Princeton University Press.

Desai, A. R. 1948. *Social Background of Indian Nationalism*. Bombay: Popular Prakashan.

Dhanagare, D. N. 1982. *Peasant Movements in India 1920-50*. Delhi: Oxford University Press.

Dirks, N. B. 2001. *Castes of Mind: Colonialism and the Making of Modern India*. Princeton: Princeton University Press.

Embree, A. T. 1989. *Imagining India: Essays on Indian History*. Delhi: Oxford University Press.

Gandhi, M. K. 1958. *The Collected Works of Mahatma Gandhi*, vol. I. Delhi: Government of India.

____. 1963. *The Collected Works of Mahatma Gandhi*, vol. XI. Delhi: Government of India.

____. 1966. *The Collected Works of Mahatma Gandhi*, vol. XXI. Delhi: Government of India.

____. 1969. *The Collected Works of Mahatma Gandhi*, vol. XXXIII. Delhi: Government of India.

____. 1970. *The Collected Works of Mahatma Gandhi*, vol. XLI. Delhi: Government of India.

____. 1972. *The Collected Works of Mahatma Gandhi*, vol. LI. Delhi: Government of India.

____. 1974. *The Collected Works of Mahatma Gandhi*, vol. LIX. Delhi: Government of India.

____. 1975. *The Collected Works of Mahatma Gandhi*, vol. LXII. Delhi: Government of India.

____. 1976. *The Collected Works of Mahatma Gandhi*, vol. LXIV. Delhi: Government of India.

____. 1977a. *The Collected Works of Mahatma Gandhi*, vol. LXVIII. Delhi: Government of India.

____. 1977b. *The Collected Works of Mahatma Gandhi*, vol. LXIX. Delhi: Government of India.

____. 1978. *The Collected Works of Mahatma Gandhi*, vol. LXXI. Delhi: Government of India.

____. 1979a. *The Collected Works of Mahatma Gandhi*, vol. LXXVI. Delhi: Government of India.

____. 1979b. *The Collected Works of Mahatma Gandhi*, vol. LXXVII. Delhi: Government of India.

____. 1980. *The Collected Works of Mahatma Gandhi*, vol. LXXX. Delhi: Government of India.

____. 1982. *The Collected Works of Mahatma Gandhi*, vol. LXXXVI. Delhi: Government of India.

Gopal, S. 1972. *Selected Works of Jawaharlal Nehru*, vol. 3 (Old Series). New Delhi: Orient Longman.

____. 1973. *Selected Works of Jawaharlal Nehru*, vol. 5 (Old Series). New Delhi: Orient Longman.

____. 1986. *Selected Works of Jawaharlal Nehru*, vol. 4 (New Series). Delhi: Oxford University Press.

____. 1997. *Selected Works of Jawaharlal Nehru*, vol. 20 (New Series). Delhi: Oxford University Press.

Habib, I. 1995. *Essays in Indian History: Towards a Marxist Perspective*. New Delhi: Tulika.

Inden, R. 1990. *Imagining India*. Oxford: Basil Blackwell.

Jodhka, Surinder S. 'From "Book View" to "Field View": Social Anthropological Constructions of the Indian Village', *Oxford Development Studies* 26 (3): 311–31.

Keer, D. 1962. *Dr Ambedkar: Life and Mission*. Bombay: Popular Prakashan.

Khilnani, S. 1998. *The Idea of India*. New York: Farrar Straus Giroux.

Mencher, J. P. 1975. 'Viewing Hierarchy from the Bottom Up'. In *Encounters and Experience: Personal Accounts of Fieldwork*, ed. A. Beteille and T. N. Madan. Delhi: Allied Publishers.

Moon, V. 1979. *Dr Babasaheb Ambedkar Writings and Speeches*, vol. 5. Bombay: Government of Maharashtra.

____. 1989. 'Untouchables or the Children of India's Ghetto'. In *Dr Babasaheb Ambedkar Writings and Speeches*, vol. 5. Bombay: Government of Maharashtra.

____. 1994. 'Draft Constitution: Discussion'. In *Dr Babasaheb Ambedkar Writings and Speeches*, vol. 13. Bombay: Government of Maharashtra.

Moore, B. Jr. 1966. *Social Origins of Dictatorship and Democracy: Lord and Peasant in the Making of Modern World*. Boston: Bacon Press.

Mukherjee, R. (ed.). 1993. *The Penguin Gandhi Reader*. New Delhi: Penguin.

Nehru, J. N. 1946. *The Discovery of India*. New York: The John Day Company.

____. 1980 [1936]. *An Autobiography*. New Delh: Oxford University Press.

____. 1954. *Jawaharlal Nehru's Speeches*, vol. II. New Delhi: Publications Division, Ministry of Information and Broadcasting, Government of India.

Parel, J. A. (ed.) 1997. *Hind Swaraj and Other Writings*. Cambridge: Cambridge University Press.

Pramanick, S. K. 1994. *Sociology of G. S. Ghurye*. Jaipur: Rawat Publications.

Sinha, S. 1972. *Aspects of Indian Culture and Society: Essays in Felicitation of Professor Nirmal Kumar Bose*. Calcutta: The Indian Anthropological Society.

Srinivas, M. N. 1955. 'Village Studies and Their Significance'. In *Village Profiles*, vol. 1, ed. D. N. Majumdar. Lucknow: Ethnographic and Folk Culture Society.

____. 1987. 'The Indian Village: Myth and Reality'. In *The Dominant Caste and Other Essays*. Delhi: Oxford University Press.

Uberoi, P. (ed.). 1993. *Family, Kinship and Marriage in India*. Delhi: Oxford University Press.

Upadhya, C. 2002. 'The Hindu Nationalist Sociology of G. S. Ghurye'. *Sociological Bulletin* 51 (1): 28–57.

Raymond, W. 1973. *The Country and the City*. New York: Oxford University Press.

Zelliot, E. 2001. 'The Meanings of Ambedkar'. In *Dalit Identity and Politics*, ed. Ghanshyam Shah. New Delhi: Sage.

Section II

Social and Cultural Life

Introduction

In popular imagination the village has often been seen as a site of 'tradition', a social and cultural system which is relatively stable and is generally governed by custom and communitarian norms. Caste and religion have been the most important customary institutions in the Indian context. This section has six chapters focusing on themes of religion, caste and traditional property regimes. Though the chapters deal with these 'traditional' structures, they do not present a static view.

Two chapters in this section reveal how the practice of religion is closely linked to everyday material life of different communities. The chapter by Pratap C. Aggarwal, interrogates the relationship of the institution of caste with religious identity in a village of Rajasthan. Though 'sanskritisation', as a process of mobility within the caste system, works in the village, it is closely determined by power equations. It is only after the local chamars got agricultural land that they could give up their traditional occupations and start imitating the upper castes and sanskritise themselves. The Meos, Muslims by religion, were well-integrated into the local caste structure as the landowning 'dominant caste' and did not fore-ground their religious identity until the 'Partition', when they lost their monopoly over agricultural land. Institutionalisation of democratic political process also encouraged other religious groups to come together as 'viable communities' for a share in the local power.

In Chapter 4, based on his study of a U.P. village, G. K. Lieten argues that the prevailing system of status/caste hierarchy and economic interest directly influences the villagers' identification with Hindutva politics. The idea of Hindu-Muslim schism in the village found its support primarily within the dominant/upper castes. Those lower down in the caste hierarchy and landownership did not find these religious identities to be of much relevance in the everyday political life of the village.

The next three chapters in this section deal with the changes and continuities in caste-based inequalities. In his study of rural Karnataka, G. K. Karanth found that the new technology has had profound influence on the traditional system of *jajmani* relations. However, while the old structure of social and economic relations had indeed undergone many changes and choices for dependent castes had grown, the hegemonic control of the dominant communities continued. They were still able to command a certain degree of authority over the 'lower' castes.

The chapter by K. L. Sharma, based on a study of six villages of Rajasthan, reinforces Karanth's argument. A majority of the caste groups were no longer employed exclusively in their traditional occupations and could easily move to a 'secular' occupation. However, the choice of a new occupation and rejection of the old one was generally based on pragmatic considerations. Some castes had discarded their caste occupations because of their polluting nature or stigma attached to them. But it did not produce equality or resulted in end caste discrimination. Only theoretically, was the process of modernisation 'open' to all. Practically, it was only the rich and dominant who were able to benefit from the new technology.

The chapter by Mukul Sharma provides a vivid account of the social and economic life of a poor Scheduled Caste community, the Musahars of rural North Bihar. Their experience of untouchability was closely associated with their economic deprivation. However, over the years, some of them had become mobile and had migrated out of the village, to Punjab and to urban centres in the rest of India in search of employment and livelihood. Though they continued to remain poor, Mukul argues, migration provided them with a sense of dignity and enabled them to earn enough for meeting basic survival needs.

The final chapter in this section presents a critique of the popular view that traditional communities 'share a close relationship with environment and have complex regulatory mechanisms of their own to conserve village resources'. Based on his study of hill villages of North India, Jishnu Das argues that 'the conservationist view over-romanticises the historical evidence on common resource management in Garhwal. Even though it might seem that regulatory and access restrictions were consciously implemented by villages, these were simply responses to the politico-economic situation during this period rather than institutions designed with an aim to conserve scarce resources'.

4

Inclusive View of Religion

A Rural Discourse in Uttar Pradesh[*]

G. K. Lieten

Muzaffarnagar is one of the richest districts in the country. The prosperity in the district is abundantly visible in the form of brick houses and mansions to live in and tractors to work on. Indicative of the polarisation as a consequence of the commercialisation of agriculture in the region is the fact that whereas one-third of the families do not even possess a bicycle, more than 40 per cent of the total sample have a television set, and 12 per cent possess a mobike. A television set in the house of a landless labourer or small peasant is still an exception. In the house of middle peasants, it has become a normal sight. For rich peasants, not only a television, but a mobike and a tractor have become integral assets.

The relative poverty of the agricultural labourers and poor peasants, on the other hand, usually does not amount to destitution. Agricultural wages are reasonably high (an equivalent of 8–10 kg of wheat), and the occasional seasonal migration helps many families to overcome the lean periods. Economic conditions of these families, contrary to what has been predicted as a consequence of the green revolution, have not worsened. Downward mobility of the agricultural labour class was experienced as frequently as upward mobility (for a more extensive treatment, see Lieten 1994a).

On one issue practically all the villagers are tuned in unison: despite the economic progress (or because of the economic progress), social quality of life is deteriorating. The changes in economic activities have had a manifold impact on social praxis. Even in the past (Patel et al. 1977: 83) solidarity (within the *viradari*) and the traditional *bhaichara* may have been more fiction than fact, but the differentiation which has occurred in the wake of the green revolution has made the break in solidarity even more tangible.

---

* This chapter has been extracted from a longer paper published by the author in the *Economic and Political Weekly* 31 (23): 1411–16, 1996.

This chapter is based on an intensive field study carried out in the Muzaffarnagar district, a BJP stronghold, in western Uttar Pradesh.

Complaints about a deterioration in mores and norms often involve references to *asuraksha*, insecurity. The discourse on insecurity and criminalisation usually deals with virtual reality. The collective assessment of decreasing cordiality and increasing insecurity is likely to be based on real stories of the immediate neighbourhood, on twisted stories of adjoining villages and on invented stories of the wider area. In the case of the dominant castes, it is probably also induced by the weakening of caste dominance. Whereas hitherto there was compliance and order, nowadays there is some defiance, and therefore, disorder. Many villagers, made insecure by varied developments, prefer to refer to the present age as the *kaliyug*. Under circumstances of injustice, disorder and misery, the memories of the *satiayug*, age of justice, honesty and rectitude can bring succour.

Political Polarisation

The area has been known as a bulwark of the various avatars of the Janata Dal . Since Charan Singh left the Congress Party in 1967, and, in 1969, started the Bharatiya Kranti Dal (BKD) and later the Bharatiya Lok Dal, which then merged into the Janata Dal, the villages in Muzaffarnagar had voted for the BKD and the Janata Dal. The bhaichara loyalty of the Jats to Charan Singh may have been real, but the allegiance to his incumbents has dissipated. Election victories of the Janata Dal in 1989, and of the Bharatiya Janata Party (BJP) in 1991 and 1993, are likely to have been helped by the fatafat factor (i.e., quick voting, in fact, stuffing of the ballot boxes), and by the process of churning which caused various swings. Yet, the strong electoral showing of the BJP remains to be explained.

Through a series of field studies, we have attempted to check the actual political preferences, castewise and classwise. This could provide us with an idea about the 'homogeneity' of the religious identity. Does Hindutva reflect inter-class homogeneity, or does it rather reflect an upper-class design?

The field studies suggest that around 10 per cent to 20 per cent of the villagers do not have political preferences. The reason, for some of them, is utter disappointment with politicians.[1] Others, usually among the poor villagers, just claim ignorance of politics, and will not be enticed into stating a political preference.[2]

Usually, the vote is decided collectively, according to the general tendency in the jat 'viradari'. In 1991, in order to reach a compromise between the Jat factions, the best solution thought of was that the 'big vote' (for New Delhi) should go to Chandrashekar's Janata Party and the 'small vote' (for Lucknow) to the BJP. At that time, such was the shrouded advice of Tikait. In view of the dissatisfaction with the Congress and the Janata Dal, the BJP at that time was looked upon as an alternative delivery system. This choice did not appear to be related to its religious appeal.

The BJP has a recent and narrow electoral base. Its ideological base, on which we shall dwell later, is even thinner. The class source of the BJP victory in the 1991 and 1993 elections in the constituency seemed clear on the basis of the village studies in early 1993: 11 out of 18 BJP supporters, in our sample were rich peasants, and all the supporters, with one exception, had made it to the grade of TV owners. The real ideological commitment to the BJP, however, came with a mobike. One write-up in *The Times of India* (24 October 1990), with a sneering reference to the upper middle-class car owners of the urban BJP support base, went under the heading 'Toyota Hinduism'. In Muzaffarnagar, the staunch BJP backers, without exception, own a motorbike.

Some of the Jat supporters defended their choice in the language of religion, but usually these very same people were also conscious of the material advantage (*labh*) which the Muslim-Hindu conflict could deliver. Although reasonably large and successful landowners, they know that their children shall have to turn to business and jobs, and that they shall have to face competition from Muslims in the labour market. Charan Singh, a rich peasant and shop owner, actually thinks only in terms of the labh which a BJP government will bring. He actually, like many Jats, is not religious, and, moreover, is of the opinion that the BJP should not interfere with temples and mosques. In his opinion, although a non-believer himself, a religious building should not be destroyed. Probably not informed by religious nationalism, and possibly for the simple reason that all other shops are owned by Muslims, he nevertheless wants the Muslims to leave for Pakistan.

> I am having a shop here, and all the other shops are owned by Muslims. They prefer Pakistan, not India. When Pakistan wins in hockey, they celebrate as if it were diwali. Now look, suppose I am living with you and have food with you, but you are in love with somebody else, what should I do? They should have gone to Pakistan.

The shift from the Congress and the Janata Dal was initiated and executed electorally by the dominant rich peasant Jats. Many of the less wealthy (ex-)voters complain, however, that since the BJP allegedly has been interested only in the temple issue, during its reign nothing has been done for the peasants. Randhir Singh is one of the middle peasants who had decided to give the BJP a chance, but he has become dissatisfied:

> Its policy on the Hindu-Muslim conflict is not good; it is bad. And also, they are not looking after the peasants. It is true that they are a Baniya party. That is why they have increased the fertiliser prices. So I cannot support them any longer and I want to shift, but it is very difficult to decide. All these parties have let us down.

The dilemma under which many middle and rich peasants had to make up their mind is epitomised in the last sentence. During the BJP administration, they had wished to shift back to the Congress, and Tikait even invited the prime minister to come and share the platform in Sisauli on conditions that the Congress would promise major concessions. The Congress, however, opted for a reiteration of the new economic policy, and the deal fell through.

The Congress, even after the exit of the Nehru *parivar* from politics in 1992, could still count on considerable support, although not a solid one. Many of the poor and landless families still remember the days of Indira Gandhi. In those days they felt that they had somebody who was concerned about them, and who tried to implement some social policies. The benefits did not necessarily reach them since between Delhi and their village, a whole battery of government officials siphoned off most of it, but her sympathy with and concern for the poor people was reassuring and promising. Many of these voters, or aspirant voters, remained with the Congress till 1992, or returned to the Congress for negative reason: there was no viable alternative as yet. They considered the BJP as a party of capitalists and traders who want to divide the people by creating chaos and religious genocide.

Of all the people in the early 1993 village sample who stated a party preference, 47 per cent opted for the Congress, 30 per cent for the Janata Dal and only 16 per cent for BJP.[3] An alternative political formation appeared to emerge in late 1993. In the 1993 state elections, the Socialist Party (SP) received 22.2 per cent of the votes, and the Janata Dal an additional 28.1 per cent. The BJP won the constituency with 39 per cent votes. And the Congress? It secured only 2.2 per cent votes.

From field reports, we got the impression that, given the division among the Jats, the 1993 elections were conducted fairly democratically. What thus appears to have occurred is a political polarisation after the demise of the multi-class Congress Party. The hypothesis that the BJP attracted the richer half and the Samajwadi Party, and to an extent the Janata Dal, the poorer half of the electorate, however, needs to be corrected.

On the basis of a survey conducted in 1994 among 213 respondents in the area (Table 4.1), we can apportion the political preferences classwise and castewise.[4] Although there was no straightforward correlation, some correlations could be established nevertheless. Whereas the votes of the landless were fairly evenly spread over various parties, one-third of the poor peasants opted for the BJP and close to 50 per cent of the middle and the rich peasants voted in favour of Janata Dal, i.e., the party of Charan Singh and his son Ajit Singh who soon afterwards defected to the Congress. The introduction of the Mandal Commission report was one of the reasons for Ajit Singh to move away from the Janata Dal. His supporters, with a few exceptions, were clear that any sort of reservation for harijans and OBCs was wrong.

TABLE 4.1: Political Preferences: Statuswise and Castewise, 1994
Percentages

	Janata	Congress	BJP	SP	None	Frequency (Absolute)
Poor	26	12	25	17	20	114
Middle	42	14	25	13	6	69
Rich	46	7	27	20	–	30
Brahmin	10	25	55	5	5	20
Jat	49	9	20	18	4	77
OBC	14	8	40	22	16	50
SC	12	24	23	14	27	42
Muslim	88	–	–	8	4	24
Total	34	12	24	16	14	213

A somewhat greater demarcation of political preferences could be observed in the case of caste. Muslims and brahmins had diametrically opposed preferences: the aversion of the former for the Congress and the BJP was matched by the affinity of the latter for these parties. The Jats were clearly with the Ajit Singh wing of Janata Dal. The preferences of the OBC and SC were spread over various parties, albeit with a specific preference for the BJP. This presumable 'popularity' of the BJP shall have to be contextualised.

The field material allows us to indicate the direction of the shift. The poor families had spread their options. Their shift towards the BJP was a swing away from the Congress and, to a lesser extent, from the Janata Dal. The gains of the SP came mainly from the Janata Dal, particularly from poor peasant households. The losses of the Janata Dal were compensated by the return of rich peasants, and even more so of middle peasants, from the BJP. It is typical of this area for various parties to count support among different socio-economic groups.

The political churning between 1991 and 1993 elections indeed caused multiple shifts: middle and rich peasants from the BJP and the Congress to the Janata Dal, agricultural labourers and poor peasants from the Janata Dal to SP, poor peasants from Congress to BJP. We did not notice any shift towards the Congress. The shift which had occurred reflects a dissatisfaction of the middle and rich peasantry with the agrarian policies of the 1991–93 BJP government, and of the poor and non-Jat households with the Jat dominance: the BJP at that time offered them an escape avenue from the local power enigma.[5] At a later stage, we shall find that this generally did not imply an ideological alliance with Hindutva.

Communalism

Many Jats explicitly state that they are not preoccupied with the 'Hindu Dharm'. Dharamvir, who has called her own sons 'a little bit chamars' for frequenting the lower caste people more than she likes, may stand as a typical example of many Jat women: caste conscious, but hardly religious. Of course, she knows the name of Ram, but she does not do anything at all (*kutch nehi*). Jats are not supposed to worship, although some people occasionally fast in honour of Durga, and some women attend a satsang. The Jats, as a culturally dominant caste, have even effected a reverse type of sanskritisation: a number of brahmins have adapted to the 'little tradition' and have de-sanskritised their religious practice.

The Hindutva storm which has been blowing over U.P. from 1990 has prompted some of the brahmins and Jats to adopt overtly religious practices. The village temple, which had been lying unused, except for an occasional visit by brahmin ladies on their fasting day, has been renovated and a loudspeaker now helps to broadcast kirtans in the morning hours. The form is religious, the content is political. It is aimed at awakening the Hindus.

Motorised BJPwallas like Kalyan Singh claim that the Hindus were asleep. Kalyan Singh has only 2.5 acres of land, but as a government employee in a strategic position, he earns a good living. The motorised Hindu speaks the ethical language of Hinduism and civilisational values. Although the interests of the kisan have been hit by the BJP, after all it is a party of businessmen, he still favours them:

> Yes, the Jats were awake, but not in religious matters. The Hindus were sleeping. The temple in the village was lying unused. That has changed now. We have purchased a sound installation, and every morning kirtans are being sung for the solace of the whole village. Mohammedans and Christians have always been conscious about their religion and have propagated it. We also should have priests to do that.

Since there is no benchmark to compare with, it is hard to infer whether the Hindus have woken or not. Some may have decided to stand up to the so-called danger of Muslim domination, but they are very few in numbers anyway. Denigrating references such as 'pseudo-secularism' (the pampering of Muslims) which are paradigmatic in the urban debate have their rural equivalents, but only on the fringe of the village idiom. The grand discussions on the Shah Bano case[6] and Pakistani agents do not cut much ice in the rural context. Muslims and Hindus belong to all classes and all castes, and have very similar life styles, an identical language (Haryanvi) and a semiotic alignment. Close-range lived-in experience has taught them the overriding commonness of culture and interests. The only aspect in which the Muslims in this area may deviate from the local social texture is in the attitude towards family planning.[7]

Straightforward communal remarks are rare. In a village sample of 149 respondents, we got statements from nine persons to the effect that Muslims should change their ways. They argued that all of those who have more sympathy for Pakistan than for India should be asked to leave. The others can be allowed to stay back, but on condition that they abide by the rules of 'Hindu Rashtra' and adhere to family planning. If they would not, the occasional respondent maintained, Hindustan may come under the domination of the Muslims. We have also noticed that even those who expressed anti-Muslim sentiments did so on various grounds. Even in their case, religion appeared to take a back seat. Surprisingly, four of these nine Muslim-baiters were specifically opposed to the destruction of the mosque at Ayodhya on the ground that a religious site should never be destroyed. Of the other five persons, one Rajput teacher and one Jat peasant, both with an allegiance to the Congress, took reactionary positions on each and every ideological issue. A brahmin doctor desired revenge for the 'minority-baiting pseudo-secularism' which he sees everywhere. The example of the Indian cricket team ('a Hindu team with a Muslim captain') is foremost in his mind. Another person had taken to the BJP line because Tikait at that time had told him to do so, but now he realises that it will be dangerous for the country if Hindus and Muslims fight each other. A Jat who is an MSc and now works on one-fifth share of 15 acres of family land, has the following explanation to make:

> Yes, I do believe in God, as an abstract power, but I don't practise or worship, and so I never go to the temple. But it was justified to demolish the mosque at Ayodhya, not because of revenge or something like that. No, it is a matter of correction of an historic injustice. Babar had taken our temple, and now we have taken it back. Now, if you ask me whether there is a difference between a mandir, a masjid and a gurudwara, I must

> say that there is no difference, and I must also say that this has been a political game which is not good for the nation. But even then I support the issue because when India was divided, the Muslims should have gone to Pakistan, and they have stayed, and now they are making more children and they are going to overtake us.

We have given the long statement for two reasons: many elements reappear in the stories others narrate, and also because Sarita Devi, his wife, has a totally different story to tell. The marital ideological discord illustrates the ongoing multivariate discourse which was thrown up in the wake of the Muslim-Hindu riots and the dramatic news coming in from Ayodhya. The happenings had engrossed everybody and had coerced them into a stand. It is an issue on which the women in our sample, with the exception of one brahmin and two Jat women, have outrightly disapproved of the masjid demolition. The stand taken by Sarita Devi, however, is typical in the sense that she not only defends the unity of Hindus and Muslims, but also opposes the caste cleavages. Hers is a religious belief which could have been taken straight from the pages of Akbar's *din-ilahi* and which is a perfect example of religious tolerance. Her testimony tells of the Indian tradition of tolerance and inclusiveness, rather than of dichotomy and dualism:

> To my mind all castes, all harijans and all Muslims are one. They are all children of God. They have one and the same blood. There is one God, and there is no need to go to mandir or masjid to worship Him. The battle for the mandir or masjid is therefore absolutely useless. Those who want to worship, they can do so anywhere. It is the purity of the soul, the willingness to do good work, not to hurt others, that is worship, that is religion. The rest is politics and fooling the people. They have raised a wall of Hindus and Muslims, and they are instigating them to kill each other. This is not a good thing. They are all sons of God.

It is unmistakably an ecumenical position. Religion is seen as an individual affair, from which government should stay away. India should remain a secular state, and Ram, Bhagwan, Khuda and Allah are all names for the same god. A mosque or a temple once constructed becomes a house of god, and should never be destroyed. The destruction of the Babri Masjid, a house of god, therefore was a sacrilegious act.

Not a Hindu State

In 1994, one and a half year after the in-depth interviews conducted in the above village sample, we conducted a survey among 213 respondents (155 males and 58 females).[8] Among others, we formulated two statements, framed positively and negatively, on the position of Hindus and Muslims in India. We got similar replies on both statements: 76 per cent of the male respondents and 72 per cent of the female respondents considered both religious communities as citizens of a multi-religious state, with equal rights and equal claims to citizenship. On the other hand, around one-fifth of the Hindu respondents were inclined to discriminate against the Muslims.

Whereas the brahmins were neatly divided on the issue, Jat and SC respondents were generally of the opinion that there should not be any discrimination between the two religious communities. As many as 34 of the 41 SC respondents were vehement in their opinion that India should not be considered a Hindu country and that Muslims should have equal rights in all respects. The OBC respondents were more ambivalent, mainly because of the opinion prevalent among the economically advantaged groups.

This actually turned out to be a general pattern: the higher the position in the socio-economic hierarchy, in terms of land-ownership, education and economic status, the more frequent the position that India belongs to the Hindu community, and that Muslims should be treated as second-class citizens. To be more precise: more than one-third of the rich Hindus rejected the idea of Hindu-Muslim equality in a secular Indian state. Among the poorest households, this idea was practically absent (Table 4.2). These findings do suggest that the zeal for Hindutva is likely to be informed by the class position.

TABLE 4.2: The Normative Character of the Indian State

Category	Hindu	Secular	Frequency
Brahmin	8	12	20
Jat	17	58	75
OBC	13	36	49
SC	7	34	41
Muslim	0	24	24
Very poor	1	19	20
Poor	14	75	89
Middle	18	50	68
Rich	5	7	12
Very rich	7	13	20

Note: Information based on 213 respondents, of which only four did not have an opinion.

Ayodhya as a divide and rule game, as 'politics of chair' as the merry-go-round of the leaders (*netao ki chak*) are crisp summaries of the stand taken not only by Muslims,[9] but by most OBCs and SCs, and by many male and female Jats as well. Nevertheless, the BJP's inflammatory message that Babar in the 16th century raided the temple which was erected on Ram Janmabhumi has spread to the nooks and corners of the country. In the regions where we conducted research, this historical interpretation fell on fertile ground. The message has convinced one out of every three Hindu males that the mandir indeed had been destroyed by Babar, and therefore it was justified to demolish the Babri Masjid. Most of them see it as a rectification of the historic wrongdoing, and some, like Bhawar Singh, a Jat middle peasant, have changed their mind: 'I do not know what proof was given of the Ram Janmabhumi. Yes, I ran behind the BJP as a fool, like a real Jat. Half of us don't have brains.' His count turned out to be a good guess: 49 per cent of the Hindus were now opposed to the construction of a temple at Ayodhya. The others did not have a shortage of brains. They used their brains differently: although the wilful destruction, for a number of them, was unpalatable, their assumption often was that since the mosque had been removed anyway, the best solution would be to construct the temple as soon as possible so as to smother the communal fire.

Whereas the brahmins were clearly in favour of temple construction, a majority of Jats were opposed. Especially, OBC males and SC males were neatly divided over the issue; their female counterparts were generally in favour of temple construction (see statements on religion in Table 4.3). They were not so much interested in the temple, as in having the problem sorted out as soon as possible. They had preferred the court to settle the issue, and in the post-demolition context, they are not pleased if only a temple were to be constructed. They proposed many alternatives: the area should have both masjid and mandir, or none, or a school and a hospital may be built because there are already enough temples in Ayodhya.

TABLE 4.3: Statements on Religion in Politics, Muzaffarnagar, 1994

	N	Temple Construction Necessary	Religion-Based Party Politics	Misuse of Ram's Name in Politics
Hindu males	136	44.8	4.5	68.4
Hindu females	49	69.4	4.1	67.3
Brahmins	20	75.0	5.0	60.0
Jats	75	38.7	4.0	77.3
OBC	49	59.2	6.5	55.1
SC	41	56.1	2.5	75.6
Muslims	24	0.0	0.0	0.0
Very poor	20	50.0	0.0	80.0
Poor	89	47.2	4.6	69.7
Middle	68	43.5	2.9	69.6
Rich	12	54.5	0.0	81.8
Very rich	20	36.8	5.6	89.5

Note: Based on 213 respondents, of which 209 cases were internally consistent. Figures close to 5.0 indicate strong agreement, on a scale from 1.0 to 5.0.

The high percentage of Hindu women (69 per cent) in favour of the construction of a temple does not necessarily signify an ex-post approval of the destruction of the Babri Masjid and of the appropriation of religious symbols for political ends. In order to get a further indication of their stand vis-à-vis religion and politics, we have confronted our respondents with a number of statements relating to the introduction of religious elements into politics. The statements used for the purpose included the expediency of organising political parties along religious lines, and the necessity of more religious leaders getting involved in politics. Both statements got by and large negative responses. Only eight Hindus thought it expedient to organise political parties along religious lines. The insignificant number suggests, as has been argued above, that the appeal of the BJP, at least in this Jat-dominated area, is related much more to secular factors than to its proclaimed defence of religion as such. We consider this to be a very significant finding, the more so since the advocates of the construction of a temple at Ayodhya were in a majority.

In its political campaigns, the BJP leadership, directly or through its VHP intermediaries, had profusely made use of the Ram icon. The reaction to the statement that the name of Ram had been misused in the political game around the Ayodhya controversy can be gauged from the response to the statements on religion (Table 4.3). The OBC respondents, it should be noted, were least inclined to agree with the statement. Particularly, Jats and SC respondents, apart from Muslims, were of the opinion that the name of Ram had been misused in the political power game. Landless Chamars and Bhangis or Valmikis have more fundamental wishes than the defence of a religious community. Fullo, in her complaints about decreasing employment opportunities and wages which do not keep level with rising prices, recollects the days of Indira Gandhi when to the poor people explicit benefits such as land distribution were still possible. Those benefits, she argues, will not come from adding more religion to politics:

> I worship the idols kept in my house, but I know that they will never provide me with bread. It is only through work that we can make a living. For that we need employment. We need factories in the villages or we need land. There is still 250 bighas of land lying vacant in this village, and so many rich people have too much land. Indira at least helped us.

The village discourse, especially in the houses of the poor folk, informs us that the simple village logic stands for practical tolerance. Revenge and punishment for misdeeds done in the distant past cannot be allowed for it would set in motion a whole process of retaliation. The stand is a note of warning against politicians who want to undo a historic wrongdoing with a new wrongdoing: the present day Muslims cannot be punished for 'misdeeds' which have occurred in a different context in history. Moreover, the plea continues, Muslims have been living here peacefully, and there is no obvious reason why the cordial relation should be disturbed after more than four decades of independent India.

Another line of argument in the village discourse against religious politics starts from the premise that a political party was behind the Hindu revival movement. Since political parties have never helped the people, and have never helped the peasants, the question then asked is: 'If politics works against the people, then how can Hindu politics work in the interests of the people?' A majority of the Hindus in the area prefer not to be fooled by *netajis* and *lalajis*, even if they get dressed up in saffron robes. Dharamvir is a small peasant with a BA degree who in 1991 had voted for the BJP, but has never swallowed their arguments:

> God has created all of us, and he is supposed to be there for the mental relief and happiness of the people, and the people are not supposed to be there for the service and happiness of God. So the BJP should make a policy not for the benefit of Ram, who is not a god anyway, but for the people, and on this point their policy is anti-people. They are trying to capture power through the backdoor in the name of religion. Some local people have supported them in their game. I did not like it, but I alone could not go against their verdict.

Conclusion

The mainstream tradition in Indian scholarship, and in Indian politics, has been the secular approach. Its many excellent historians (Romila Thapar, R. S. Sharma, Irfan Habib, Sumit Sarkar, Bipan Chandra, Barun De, to name only a few) and a plethora of other stalwarts in their slipstream have analysed the emergence of the Indian subcontinent in terms of a secular process. The Indian nation which came to be established was conceived in the context of a secular and democratic state. It embodied the ideals which had wafted in from the enlightenment era.

This analysis has drawn flak from authors in the post-modernist school who, in a neo-orientalist appraisal, have come to the conclusion that India cannot but be steeped in a religious discourse and frame of mind. From afar and from above, the people down below are projected as basically being replica of the people who were described as religious, spiritual and transcendental by the nineteenth century orientalists.

At a general level, the neo-orientalist approach is an unequivocal denial of the probability and the desirability of universal values, ambitions and aspirations. The abandonment of the ideal of secularism presumably has a class echo to it. It is probably not those who are suffering from injustice and exploitation, who have abandoned secularism. In the words of O'Neill (1995: 1): 'No, it is not these people who have abandoned idealism, universalism, truth and justice. It is those who already enjoy these things who have denounced them on behalf of the others.'

The postulates at the general level have been tested in the local environment. We have chosen an area in which the BJP had a strong electoral showing and in which the rural poor, inclusive of the SC segment, unlike in many other areas of U.P., had voted for the BJP. The field data have thrown up a number of interesting findings relevant to the debate on the role of religion and of political parties riding on religious symbols and values. They basically confirm earlier findings in Lieten (1996) on other areas in Uttar Pradesh, and support the general views held in Engineer (1989, 1995), Graham (1993), Gopal (1991), Balasubramanian (1992), and a host of others, including a newly emerging post-modernist interpretation, such as Ashis Nandy et al. (1995). The latter (1995: 78) consider Hindu nationalism as 'an illegitimate child of modern India, not of Hindu traditions', and as a political movement with an instrumental use of religion as an ideology the roots of which 'lay primarily in the Brahmanic, westernised tertiary sector' (1995: 82).

In Muzaffarnagar, despite the restraints on civic freedom, new ideologies have been wafting in and have affected the individuals in different ways. A redefinition of each individual's position on caste, class, gender, religion, nation, and so many other categories which demand a normative stand, is continuing. In this process, Hindutva for most of the villagers is an alien concept. Theirs is a discourse on much more mundane issues. The conclusions on the three issues, which we have reported from a BJP stronghold, are diametrically opposed to the Sangh parivar ideology: the Indian nation continues to be conceived as secular; secularism (and religious tolerance) are distinctly considered as valuable, and religion is experienced as having been misused for political purposes by the socio-economic elite.

Notes

1. They claim that criminals and politicians are 'two hands on one stomach' and that the more important the politician the bigger the stomach. One such disappointed Jat, an MSc from a small peasant background, explains, in an intellectual fashion that 'the sovereignty of the people exists on paper only. Actually it resides with the criminals and the big businessmen.'

2. Their ignorance is very much related to the democratic deficit in the villages: 'We do not have voting rights. We are like the *gulam* of the Jats. Lucknow and Delhi are far away. Here we have a Jat government. So what is the use of telling you our political party preference.' Coercion and ballot box stuffing are common features of the election process in the area (see also Jagpal Singh 1992: 133 ff) and the election results may only vaguely reflect the political preferences.

3. Mulayam Singh Yadav and the BSP, the overall winners of the state legislative elections in late 1993, and the communist parties–the CPI(M) won Bijnor constituency–could count on only a few supporters.

4. Our sample does not tally with the actual election results. The difference can be explained by three factors: we covered only a part of the constituency; we asked the respondents for their actual preferences, even if they had not voted, or had not been allowed to vote; our sample was intentionally biased, giving a higher weightage to poor villagers.

5. The Communist Party and Kanshi Ram's BSP are names which scheduled castes, backward castes and Muslims occasionally refer to as parties which have taken up the cudgel against caste suppression, but since none of them is really active in the area, the poor villagers are left to lament: 'We are helpless'.

6. In 1985, the Rajiv Gandhi government decided that Muslim women, after divorce, should not be paid allowance by the ex-husband. The case can be construed as one of pampering the conservative Muslim males, but not the Muslims in general, and certainly not the women.

7. Whereas most Hindus do accept a restriction on the number of children, and the younger couples have generally started practising it, many Muslim males and females in the area still accept progeny as a natural process which should not be interfered with. It is an attitude which, it should be added, is common for poorer segments of rural society, and which is also prevalent among Hindu lower castes.

8. The samples were drawn differently. The 1993 sample covered two villages, and although randomly selected, gave a high weightage to the poorer neighbourhoods. The 1994 survey covered the village in the *nyaya* panchayat and included comparable size groups from

each caste or class. The findings may therefore differ because of a methodological variation. The intervening time period may also have shifted opinions.

9. For Muslims, the terms of the debate are not set by the historical record, but by the political and social meaning of the agitation. The fact is, they claim, that Hindus and Muslims have been living together peacefully, and that the opportunist political game of the 'goonda party' (the BJP) has succeeded in provoking the Hindus.

References

Balasubramanian. R. (ed.). 1992. *Tolerance in Indian Culture*. New Delhi: Indian Council of Philosophical Research.

Basu, Amrita. 1994. 'When Local Riots Are Not Merely Local: Bringing the State Back in, Bijnor 1988–92'. *Economic and Political Weekly* 29 (40): 2605–21, 1 October.

Chatterjee, Partha. 1993. *The Nation and Its Fragments: Colonial and Postcolonial Histories*. Princeton: Princeton University Press.

Engineer, Asghar Ali. 1989. *Communalism and Communal Violence in India: An Analytical Approach to Hindu-Muslim Conflict*. New Delhi: Ajanta.

_____. 1995. *Communalism in India: A Historical and Empirical Study*. New Delhi: Vikas Publishing House.

Gopal, S. (ed.). 1991. *Anatomy of a Confrontation: The Babri Masjid-Ram Janmabhumi Issue*. New Delhi: Penguin Books.

Graham, Bruce. 1993. *Hindu Nationalism and Indian Politics*. New Delhi: Cambridge University Press.

Joshi, P. C. 1995. *Secularism and Development: The Indian Experience*. New Delhi: Vikas Publishing House.

Lieten, G. K. 1994a. 'The North Indian Kulak Farmer and His Deficient Democracy'. Indo-Dutch Programme on Alternatives in Development (IDPAD), New Delhi and The Hague.

_____. 1994b. 'On Casteism and Communalism in Uttar Pradesh'. *Economic and Political Weekly* 29 (14): 777–81, 2 April.

_____. 1996. 'Hindu Communalism between Caste and Class'. *Journal of Contemporary Asia*, No 2.

Lieten, G. K. and Ravi Srivastava. 1999. *Unequal Partners: Power Relations, Devolution and Development in Uttar Pradesh*. New Delhi: Sage.

Madan, T. N. 1987. 'Secularism in Its Place'. In *Religion in India*, ed. T. N. Madan. Delhi: Oxford University Press.

Nandy, Ashis et al. 1995. *Creating a Nationality: The Ram Janmabhumi and Fear of the Self*. Delhi: Oxford University Press.

Pandey, Gyanendra. 1989. 'The Colonial Construction of "Communalism": British Writings on Benares in the Nineteenth Century'. In *Subaltern Studies VI*, ed. Ranajit Guha. Delhi: Oxford University Press.

O'Neill, John. 1995. *The Poverty of Post-Modernism*. London: Routledge.

Sarkar, Sumit. 1993. 'The Fascism of the Sangh Parivar'. *Economic and Political Weekly* 27 (5): 163–67, 30 January.

Van der Veer, Peter. 1994. *Religious Nationalism: Hindus and Muslims in India*. Berkeley: University of California Press.

5

Modernisation and Rural Stratification

An Application at the Micro-Level*

K. L. Sharma

As we understand it, modernisation results in a high level of structural differentiation and social mobilisation—in terms of large-scale unified and centralised institutions and establishment of viable, flexible and yet effective symbolic and organisational centres that are responsive to the continuous problems of modernisation and to the regulation of them (Eisenstadt 1965, 1966). To what extent the new role structures have come up as a result of this process, how far their nature is particularistic or generalised, and whether they are viable and flexible adaptations, are some of the major questions to be examined on the basis of data gathered for the above referred study. An examination of the following aspects enables evaluation of the kind required by these questions.

Occupation

The data reveal that the traditional occupational structure continues to exist to a great extent alongside the emergent economic role structures. The present occupational structure in the six villages is a conglomeration of the two structures, e.g., traditional (caste-based) and secular (non-caste based). Today, the majority of the castes do not exclusively carry out either the traditional occupations or the secular occupations (Sharma 1968). The choice of the new occupations and the rejection of the old ones is pragmatic and selective in character. There are castes which have discarded traditional occupations because they were considered 'impure' or 'unclean' or 'lower'

---

* This chapter has been extracted from a longer paper published by the author in the *Economic and Political Weekly* 5 (37): 1537–43, 12 September 1970.

This chapter is based on a field study conducted by the author during 1965–66 in three districts of Rajasthan, namely, Sikar, Jaipur and Bharatpur. A total of six villages, two from each of the districts, were selected for the study.

or 'Kamin', i.e., because of the stigma about the polluting nature of their traditional occupations. These castes even had to face some initial economic hardships, as the rejection resulted in unemployment and imbalances in their economic standards.

On the other hand, there are certain caste groups, particularly the ex-zamindars, who have been forced to take up certain lower and degrading occupations, such as, manual labour, peonship, and domestic work. This drastic change is a result of the structural changes that took place with the abolition of the jagirdari and zamindari systems.

The continuity of tradition with modernity in the occupational field is evident from Table 5.1.

TABLE 5.1: Distribution of Traditional or Caste-based Occupations (Pure and Impure) and Secular or Non-caste Occupations

Caste	Traditional or Caste-based Occupations (Pure and Impure)	Secular or Non-caste Occupations	Total
Upper	203 (54.0)	173 (46.0)	376 (100.0)
Intermediate	751 (88.4)	98 (11.6)	849 (100.0)
Lower and Untouchables	519 (90.7)	53 (9.3)	572 (100.0)
Muslims	50 (48.5)	53 (51.5)	103 (100.0)
Total	1,523 (80.1)	377 (19.9)	1,900 (100.0)

Note: Chi $^2/_3$ = 301.4 P .001

Out of 1,900 male workers, 20 per cent are engaged in secular occupations. The upper castes have adopted new or secular occupations more than the lower castes have done. Of them, 46 per cent have taken up secular occupations, whereas among the intermediate and the lower castes the corresponding percentage is 11.6 and 9.3, respectively. One reason for this simultaneity of traditional and secular (modern) occupations is that the village does not provide employment to all the members who were in the traditional occupations before, and consequently a few of them have to seek alternatives either in the village or outside it. The other reason is that some persons are willing to discard the traditional occupations but do not find suitably remunerative jobs; they therefore stick to the traditional ones in the absence of suitable alternatives. Some persons still continue to derive gainful remunerations from the traditional occupations. Others have discarded these callings even at economic loss or hardship on account of leaving them (Sharma 1969). Thus the nature of the existing continuity of tradition and modernity in the occupational realm is diverse, selective, pragmatically-oriented and circumstantial.

TABLE 5.2: Secular or Non-caste Occupations which did not Exist Three Decades Ago

Occupations	Upper	Intermediate	Lower and Untouchable	Muslim	Total
1 Industrial labourer	14	26	20	1	61
2 Teacher and clerk	38	11	1	–	50
3 Peon	4	7	2	3	16
4 Wineseller	2	–	–	–	2
5 Teashopman	8	3	–	–	11
6 Police and armyman	34	33	6	43	116
7 Railway gangman, jamadar and inspector	–	2	16	–	18
8 Milkseller	1	3	1	–	5
9 Panchayat samiti extension officer	2	4	–	–	6
10 Excise inspector	–	1	–	–	1
11 Motor driver	1	4	1	2	8
12 Shop assistant and accountant	52	2	2	1	57
13 Patwari	4	–	–	–	4
14 Laboratory assistant	1	–	–	–	1
15 Khalasi (motor cleaner)	–	–	–	1	1
16 Bus conductor	–	–	–	2	2
17 Forest officer	1	–	–	–	1
18 Vaidya (ayurved doctor)	6	–	–	–	6
19 Telephone operator	2	–	1	–	3
20 Postmaster	1	–	–	–	1
21 Vaccinator	–	2	–	–	2
22 Postman	1	–	–	–	1
23 Tonga driver	–	–	3	–	3
24 Engineer	1	–	–	–	1
Total	173 (46.00)	98 (26.0)	53 (14.0)	53 (14.0)	377 (100.0)

The factors responsible for occupational diversification (cutting it off from the association of caste) are both structural and cultural. These factors have, however, not resulted in 'equalitarianisation' or 'distributive justice' in the six villages. The prestigious secular occupations are being virtually monopolised by the ex-privileged castes. This is because the earlier privileged positions of the upper castes enable them to acquire the new bases of higher social, economic and political positions. The non-privileged castes are unable to afford the cost of acquiring these new bases of prestige and power which are higher education, white collar jobs and formal offices of power, such as the Panch and the Sarpanch. These lower sections of the village population imitate what the higher castes discard deliberately and what they are even reluctant to take note of as imitation by the lower castes. In fact, the upper castes are in a position to preserve the prestigeous elements of status determination from the traditional stock and to add to it from the new avenues, such as, modern education, village panchayat system, white collar occupations, and outside contacts.

An analysis of the distribution of secular (non-caste) occupations reveals (see Table 5.2) that the upper castes have a near monopoly over the more income, prestige and power-providing occupations and avenues.

Though the male workers from among the upper castes constitute about 20 per cent of all workers, yet they are 46 per cent of the total secular job-doers. Most of the white-collar job-doers in these villages are from the upper castes. This is due to the fact that these jobs are a regular source of cash income. These occupations involve less, or no, manual labour. As such, the upper castes not only have higher income, but are in a position to maintain certain styles of life in the changed circumstances. In this context we observe a lack of distributive justice. Theoretically, modernisation is open to all—in terms of exercise of fundamental rights of receiving higher and professional education, migration and taking up of jobs of one's liking, etc.—but practically the doors are open only to a small minority. The capacity for adaptability is differential. Taking secular occupations as one index, it can be said that the higher castes are more 'modernised' than the lower castes.

Education

Education is one of the most significant determinants of status in the present-day village community. Modern education, and particularly higher education, is again virtually a monopoly of the higher castes. It is college and university education which extends the horizon of occupational possibilities by providing the formal qualifications required for superior occupations and intellectual superiority to those who achieve it.

An analysis of the data about graduates (including intermediates) shows that, about three decades ago, there was not even a single graduate in these six villages. Today, there are 29 graduates and 74 matriculates, who, invariably, in all the six villages, are from among the brahmins, Rajputs, Banias and Jats. There is besides a tendency among the upper castes to send boys for technical and medical education. Two engineering graduates, one medical graduate and all the graduates in science, arts and commerce are from among these higher castes.

Besides the coincidence of caste rank and educational achievements, class position is also associated with attainments in the educational field. This is because of the considerable congruence between caste and class ranks. Table 5.3 shows the relationship between class and education.

It is evident that the ex-better-off class groups can afford the expensive higher education, whereas these opportunities are virtually closed to the lower classes because of their economic incapability to bear the expenses of modern professional and university education.

We find that there is not one graduate from among the lower classes. More than two-thirds of the total number of graduates come from the higher classes and castes. There is one graduate and one matriculate among the higher classes to every 5 and 2.5 families, respectively. The proportion of the graduates and matriculates is very low among the middle and lower classes. Among the middle class people there is one graduate to every 19 households and one matriculate to every 6.3 households. This proportion is still lower among the lower classes, where there is one matriculate to 127 households.

TABLE 5.3: Class Position and Educational Achievements

Class	Graduates	Matriculates	Total
High	20 (33.3)	40 (66.7)	60 (100.0)
Middle	9 (25.0)	27 (75.0)	36 (100.0)
Low	–	7 (100.0)	7 (100.0)
Total	29 (28.1)	74 (71.9)	103 (100.0)

These discrepancies in achievement of educational standards falsify the universal approachability to educational opportunities for the various castes and class groups. Aspects of modernisation, which provide high scores on the prestige-scale, are accessible almost in a monopolistic way to the upper sections of the population. Thus in education, too, we do not find 'distributive justice' which aims to minimise the inequalities between different sections of the population. On the contrary, status inequalities have been increasing on the non-sacred hierarchical lines under these emerging, modernising forces of status and prestige. The higher castes and class people centralise their efforts for achievement of these determinants; and in course of time they conserve and sanctify these attributes or, in other words, they traditionalise them.

POWER

A hierarchy of power relations coincides with the caste and class stratification in the six villages. The ex-landlords have a decisive command both over the formal positions as well as the informal decision-making process. They are the key influentials in these villages. In both the villages of Bharatpur sub-region, the Jat ex-landlords hold the key offices of Sarpanch (head of the village panchayat), Chairman of the judicial panchayat, President and the Secretary of the cooperative society, etc. These offices in other villages have been held by the upper castes, such as Brahmins, Charans and Rajputs. In two of the villages, viz., Sabalpura and Bhutera, where the Jats constitute a single overwhelming numerical strength, they have superceded their upper caste rivals. The latter, however, put up a formidable opposition to the Jats in these two villages.

An analysis of 76 influentials reveals that 41 per cent are from among the upper castes, whereas they constitute only 18 per cent of the total households in these villages. Among the intermediate castes, the Jats (who are also ex-zamindars in Bharatpur district) have occupied these offices of power more than the Jats of the villages of Sikar and Jaipur districts, who are ex-tenant peasants today. The lower castes comprise 32 per cent of the total households, but have taken up only 4 per cent of the total positions of power since the introduction of panchayati raj on 2 October 1959.

An analysis of class positions reveals a similar trend of association between class and power. Numerically, 77 per cent of families belong to the lower class, but only 9 per cent of the key influentials are from among them. Of the influentials, 46 per cent are from among the middle class groups, which comprise only 15 per cent of the total households. The high influentials share 45 per cent of the total strength of them, but they are only 8 per cent of the total households.

Out of 11 sarpanches, nine have come from the upper class and two from the middle class. Even the latter two were social workers from the upper castes. All the sarpanches are from among the brahmins, Rajputs, Charans and Jats. No sarpanch has been elected so far from among the other 30 castes in the six villages. The other significant fact is that the rivalries, mutual hatreds and bickerings for status and power are either between the influential and well-to-do families of the same caste or among the marginally higher and lower castes which generally have the same economic position. The rivalries for power in the two villages of Bharatpur so far have been between the ex-zamindar families of the Jats. This is an intra-class friction, resulting from the structural changes in the village community. In Roopgarh, it is among the Brahmin families. In Sabalpura and Bhutera it is between the Rajputs and the Jats; and in Harmara the Charans, Brahmins and Banias form the rival groups.

It is evident from the above analysis of the power-structure that there is a positive relationship between caste, class and power ranks. As such, decentralisation of power through panchayati raj has not in fact succeeded; rather it has provided a ground where the privilegecl sections can centralise and consolidate their positions with new means and in a disguised form. The process of bringing down the status of the ex-landlords through land reforms and, by the same means, upgrading the positions of the ex-tenants, particularly in the Jagirdari villages, cannot be denied. The process of upgrading the status, from lower to higher rank, has been designated as 'bourgeoisiefication' while the opposite process, of degrading status, is called 'proletarianisation' (Sharma 1969). These processes are of immense significance in understanding the outcome of some of the structural changes such as land reforms, Panchayati Raj and Adult Suffrage, etc.; however, they have affected the traditional structure in a very limited way. Their effects are minimised by the privileged sections by 'seeking out' some new bases of power and prestige and by extracting maximum benefits out of these new avenues introduced for achievement of an egalitarian and equalitarian society.

STYLES OF LIFE

The families from among the upper castes and class again have superior styles of life compared to the families of the lower and intermediate castes and class. Their styles of life are better in terms of expenditure on clothing, food, house, marriage, education, etc. There are families from these privileged sections, which have spent up to Rs 20,000 on the marriages of the girls in recent years. It is these families which use stainless steel utensils, crockery, carpets, chairs, tables, costly garments and gold ornaments. Other goods, such as, watches and transistor radio sets are also coming into use by them. Some of these elite families in the villages maintain drawing rooms, decorated with photos, carpets, chairs, etc.

It is also that these families are innovators in the villages. In Bharatpur villages six families of the ex-zamindar Jats own tractors as well as the other items referred to above. Similarly, in four other villages, tractors, for example, are owned by the ex-landlords and the bourgeoisiefied ex-tenants.

Not only are these cultural distinctions clear between the privileged and the non-privileged sections, but they also accentuate and widen the gulf between these polar sections of the village commtunity. This is indeed sometimes why the upper castes conspicuously spend on marriages and other occasions, seeking higher prestige and status. They can afford expenses on these cultural items, as they are in a position to do so because of their changing adaptability to the challenges, and situations thrown out by the structural changes. Thus, we find a great gap between the cultural styles of the privileged minority and the non-privileged majority.

Because of these divergences, the lower castes and class people are less informed, have no contacts with leaders other than the leaders of their respective villages, and are almost unaware of the political set-up of the country. They have no clear-cut knowledge about the ideologies and programmes of the political parties. They have only a faint idea about personalities like Mahatma Gandhi, Jawaharlal Nehru and Mohan Lal Sukhadia. Indira Gandhi, being the daughter of the late Nehru and a lady Prime Minister, is known by the people in terms of recognising how times have changed so that a lady rules over them.

The upper sections of the village population are more aware of the present-day structure of the country and of their surroundings. The obvious reasons for this are their educational attainments, their white-collar jobs, migration and contacts with the block and district level leaders.

The changing character of styles of life among the elites supports their pragmatic orientation for maintaining the status quo or for raising the present status and prestige to a higher level. The wearing of Khadi and the acceptance of Kucha food, water and tea from the Jats by the Brahmin leaders, are some of the examples of this. Touching an 'untouchable' on the farm when the upper caste men and the former work together is not considered polluting. But on certain occasions acceptance of

Kucha food from the Jats and touching 'untouchables' in public is still considered impure. Similarly, carrying out of certain rituals and practices is considered useful as these still provide prestige but certain other rituals have been dropped as they either no longer contribute to status upgrading or negatively affect the status of the practitioners.

An analysis of the status structure of the six villages on the basis of selected criteria, viz., land-holding, income, house-type, and caste rank, reveals that 'composite status' and caste rank do not differ significantly. The ranking of families on the basis of these four factors (see Table 5.4) at three kinds of significance (high, medium, low) was worked out. The families were thus classified into four status groups on the basis of their respective total scores on these four factors.

TABLE 5.4: Composite Status Ranking of Different Castes

Caste	Lower	Middle	Upper Middle	Upper	Total
	(3–4)	(5)	(6–7)	(8–12)	
Upper	–	7(3.1)	81(36.2)	136(60.7)	224 (100.0)
	–3	(3.0)	(28.4)	(52.3)	(20.5)
Intermediate	39 (7.8)	160 (31.9)	183(36.4)	120(23.9)	502 (100.0)
	(12.3)	(68.7)	(64.2)	(46.2)	(45.8)
Lower and 'untouchable'	278 (75.3)	66 (17.9)	21 (5.7)	4 (1.1)	369 (100.0)
	(87.7)	(28.3)	(7.4)	(1.5)	(33.7)
Total	317 (28.9)	233 (21.3)	–285 (26.0)	260 (23.8)	1,095 (100.0)
	(100.0)	(100.0)	(100.0)	(100.0)	(100.0)

Note:

Status score	1 to 12	Lower status scores	3 and 4
First quartile at	4	Middle status score	5
Second quartile at	5	Upper middle status scores	6 and 7
Third quartile at	7	Upper status scores	8 to 12

An overwhelming majority (61 per cent) of the upper castes belong to the 'upper composite status' rank. Only 36 per cent of them have 'upper middle status'. No family from the upper castes belongs to the 'lower status' rank. Only 3 per cent have 'middle status' rank. On the other hand, 70 per cent of the lower castes belong to the 'lower status' rank, whereas only one and 6 per cent of them belong to the upper and the upper middle status ranks, respectively. The intermediate castes are mainly in the upper and upper middle status ranks. Only 8 per cent of them have lower status rank. This shift is an indication of their upward status mobility. The lower castes have not improved significantly, as 86 per cent of them possess lower status rank and only 28 per cent of them have middle status rank whereas 69 per cent of the intermediate castes have middle status rank.

This overwhelming association between caste rank and composite status rank also supports our analysis of the relation between stratification and modernisation on the basis of the indices of occupation, education, power and cultural styles of living.

The minor fluctuations in the rural stratification system are not strong enough to challenge its basic foundation at least in the existing circumstances. As such, we cannot expect major overhauling of our stratification system with the existing forces of modernisation. These forces rather help mainly those who are already better-off. In other words, only the well-off sections can exploit and benefit from these emerging avenues of modernisation. On the basis of these observations at various levels we wish to arrive at certain analytical clues in the following concluding section of this paper.

Overall Analysis

Modernisation depends upon two basic characteristics of society, viz., institutionalisation of modern values and adaptability of the society concerned. These two interrelated attributes are closely associated with the two basic universals of Talcott Parsons, that is, of social stratification and cultural legitimation (1964). The nature of social stratification (relatively open or relatively closed in practice) may make the growth of the process of modernisation particularistic, narrow and limited to a minority of the members of society. This process may be universalistic in character if there are no hurdles from the side of existing stratification system. The nature of our stratification system is segmental and hierarchical based on certain historical forces. The difficulty is not in changing the values of this system; there is a pervasive and acute lack of means for the non-privileged castes and groups and families to adopt and internalise the modern values. The privileged groups are in a position to adopt these values, and as such they are able to maintain qualitatively the same status distinctions in relation to the non-privileged sections though on the basis of new factors such as education, office, economic position, white-collar jobs, outside contacts and styles of life.

S. C. Dube emphasises the need for emergence, which implies 'value-change' for institutional rearrangement considered essential for modernisation. Some of the difficulties pointed out by him include the vast gap between the elite and the masses, sacred and secular, ascription and achievement, self-orientation and collective-orientation and particularistic and universalistic values associated with our social system. These dichotomies of values are a product of the basic values of Hindu social organisation, such as, *karma*, *dharma*, *purusharthas*, *aparigraha*, etc. (Dube 1967).

But we have analysed earlier that value-change does not come as a barrier in the process of modernisation. It is the inequal or differential accessibility to the attributes of modernisation which is the barrier and which is basically due to the particularistic nature of our stratification system. Because of this, institutionalisation and legitimation of modern values are partial, limited and un-universalistic. Gunnar Myrdal's suggestion that caste is an obstacle in the development of India and egalitarian ideology, cannot be accepted by us (Myrdal 1968; for a review of Myrdal's *Asian Drama* see Madan 1969). The problems before us are not, as suggested by Myrdal, of changing attitudes and institutions, abolition of the caste, or killing of the cows, etc. As Yogendra Singh suggests, change is necessary in the instrumental or non-categorical values of the society facing modernisation (Singh 1969). The caste and other religious values constitute a categorical part of the value-system of our culture. These categorical values are not hurdles in the way of modernisation. This we witness in the case of the modernising sections of the village community. The privileged castes and class people have adopted instrumental values either to enhance or to maintain their status quo in the wake of the emerging structural forces of change. This does not mean that they have discarded what they inherited from the past. The two sets of values go together, without conflicting or weakening each other. The two serve in different contexts, in different ways, and also jointly, but for the same end which is status enhancement or maintaining of it. Those who fail to achieve a balanced on-going coincidence of the two value-sets suffer on the status-hierarchy in the village community. As such, modernisation is an integrative, cohesive, and adjustive process.

The classification of the 'modern, transitional and traditional' societies does not apply to our context. The 'psychic' element for mobility in the direction of modernisation may be very much there (Lerner 1958: 43–45). But availability of resources to satisfy that 'psychic' element is a foremost prerequisite for modernisation. The people express their desire to have office, a high standard of living, education for their children, but fail to translate these aspirations into reality. This proves our proposition that differential nature of social groups (in terms of resources) does not allow modernisation to result with 'distributive justice', irrespective of structural differentiation. In other words, the fruits of modernisation are not available for consumption to the rank and file in the present day social set-up.

Another point we wish to refer to in conclusion is that modernisation of the economy, or discarding of the traditional rituals and practices, will not necessarily result in secularisation of the norms of society. Scarlett Epstein's comparative study of two south Indian villages proves that irrigation of fields brings economic prosperity and this results in strengthening the traditional system in terms of caste hierarchy, rituals and Jajmani system. The dry village induces multiple changes such as education, migration, occupational differentiation and weakening of norms of caste and jajmani svstems (Epstein 1962; see also Deva 1966 and Gusfield 1967).[1] Similarly sanskritisation does not touch upon instrumental values and it results generally in horizontal mobility without disturbing the vertical arrangement or structure of caste system. Sanskritisation is basically related to changes in the notions of pollution-purity, untouchability and ritual hierarchy, etc.

Thus, modernisation is an adaptive, integrative and continuous process which does not necessarily oppose or weaken 'tradition'. Every society is an on-going system of tradition and modernity. But modernity is found in certain societies not on a universalistic pattern, in terms of resources and 'distributive justice'. In societies where the nature of modernisation is particularistic, inequitable and discriminatory, it results in strengthening and consolidating the position of the traditionally privileged and elite groups and in weakening the position of the expropriated; it thus increases the gulf between the higher and lower strata. The indices of modernisation—occupation, education, power and cultural styles of life—support the view that modernisation in the village community so far has been confined to the privileged castes and class families. Consequently, modernisation does not result in 'distributive justice', as the role differentiation is confined within the upper segments of the rural society.

Notes

1. For Deva (1966) social change takes place not always in relation to economic and technological development. He takes the case of India where socio-cultural changes are ahead of industrial and technological progress. This has not happened in many of the western countries where the industrial revolution was rather rapid compared to the changes in cultural traditions. Gusfield (1967) states that modernisation has rather strengthened traditional norms in Indian society. He cites the case of Hindu joint family. The examples referred to are of the big industrialists of India who maintain big joint families. The field study of the author in the six villages of Rajasthan also supports the view that the joint family organisation is not weakened by modernisation, in terms of education, migration, white-collar jobs and economic prosperity. The big joint families in the six villages are of the economically well off, upper castes and classes, and educated people.

Reference

Deva, Indra. 1966. 'The Course of Social Change: A Hypothesis', *Diogenes*. No. 56. Winter.

Dube, S. C. 1967. 'Modernisation and its Adaptive Demands on Indian Society'. In *Papers in the Sociology of Education in India*, ed. M. S. Gore, I. P. Desai and Suma Chitnis. 33–71. New Delhi: NCERT.

Eisenstadt, S. N. 1965. 'The MacIver Lecture: Social Transformation in Modernisation'. *American Sociological Review* 30 (5): 659–73, October

Eisenstadt, S. N. 1966. *Modernisation: Protest and Change*, Englewoods Cliffs N. J.: Prentice-Hall.

Epstein, T. Scarlett. 1962. *Economic Development and Social Change in South India*. Bombay: Oxford University Press.

Gusfield, Joseph R. 1967. 'Tradition and Modernity: Misplaced Polarities in the Study of Social Change', *The American Journal of Sociology* 72 (4): 351–62, January.

Lerner, Daniel. 1958. *The Passing of Traditional Society*. Illinois: The Free Press.

Madan, T. N. 1969. 'Caste and Economic Development' *Economic and Political Weekly* 4 (5): 285–89, 1 February.

Myrdal, Gunnar. 1968. *Asian Drama: An Inquiry into the Poverty of Nations*. 3 vols. New York: Pantheon.

Parsons, Talcott. 1964. 'Evolutionary Universals in Society'. *American Sociological Review* 29 (3), June.

Sharma, K. L. 1968. 'Occupational Mobility and Class Structure'. *Man in India* 48 (2): 106–44, April–June.

Sharma, K. L. 1969. 'Stresses in Caste Stratification: A Study of Six Villages in Rajasthan'. *Economic and Political Weekly* 4 (3): 217–22, 18 January.

Singh, Yogendra. 1969. 'Historicity of Modernisation'. Paper presented at the seminar on Tradition and Modernity in India, Indian Institute of Technology, New Delhi, 3–6 February.

6

THE UNTOUCHABLE PRESENT

*Everyday Life of Musahars in North Bihar**

MUKUL SHARMA

The musahars belong to the scheduled castes and populate several districts of north Bihar. How is this untouchable caste coping with the social and economic changes being forced on them? How are their own institutions engaging with the dominant discourse—changing it and being changed in return, producing new social spaces?[...]

DISAPPEARING WORK

April 1998. Sitting idle in his village Sirpur mushhari, six km away from the town of Jhanjharpur in north Bihar, Asharfi Sadai was saying, 'We are two in one–musahars and 'mitti' (soil). Digging soil is like a physical exercise for us, much better than sitting or lying. When we don't do it, then we feel tired.' Musahars dig deeper and faster. They have carried on the skill of measuring and assessing the quality of soil for generations. Asharfi Sadai is a representative of many thousands in the area, who take pride in their traditional skills. He does not need an inch-tape, any modern measuring devise or the advice of an engineer. He does not remember now those large number of dams, ponds, bridges or multi-storeyed buildings, where his skills and labour have been applied–in assessing, in digging, or in measuring the soil.

But now he gets less work related with soil. Since he, like many others, has no land, and most of his life has passed working with soil, his choices are very limited. However, always enterprising, and not afraid of learning new things, Asharfi has now started weaving baskets. But the going is tough. Says he, 'Bamboo trees are not mine: they belong to somebody else. The Basket market is not certain. If somebody gives me the bamboo, I weave it for them.' Other than this Asharfi looks here and there for soil work. Asharfi goes to cities, like Darbangha, Samastipur, Muzaffarpur and sometimes even to Patna, the capital of the state. There is less and less demand

* This chapter has been extracted from a longer paper published by the author in the *Economic and Political Weekly* 34 (49): 3465–70, 4 December 1999.

for labour like his, in spite of various ongoing construction activities. 'I see that for an activity like assessment and measurement, we are no longer required. Further, the digging work in big project works is being done by the machines', he explains.

The musahars' traditional job market has been squeezed by some other hidden ways, especially in the recent years. In village level developmental works, under the Jawahar Rozgar Yojana or other schemes, these are a number of works, somewhere related to digging and carrying of soil. These were all being done by musahars before, but not now.

Harhar Sadai, of the same village says, 'We do the digging. But that is all. The loading, unloading and carrying of the soil–all is now being done by trucks and tractors, contractors and their labourers. Here commissions rule the game.' Surya Narayan Sadai of village Bheja in Madhapur Block complains of similar incidents, 'Trolleys and contractors have taken over the scenario, leaving less space for us'. In the recent past, the dispossession of musahars from rural land and employment has taken new turns. Since the last four-five years, landlords in Bakunia have purchased three tractors. They also hire tractors from outside as well. A landlord rents it to another for ploughing, at the rate of Rs 150–170 per bigha. 'It has become easier for landlords, as now they do not require labour, cattle or plough for a major part of their farming', says Tithar Sadai.

Thus now there is work available locally only for three four months and that too primarily for womenfolk. Bindo Sadai, another musahar labourer in the village, confirms, 'Sowing and harvesting, and in between, some other work related to standing crops, are barely enough for the womenfolk. Musahar men are becoming more and more unemployed. The new landlords, the yadavs, do not want us anymore on a longer basis.' Musahar men and women work from 6 o'clock in the morning to 1 in the afternoon. They get a breakfast of two rotis at 8–9 am, and their daily wages are 2–3 kg of maize or wheat, which costs approximately Rs 12–13. Earlier, there was a variety of other work available in the village vicinity: making of paper packets, knitting of ropes, weaving of baskets, stitching of leaf plates, husking of rice and preparing eatables from it. But these opportunities of employment have disappeared today. 'Rice mills have opened both in the village and at the block. Their owners are not musahars or other poor. So landlords prefer to go to these mills, rather than calling musahars to their houses, or giving gears to them for manual processing', says Surya Narayan Sadai in Bheja village.

Similarly, Ashrafi talks about the problems of basket making and marketing. Paper packets have now virtually vanished. In the district town of Muzaffarpur, the refugee colony at Ganipur Muhalla and the old market Kali Kothi Muhalla, were once known for making of paper packets. In these two areas, around 250 families were totally dependent on this work, and among them, there were some musahar families too. They used to make 100 to 200 paper packets a day and were earning Rs 20 to 35 per day. But the coming of polythene bags, has changed the market for paper packets. 35-year-old Saumitra Das of Refugee Colony says that now they are able to earn only Rs 10–15 a day. Thus most of the families have started going for daily job market in search of any work.[...]

Out-Migration

In May 1998, there is one sight, strikingly common, in all nusahar villages. You see women, young and old, children of all ages and old men, but young/middle aged men are hardly to be seen. Those visible, can be counted instantly by the villagers. The unseen ones, everybody knows, are somewhere in Gurdaspur, Batala, Pathankoth, Chandigarh, Panipat, Sonipat, Deenanagar in Punjab and Haryana states.[...]

Every year, in December-January, they start moving out to Punjab, Haryana or Uttar Pradesh. They do wheat harvesting and rice sowing there. By June end, they come back and go again in September. Then they do rice harvesting. They get wages at the rate of Rs 40 to 50 per day. Thus they work primarily as agricultural labourers for six-seven months a year. But some of them, like Domi Sadai of village Partaha, work in the rice mills of Chandigarh. He also takes some villagers along with him for working in the same mills. Then there is Hadi, who works as a night watchman in a farm of Gurdaspur.

Large-scale migration of musahars has a recent history, starting largely from the early nineties. Villages are now found totally deserted of young-middle male members during most of the agricultural seasons. It enables musahars to survive, but it makes moneylenders more accumulative and exploitative. It also releases the musahars' sense of deep humiliation and reflects the changes that are taking place between high-middle caste landowners and musahar agricultural labourers. Mallu Sadai, Rameshwar Sadai and others in Bakunia Bichali village recollect that some years back, say 10–12 years before, only two, three or four from the village were going to Punjab as labourers, and the rest were working as labour in and around the village. But now, only a few remain here in the working season. Old Subodh Sadai of Bakunia Purabi village is a father of five sons. All the three adult sons have been working in Punjab since the last seven years. He says, 'They used to work here as agricultural labourers or sharecroppers before. Now they come, stay for a few months and go back again. They send us money from there through cheques or bank drafts. Their families are our responsibility. In place of them, their wives now work in the fields for some months.'

This migration helps in meeting the basic survival needs, but it is not enough to counter the blood sucking moneylenders, who have an overpowering presence in the area. Whenever they go, they normally have to take loans from the local landowners, turned moneylenders, at the rate of 10 to 12 per cent per hundred per month. Mohan Ram takes a loan of Rs 600 everytime he has to go. If he pays back within three months, he pays an interest of 10 per cent. If he does not, then the interest amount gets integrated into the main loan amount and he pays interest on that amount.[...]

This new course of migration among musahars is going to continue. Hari Narayan Harsh, a known activist of the area, characterises this trend as one with contradictory implications, 'On the one hand it involves tremendous pain which is almost like a running sore–of constant seperation, of increasing burden on women, of new exploitative mechanisms. On the other, it provides musahars with some bargaining power, gives basic sustanance to their families and has lead to changing relations in the village, where they are able to escape relatively the constant work humiliation inflicted on them locally. Degradation is there as well, but it is outside their society, which cannot be "seen".'

This musahar who migrates, is a new untouchable, who is away from his traditional skill, and is now in a place where cash income is the centre of his activity. He is primarily involved with an economic activity which is highly competitive and also integrated with the national and the global market. Not only is his social activity severely limited, even the dominant economic activity has not been able to take root in the social and cultural systems. They are victims of a social polarisation where they cannot get integrated, and are also victims of a dicotomy between the economic and the social activity. Nevertheless they are creating a new social space, for whatever reasons, be it because of survival needs or social justice or due to the mobile and flexible character of their work. Socially invisible they may be but they are creating their own limited arenas.

CHILD LABOUR

Parthaha, a village of scheduled caste community in the Navahatta block of Saharsa district in Bihar, is known for child labourers. Only a few years ago, 24 children of the village were found working in the carpet factories of Bhadohi, Uttar Pradesh. Now, amongst them, only one works there, but the rest are also not in the village. They are all in Punjab. Kamala, a middle-aged woman in the village, gets scared when one talks to her, asking her name, age and the work her child does. 'My son is in Punjab now and he is working in some farm along with the adults of the village. He was in Bhadohi before. But here there is no work, no food, no school', says she in a hush-hush manner. Similar is the case with 12–13 year old Sikander Sadai. He too was going to Bhadohi, but since the last two years, he goes to the villages of Punjab, to work in the rice and paddy fields, for at least five-six months every year.

The village, it soon becomes clear, does not want to open its mouth much in this regard. Incidentally, we meet the 12-year-old Brahmadev, who had returned from Punjab only 10 days ago. He went to school only for a few months at the age of seven-eight years. Unable to read and write, he has now learnt how to sign. Says he, 'I go either to Punjab or to Delhi, work in the rice mills and carrying sacks. Gyani Kumar (14) has also been going to Punjab for the last two years. 'I had nothing, not even a pen, paper or book. That is why I had to leave the school. After that I used to sit idle at home. When other children of the village started going, I decided to follow them. I usually earn about Rs 500 a month for loading-unloading of sacks', narrates he.

Children continue to work in many hazardous industries. Samajik Shaikshanik Vikas Kendra, a social organisation working in the villages of north Bihar, gives details of a survey on the status of child labour conducted in November 1997 by the organisation, in Navahatta Block of Saharsa district: 10-year-old Dukhi Sadai, son of Kamal Sadai of Bakunia Purabi village, was working in a carpet weaving unit of Allahabad. He died there, but his father does not know much about it. His second son, 13–14 year old Surindra Sadai, continues to work in a carpet weaving unit at Bhiti Baraut, Allahabad. Three more children–Bijali Sadai, Ramu Sadai and Ghuran Sadai of the same parent had gone to a village near Allahabad in early 1997 to work in the carpet sector, and a middleman Suraj Yadav gave Rs 1,500 as an 'advance' to them.

The survey identifies a total of 1,704 cases of child labour in 20 villages of Navahatta Block, of which 650 are female child labour. The need for repayment of debt to the landowners or the moneylenders is the main reason for the prevalence of this labour.

In village Sohrai, block Lakhnaur, district Madhubani, lives Fulia. She had sent her 10-year-old child Dadu, to work in a rice mill of Haryana in November 1997. 'From here, a large number of children, aged between 6 to 12 years, are going to Punjab, Haryana and Delhi. Nobody goes to Bhadohi any longer', confirms Somani Devi, another woman sitting alongside Fulia.

In the Bakunia Bichali village, some cases of child labour come to light, who had gone to work in the carpet weaving units of Allahabad district, but have been missing since the last few years. Bindo Sadai is the father of 10-year-old Gugali. 'My son went to work at the Allahabad district in 1996, but now there is no information about him', narrates the worried father. Another father Bhannu Sadai says almost the same thing. His nine-year-old son Manoj Kumar went to Bhadohi in 1994–95 and thereafter, he lost touch with his son. The local middleman, through whom the children had been taken there, has disappeared, and the parents do not know what to do in this situation. Though some child labourers have disappeared, that does not deter parents from sending their wards to the same carpet weaving units in Bhadohi and Allahabad areas. Mallu Sadai sent his 10-year-old son, Sanjay, to Kurmecha, Allahabad in May 1997 to work in a carpet weaving unit and in return he received Rs 1,000 in four instalments from the middleman.[...]

Caste Violence and Assertion

In mid June 1998, Tilaya Devi and her Khairi village witnessed an armed attack, something they had never experienced in their life time on such a scale. Around 40–50 yadavs of the same village attacked the village and left in an hour. After the incident, Tilaya Devi, has been unable to come back to her village. Her family members and other musahars of the village are shocked and shattered.

Khairi, a village of 100 and 70 houses of yadavs and musahars respectively, is barely 12 km away from Jhanjharpur town of Madhubani district. Musahars live in small thatched huts in one corner of the village. Tin roofs are an exception. These huts have been built on a stretch of land that appeared a few years ago from under the flood waters. All around the houses of musahars are vast fields of rice that do not belong to them. 'It was around 8 am, when the yadavs came with 'pharsas', sickles and spades and started beating up everyone–women and children, young and old. They damaged our 'kaccha' louses, utensils, and other items, spoiled the grain, took away all the valuable belongings, even cows, oxen, buffaloes. They were vociferously threatening to kill every musahar of the village', recount Vaidhyanath, Mahakant,

Amolia, Lichia, Bachla Sadai, Marani Devi and many others of the village. Some of them show their injuries with bandages and plasters.

Yadavs were indiscriminate in their attack, but were specifically asking for Tilaya Devi. When they found out that she and her family members were not in the village, not only did they destroy her hut completely, they also took away a buffalo belonging to her. While leaving, they declared that they would teach more 'lessons' to Tilaya, if she continued to defy and agitate against them. In the village, Lichia asks in anger, 'Why do they want to kill us like this, when we are the ones who work in their fields? Other villages also have musahar labourers and yadav landowners, but why are the landowners here acting in this manner?' Moreover, the yadavs have stopped employing them this year and thus they have been forced to go to other villages for work. Tilaya has taken shelter in the office of Lok Sakti Sangathan in Balbhadrapur village. Looking sad and pale, she prays for more rain and darkness, so that she can go to her village someday, to see for herself the condition of her house. She was fearing attacks from yadavs since many months. One day she even went to the local Lakhnaur police station, but the police neither recorded her statement, nor lodged any complaint. Instead, she was humiliated.

Small-built and simply dressed in a sari, Tilaya calls herself a musahar and names her husband as Nayal Sadai. She works continuously, sometimes as agricultural labourer, and sometimes as maker and seller of leaf packets in the local market. She is also a well-known activist of musahars. She has been working in the fields since her childhood. She got married at an early age and has never gone to a school. 'Nobody in the community was going to school, nobody realised then the importance of education. Also, the rich and the powerful were not willing to impart education to us', says she, matter-of-factly.

When for the first time, the musahars tried to take control of some 'gairmazarua' (ceiling surplus or public commons) land for their housing, the deep-rooted unwillingness of the rich to share any resources with the musahars became apparent and made Tilaya acknowledge the threat of attacks from the landlords of the village. 'The whole land area surrounding Khairi, approximately 150–170 bighas, is owned by Lokpati Singh, alias 'Babu Sahib' of Lakhnaur. The land is of different kinds–ceiling, bhoodani, governmental–but he is the owner of all, and the musahars used to do sharecropping on this. We live in a small corner in the village and were finding it hard to accommodate our growing families there. Thus we decided to build our houses in a small plot of 13 bighas, which was a gairmazarua land. A year ago, we built our houses there, and that entirely changed the attitude of landowners', she says.

Everybody in the village listens to Tilaya, and follows her, as their leader. She was the one who had taken the initiative in taking control of the land. 'I have been working in the fields since long, but that was not the case with so many other musahar women. Now more and more women work, because of increasing economic pressure and migration of the menfolk to Punjab-Haryana. We have to bear so many burdens now. We have to decide things for our houses', says she, regarding her involvement in the work of the organisation. Tilaya's involvement in the organisational work started a few years ago, when the idea of a 'gram kosh' came to the region. She started collecting Rs 5 per family, in spite of the resentment shown by the males. Once her husband beat her up mercilessly, but women were very supportive, especially Pagia Bai. Slowly the gram kosh became a success and it was the males who got the much-needed support from the kosh at the time of their going to Punjab. When Tilaya was accepted among the male members, she started going to other villages with the Sangathan activists. The Sangathan became stronger and vibrant in Khairi and its annual conference took place there in May 1998. More than 2,000 musahars of the region gathered there, to give the organisation more strength.

With all these activities, Tilaya was getting more confident about herself, about the strength of the organisation. When a few months ago, landlords of Khairi village offered her some land as a bribe, to keep her out of organisational work, she not only refused, but also saw it this as a vindication of her suspicious. But now, the brutal attack and the threat over her life and family has pained her immensely, and she silently asks many questions: Why has nothing happened to the aggressors in spite of the new-expressed strength of musahars? Why she has to live in hiding? What will happen to her? Who will take care of her damaged house and replace the stolen cattle, which provided 6–7 litres of milk a day for sale? Will she be able to survive and the organisation able to withstand the pressure?

The attack on Tiliya Devi in the face of her assertion, and her dilemmas, struggles and strengths can give us multiple readings. Male migration has widened the spatial gaps in local families and household, leading to increasing stresses and hardships in the lives of many musahar women. There has been a feminisation of the local workforce. At the same time, musahar women are now much more visible both within the household and outside it. They now have more decision-making powers. This change and rupture has often made them more aware of their oppression, giving them a new strength to assert themselves. Their involvement with the local organisation has grown. They are increasingly seeking to disrupt the social order by reworking their own space and asserting their agency. Even the landlords who attacked Tiliya Devi, and musahar men themselves are forced to recognise this increasing visibility of women. Thus disorder has crept into the moral order. Existing locations of gender and caste hierarchies have been slightly dislocated in this scenario.

It is Moghlaha village of Madhubani district in July 1998. Here brahmins, rajputs, bhumihars and yadavs are in a majority; and mallahs, doms and musahars are few, around 30, in number. All dalits are agricultural, migrant or construction labourers. At the same time, within the village, they have also been doing some work traditionally. Suppose a cattle dies in the village, it is the duty of a musahar to lift the dead body and throw it away, outside the village. If there is a feast at the time of marriage or last rites, doms clean up the mess after food is served and eaten.

An incident occurred a year ago regarding this traditional work, a villager remembers. A brahmin was constructing his house and he asked a musahar to come for a day's work. That day, the musahar had to go to some other village to see his relatives and he expressed his inability to come. The brahmin was furious and he called a meeting of all brahmins of the village that day where three decisions were taken. Musahars will not be given any work; their cattle will not be allowed in brahmin's fields; and their women will not be allowed to cut grass or to collect dry leaves in the fields and lands of brahmins.

The musahars were terrified at this course of development. They also faced several difficulties day-to-day. For instance, a brahmin's buffalo died in the village. The musahars then refused to throw it away outside the village, and nobody else in the village was ready to perform the work. This was seen as a crisis among the village elders and thus a meeting of the villagers was called. By that time, all the dalits had begun to see that they would suffer immensely if they were scattered, and in the meeting they all said in one voice that brahmins' unilateral decision to boycott the musahars was unjust and the traditional ways of village living, where one needs another, should be restored again. Whether the brahmins got scared, or they had an urgent need, or some of them thought that the death of a buffalo was god's punishment for a wrong decision, the meeting decided to lift the boycott on musahars.

But this was not the end. Some time after this episode came the elections. This time as in the past also, brahmins and Bhumihars started capturing the polling booths. However, they were met with some resistance by a few of the rich among the yadavs. There were violent clashes, where both sides seemed prepared with arms and ammunitions. The brahmins and bhumihars left the scene, but before leaving, some of their youth blasted a bomb, though without any damage. The police came and the brahmins lodged complaints against the yadavs and the dalits, both.

Some youths of the backward castes came forward at this time. They assured the dalits that the village would collectively fight for their cases. For this purpose, they even formed a 'Nav Nirman Kalyan Samiti' for collection of funds. The Samiti collected funds and started taking up other issues, like installing of tubewells for drinking water, hiring of unemployed youth to impart education to village children, etc. The Samiti also started organising Hindu festivals and ceremonies.

The brahmins and Bhumihars got restive on seeing the activities of the Samiti and decided on their part to construct a Hanuman temple. The construction began with a ceremony, but soon there was a dearth of funds. They approached the Samiti for collaboration in the temple building, with the promise that the name of the Samiti would be displayed in the temple. The Samiti accepted this and supported the construction in all possible manner.

The temple was built. The statue of Hanuman was installed. But the name of the Samiti was not displayed there. Dalits say that in spite of their repeated requests, the brahmins always evaded this. They felt cheated and sharp differences surfaced within the Samiti regarding the future course of action. The Samiti also became defunct in this meanwhile.

Identities of various castes and communities are being negotiated in multiple ways in this village, depending on social and economic needs. 'Musahars have always been considered impure, and brahmins would not like to be touched even by their shadows', complains a local villager. But then I saw a brahmin landowner touching the body of a musahar, while having a conversation with him in the same village. I wondered and asked the brahmin, 'Have things changed here?' He replied, 'Now there is no labourer found in the village. Everybody goes out. If I behave like this, they are happy and only then do they come to work.'

A young dalit of the same village says that he would never take up the job being done by his father, i.e., lifting and throwing away the bodies of cattle carcases. The old father contests him and says that he would have to do it after his death. Otherwise from where else would he get Rs 150–200 for a work like this. The son however shows his clear disapproval and says that he would prefer to go to Patna or Muzzafarpur to pull a rickshaw, than to lift a dead cattle.

Khairi village under Lakhanaur police station stands shattered, as armed yadav landlords attacked the musahars there, ransacked their huts and took away whatever cattle wealth and other belongings they had. The musahars and the yadavs, both lodged police complaints against each other, alleging provocation and attack by the other. The police did not come earlier, in spite of the musahars' reported fears of being attacked. Now there is a police camp in the village, but they are arresting people from both sides and there has been no recovery of looted cattle or other goods.

One hears contradictory voices from the musahars. Charitra Sadai, who was seriously injured in the attack, says in a disillusioned tone that it was the people of the Lok Sakti Sangathan, and not the police, who took the injured to Darbhanga hospital and arranged food and necessary things for them. At the same time, a local activist comments, 'the police came and they are now camping here. We have lodged our complaint with them. All this is happening because of Laloo Yadav's regime. Otherwise we would have got a worse deal, as was happening in the previous regimes.' He gets wide nods from other villagers gathered there.

Bakunia Bichali village is in Saharsa district, very far from Khairi. But the musahars there know about the Khari incident and plan to take part in the forthcoming protest programmes of the musahars. In one of their meetings organised in the village, they sit under two flags, hoisted on two long bamboos; the two flags symbolise their two gods—Deena and Bhadri, who were brothers. The two musahar brothers sacrificed for the cause of their community in an ancient time. 'Every year in June, we remember Deena-Bhadri. In small groups, we go from house-to-house, village-to-village to collect rice or paddy, so that their memory is kept alive. They are remembered because they suffered and sacrificed. They are our only gods. Their sacrifice is our's. The suffering of Khairi is our's', says Domi Sadai in a forthright manner.

The musahars' own symbols and idioms are much more visible today in the social and cultural landscape of the region. They are today trying to evolve diverse mediums to strengthen processes of social questioning and offering parallel structures to the past and present social order. An emergence of a new symbolic order is there, where what was defiled till now, is being turning into an instrument of worship, and what was considered as pure, is being rejected and questioned. Within this socio-cultural milieu lie the consciousness, contradictions and dichotomies of the musahars. The ways in which it reveals itself in daily lives, directing local contexts of culture and association, is a reflection of changing location and distribution of power in society.

Though not very visible and not much heard about, the musahars are causing fissures in the caste, gender and ritual hierarchies of the region. Several dynamics are at work, at the village, leading them to a situation in which they seek to disrupt a prevailing order, and want to create their own, though some forms of acquiescence with the present also continue. The musahars were musahars because of the location of their caste, occupation and place, which acted as fundamental signs of their identities. Today however, some of these signs are getting dislocated and are vanishing. Their previous identity as untouchables and rat seekers is shifting into the periphery. More visible today are issues of their survival, their economic and social aspirations, their demands and struggles. At the same time, this new image represents more of aspiration, and less of an achieved entity. It is in the process of formation, without yet reaching full realisation. It is moving and transitory, and yet provides alternative grounds for the society.

7

New Technology and Traditional Rural Institutions

Case of Jajmani *Relations in Karnataka*[*]

G. K. Karanth

Sociologists and social anthropologists owe a debt to the pioneering work by W. H. Wiser (1936) which gave a systematic exposition of the concept of *jajmani* relations, and to T. O. Beidelman (1959) for a comparative analysis. While the term jajmani is mainly applicable to the Hindi-speaking parts of India, the network of relations subsumed under the system has been known by different names in different parts of the country: *ayam*, *adade*, *baluti*, etc. Some scholars familiar only with the term jajmani have wrongly concluded that the institution is absent in the non-Hindi regions because they did, not come across the term (see for example, Hill 1979).

A second clarification needs to be made regarding a view which considers jajmani relations as much an aspect of agrarian relations as of inter-caste relations. Some argue that the term jajmani is to be applied only to such relations in the realm of ritual (Pocock 1962). But, by narrowing the term's scope only to ritual, we tend to ignore an important aspect of the hereditary inter-caste service-relationships; namely their secular characteristic. Such secular services, significantly, are also included by the people themselves under the jajmani system, and they are exchanged for grain and fodder under the same principle as in the religious aspect of jajmani relations. Dumont (1972: 140), for instance, recognises this secular nature of jajmani relations. As can be seen from the present study, there are some specialists who render both 'secular' and 'religious' services as part of jajmani relations.

---

* This chapter has been extracted from a longer paper published by the author in the *Economic and Political Weekly* 22 (51): 2217–24, 19 December 1987.

This paper is a by-product of my doctoral dissertation. I am grateful to T. K. Oommen, M. N. Srinivas, A. M. Shah, B. R. Chauhan, V. S. Parthasarathy, C. N. Ramachandran and R. Sivaprasad for their comments.

A broader, view of jajmani relations is justified when we take note of another important feature. The exchange of goods and services exists between the specialists on the one hand, and the patrons who own the land, on the other. Such patrons are also members of specific castes with a superior ritual status. In other words, jajmani relations do not involve patrons who do not own land, even if they are eligible to receive goods and services by virtue of their superior caste status. This emphasis on landownership can be readily explained. While exchange of goods and services makes it obligatory for the patron to make annual payments in kind to the specialists, a landless 'patron' can only provide his labour, which is not necessarily skilled, or that required by a given specialist. If the norms of caste purity and pollution permit, a landless patron can obtain the services of a specialist by paying for them in cash. But such a relationship does not amount to a jajmani relationship, for in the former instance there is, on the one hand, a right to be served and the duty to serve, and on the other, a periodic grain payment to be made by the patron for goods and services.... A third clarification needs to be made with reference to the hereditary character of jajmani relationships. What sort of a stable or hereditary relationship can be considered to constitute a jajmani relation? That is, do we consider a relationship between a landowner and his indentured servant, lasting over a few generations, as jajmani? For example, Harper (1959) considers the permanently indentured servants also as part of the jajmani system (which he terms as 'Malnad system'). Similarly, Beidelman (1959) equates the employer or jajman with the landlord and the specialist or *kamin* with agricultural labourers. Breman (1974) finds that servitude as a form of unfree labour fits completely with an interpretation of jajmani system as compulsory exchange on unequal terms.

It is, therefore, necessary to lay down certain criteria to distinguish jajmani relations from other, apparently similar relations. In order to distinguish jajmani relations from other forms of agricultural labour relations we need to ask: what is the caste of the indentured or the agricultural labourers? It is necessary to view indentured and agricultural labourers from the perspective of caste, since caste membership is a vital element for participation in the jajmani relationship either as a patron or as a specialist. Members of almost any caste could be indentured or agricultural labourers (with the exception of ritually high castes, in the past). Elsewhere I have shown that agricultural labourers and bonded or indentured servants, in the past as well as at present, came from the dominant and upper castes as well as from the lower castes (Karanth 1984). Mere continuity of indentured relations or landowner-labourer relations over a long period does not necessarily amount to jajmani relations. It would be more appropriate to consider them as 'patron-client relations' (Srinivas 1976), which may include jajmani and other relations of mutual interdependence.

Fourth, description of the jajmani system by most scholars seem to assume that it has remained unchanged from time immemorial, and that the changes which have occurred in it are modern phenomena. However, it is more likely that the system has undergone changes over time as well as space. A careful examination of the jajmani relations in the past would reveal instances of new members inducted into the system while some others are excluded, or a specialist replacing another or even competing with another in the same craft or service and also of changes in the mode and quantity of grain to be paid, etc., (see for example, Harper 1959; Epstein 1962).

Finally, almost all studies of jajmani relations have been silent about one important aspect, namely, the quantity of grain paid to the specialists and the manner in which this is determined.[1] An examination of the determinants of the quantity of grain to be paid may throw new light on the issue of distributive justice to the specialists. This study reveals that in most jajmani relationships the patrons have a formula that determines the quantity of grains to be paid to the specialists, although the actual quantity paid may not be sufficient for the specialist's survival.

The Village Setting

Rajapura[2] is about 60 kilometres from Bangalore city, the capital of Karnataka.[3] During 1978–79, the population of the village was 995 distributed among 183 households of 12 different castes. Okkaligas are the politically, economically and socially dominant caste. They own the bulk of agricultural land, while the incidence of landlessness is relatively high among the other castes (see Table 7.1). All the castes engage in agriculture, although some of them have other occupations. The main crops grown are ragi, mulberry, pulses, groundnuts, and paddy. Except among the big farmers, production of food crops is mainly for subsistence. However, some products like mustard, sesame, castor seeds, field-beans (avarekai), and lentils, in addition to ragi, often serve as sources of cash income. From the point of view of cash income, mulberry-growing and silkworm-rearing are of primary importance.[4] Farmers buy the silkworm eggs (layings) from the sericulture department of the government of Karnataka. When the eggs are hatched, the silkworms are fed with mulberry leaves, which are grown on either dry or garden land. This being a 'seed area', the cocoons are sold to the grainage of the marketing centre of the sericulture department, in the neighbouring village of Doddi, or to private buyers with the permission of the officials.[5]

Sericulture in Rajapura prior to 1967 was only an agriculturally slack season activity that too on a negligible scale. Farmers had to go to far away places to sell the small harvest of cocoons. The opening of a grainage and silk cocoon market in 1967 in Doddi village facilitated mulberry-growing and silkworm-rearing in Rajapura on a comparatively large scale. The number of households engaged in sericulture rose from about 45 during 1970 to 199 by the end of 1980. The coming of sericulture was a boon to the dry-land farmers in the region. Whereas earlier the farmers sold their crop annually or biannually, they now could harvest and sell silk-cocoons every two months,[6] and thus have a more and frequent cash income.

By the very nature of its technology, sericulture[7] is a labour intensive activity, with extensive use of female labour in particular. [...]

From the point of view of the present paper, the most important impact of sericulture was the increased demand for the services of craftsmen: basket-maker, potter, ironsmith and carpenter. Sericulture requires many appliances that are to be made and repaired by these craftsmen. Bamboo baskets, trays and mounts which are used for carrying mulberry leaves and keeping the silkworms; wooden stands to store the wormrearing trays; watering the garden with earthen pots; and making and repairing tools, etc., were some of the goods and services now required of these specialists. Instead of buying these goods from urban markets, farmers patronised local craftsmen. Thus, while prior to 1970 some members from artisan households had migrated to other places in search of work, during the post-sericulture period there was not only a halt on migration, but a reverse flow also.

JAJMANI RELATIONS IN RAJAPURA: THE ADADE SYSTEM

The local term for jajmani is adade, while the service of craft specialists are known as Kasabudararu and landowners as adade kula,[8] or as okkalu. Adade also means grain payment, while some specialists (musicians, and the village servants) refer to it as acreragi. Adade relationships exist between patrons who are landowning members of high castes on the one hand, and the priests, village servants, blacksmiths, washermen, barbers and musicians on the other. About 15 years ago the network of adade relations included an astrologer and a potter also. When the old astrologer, a brahmin from the nearby town of Magadi, died none of his children showed any interest in succeeding to his father's role. Similarly when the old potter died, his two sons were not old enough for adade relationship. Subsequently one of the sons learnt the traditional craft, and is now active selling pots for grain, but not as part of adade relation.[...]

While there are certain specialists who serve only families in the village, others serve both particular families and the village, as a whole, and yet others serve only the village as a corporate body. Accordingly, the specialists' status vary as do the mode of payment. The position of various castes in the local hierarchy is also found to be influencing, and influenced by, the variations listed above.[...]

Village-oriented Services

The distinguishing feature of this category of services is that the specialists render their services to *the village as a corporate whole*. In return they are generally given a plot of land for cultivation. Payment by gift of land stands higher than periodical grain payment. In addition to the land given, particular landowning households pay the functionaries a quantity of grain and a bundle of straw

Priests (A)

It is necessary to identify the groups of priests with a suffix (A) to distinguish them from the others also referred to as priests. Of the three temples in the village, one is of the presiding deity of the village, *Hatti Maramma*. The eldest male member of the households belonging to the lineage of the former *patel* is the hereditary priest of this temple. During my fieldwork period there were three such priestly households, each serving for a year in rotation. The temple has been endowed with 18 acres of land by the earliest settlers of the village. The three households enjoy this land among themselves. The deity has to be offered special prayers every Tuesday, while on other days merely the temple lamp is lit. The major event is the annual festival in April–May, the expenses of which are met by the priest.[9] But, a devotee may undertake a vow to have the image of the goddess taken out and on such occasions the cost is borne by the devotee himself.

By definition, the services of the priests are oriented towards the entire village. The priests officiate for everyone by accepting their offering, and distributing flowers (*prasada*) sanctified by being offered to the goddess. There is, however, a discrimination against the members of the former untouchable castes of Holeya and Madiga. Their offerings of fruits and flowers are accepted only after the higher castes make their offerings and prasada is given to them. The deity's procession is taken only till the outskirts of the Holeya and Madiga quarters.

Astrologer

No astrologer exists now in Rajapura, but when one did he lived in the town of Magadi. He used to visit the village with his almanac during the Hindu New Year (Ugadi) festival (March–April). The astrologer traditionally read out to the villagers the forecast for the year contained in the almanac (panchanga) about the adequacy of rains and which crop would fare better. He also indicated times auspicious for commencement of certain important tasks such as ploughing, sowing and bringing the harvest home. The farmers also used to consult the astrologer in the town to find out auspicious time for the digging of a well or construction of houses, going out looking for a bride, where to look for a missing cow, etc.[10] On each of these occasions a payment in cash and kind was made to him.

In some villages of the region, the astrologer was given a plot of land for his services. But in Rajapura each landowning household gave him a measure of ragi, pulses, jaggery, fruits and vegetables. The washerman provided donkeys to carry the grains to Magadi town.

Although the role of the village astrologer does not form a part of the present day network of adade relations in the village, the villagers have not lost faith in astrology. For astrological consultations they now go to a smith in a neighbouring village. Payment for him is exclusively in cash. Some peripatetic groups also give predictions about future for the villagers in addition to medicine to the sick. Most of the villagers, who are able to read now buy a pocket-calendar or a popular almanac which gives them the information formerly given by astrologers.[11] Lack of interest on the part of the village astrologers themselves has contributed to the decline in their role in *adade* relations.

TABLE 7.1: Types of Jajmani Relations in Rajapura (Services)

I Village-Oriented	II Family-Oriented	III Village-and-Family-Oriented
(1) Priests (A)	(1) Priests (B)	(1) Priests (C)
(2) Astrologer	(2) Smiths	(2) Washermen
(3) Village servants	(3) Barber	(3) Musicians

Village servant (Thoti)

This office is held by members of the Madiga caste, which was formerly an untouchable caste. The thoti serves the entire village. Traditionally his duties were to accompany and assist the patel and shanubhog (that is, headman and accountant) in performing their duties. For instance, the thoti accompanied the shanubhog during the time of assessment and recovery of land revenue from the farmers. He also accompanied the patel during his official visits in the village or outside. The thoti also had to be present during the meeting of the village council, for it was his duty to inform each member to attend the meeting, and summon the members of various families whose presence was necessary. He continues to function as the village broadcaster: All important announcements are made by him to the accompaniment of the drum-beat. He might be asked to announce the date of the accountant's visit to the village to collect revenue, the need for volunteers to repair a part of the temple, or contributions to be made by each household to a village festival.

Ideally, the thoti was expected to know the details of every dispute settled by the council and to provide the facts to the members on future occasion, if necessary. He was also expected to know the extent of land owned by each villager, and point out to the stones marking each boundary when a need arose. He was also the watchman of the village and crops and as such he had to take possession of stray animals that entered the village or its fields, and hand them over to their owners after collecting fines. Finally he removed the carcasses of cattle, the skins of which he was free to sell or make drums with.

The thoti had also duties on ceremonial occasions such as the festival of the village deity when, for instance, he had to sprinkle the blood of the sacrificed goat in the eight directions to propitiate the spirits inhabiting each.[12] He was also one of the party of musicians to accompany a corpse to the burial ground.

In return for his services, the thoti got a reward of land, referred to as *thoti-inamti*. In addition to this, from each landowning household he received a measure of grain (*acre-ragi*) as payment and a bundle of straw. Grain payment was made to the scale of two seers per acre owned by patrons.

There are two thotis now in Rajapura. They have married sisters, and between themselves have divided the land that goes with the office. They serve the village by turns. Thotis continue to serve even though the office has been formally abolished by the government along with the offices of hereditary headman and accountant.[13]

In recent years there have been some strains and changes in the adade relations involving the thoti. The number of farmers paying acre-ragi has been declining. The payment is no longer related to the extent of land owned. During 1978–79, the thoti and other musicians refused to perform at the annual festival on the grounds that annual payments were not being made regularly by many landowners. The thotis complained that they could not pay Rs 5 to the other drummers who were part of the band of musicians. But the village elders were able to persuade the musicians to perform, and some farmers to pay up their dues.

One important sociological point not to be missed here is that some traditional institutions are so strong that government's abolition is an inadequate cause for its decline and disappearance. The thotis themselves explained that they were willing to serve the village as long as their services were needed. This does not suggest that they are happy to serve the village under the prevailing conditions of declining number of people paying acre-ragi.

Some farmers, however, point out to the irrelevance of thotis' services as causes for their not making grain payment. It was also felt that the thotis were suitably rewarded with land for whatever services they now rendered.

In spite of the declining payment, the thotis continue to serve the village as in the past. They now accompany the newly appointed village accountant, and officials of the police and revenue departments during their visits to the village. Their role in the present day village council is insignificant, but they do render their services if asked for. The important reasons for their (continuing to serve the village seem to be the grant of land and the power of village elders in persuading them to work. The villagers also, by and large, continue to consider the role of the thoti in the same way as before. 'A village without a thoti is like a jungle' is a saying which the people recall whenever the thotis neglect their duties.

Family-oriented Services

As already mentioned, the specialists in this category perform certain specified tasks for patron-households. The specialists are paid fixed quantities of grain and straw. They are not given a gift of land as in the first category.

Priests (B)

Most households in Rajapura have a house-deity located generally in the village from which they or their ancestors migrated. The household refers to itself as the okkalu of such and such a deity. The priests officiating in these temples serve the client households of the deity. The client households periodically visit the patron deities and the priests of the temple serve as chaplains.

The priests of these temples also used to visit Rajapura annually to collect grain (adade) and other gifts from devotees. Where the temples were far away or the local devotees too few, the latter themselves carried a measure of ragi and other gifts during their annual visit to such temples. Frequently they gave money in lieu of the kind payment.

In recent times there has been a decline in the frequency of the visits by the priests to village. The devotees, however, visit the temples at least once in three-four years. But the relationship between the priests of this category and okkalu devotees is not as in the past. Not only do the priests not know accurately the geographical distribution of okkalu devotees, the latter have frequently accepted new temples as their family-deities. However, a few priests and devotees do maintain a adade relationship, particularly the older families in the village.

Blacksmith

There are three households of blacksmiths in Rajapura. About 35 years ago the village had only one smith who served all the households in the village for adade. After his death three of his sons left the village to work as labourers elsewhere, entrusting one brother with the caste-occupation. After a few years, the latter invited his sister's husband to assist him. Soon the sister's husband established himself independently as a smith and the villagers seemed to find the latter's workmanship better than that of the former.

In 1952 another smith migrated into the village as a tenant. Following a dispute with the old smiths of the village, a few patrons engaged the new smith. Neither the caste nor the village panchayats were able to enforce the norm of exclusive right of the old smiths to serve the households in the village. The precedence of the old Smith's brother-in-law entering into adade relation was one of the factors which helped the new smith. He was successful in gaining acceptance also by virtue of his skill and, later, by professing his loyaly to the dominant faction of the village council. The entry of new specialists into adade relations is to be viewed here with reference to the argument made earlier; namely, that the system is flexible and hereditary rights to the office are not always strictly followed.

The smith's duties consist of making, repairing, and sharpening such tools as sickles, chisels, crowbars, ploughs, etc. There are rules and conventions governing when a new tool is to be provided and when an old one is to be repaired. In making a new tool, for example, the farmer has to provide the required material. Making and repairing the tools are generally prior to the commencement of the agricultural season, and again, during harvest operations.

Traditionally the quantity of grain paid to the smith was related to the number of the ploughs owned by a landowner. For two ploughs owned a farmer paid 16 seers of ragi and two bundles of straw, and for every additional plough, eight seers of ragi. The number of ploughs used by a man was related to the extent of land owned by him. Thus different classes of landowners (big or small) paid the smith in accordance to their wealth.

For two reasons, mainly, this formula is not strictly followed in recent times. First, the smith does not verify the number of ploughs used or owned by his patrons. Formerly he knew it as he himself would have fashioned the ploughs. Nowadays many farmers themselves have acquired the skills of fashioning the ploughs, and they also lend their services to their fellow-farmers. In the absence of an exclusive right to their duties, the smiths now fail to keep track of the number of ploughs in possession of patrons. Secondly, the practice of plough sharing and mutual exchange of labour involved in ploughing renders the calculation difficult.

With the introduction of sericulture, the range of tools the smiths have to make has greatly increased. For such additional services they collect a cash fee. In either form of payment, i.e., adade or cash, the farmer is required to provide charcoal to be used as fuel for the kiln, and assist the smith in bellowing. Some other changes have occurred in the adade relations between the smiths and their patrons. For example, with the inclusion of new smiths in the network of jajmani relations, the patrons now change their smiths frequently. Not all the farmers have been prompt in settling their adade dues with the smith, which situation has been largely responsible for frequent shifts in patron-client relations.

Barber

Rajapura does not have a resident barber. A barber comes everyday from a neighbouring village. In his shop he serves all except harijans. There is pressure on him from the higher castes not to extend his services to harijans while serving in Rajapura. But at the annual cattle-fair at Magadi and elsewhere, where he puts up a temporary shop, he serves all the castes.

The barber receives an annual payment of eight seers of ragi and a bundle of straw for serving every adult and married male member of a household. For serving other male members he gets only eight seers of ragi per head. If a household has more than four adult male members, payment for serving one member is waived. He does not collect grain for cutting the hair of young children of his patrons. The number of adult male members includes bonded labourers of a given household, if they are not harijans. Adade patrons are entitled to one haircut and one shave a month. For additional services the barber collects 50 paise and 25 paise, respectively. Non-adade patrons also have to pay these rates for the barber's services.

The *adade*-barberh as also ritual duties to perform. He has the right to bring *basinga*, a forehead-ornament worn by a bridegroom and bride during marriage. In return he is given a gift of Rs 5, one cube of jaggery, betel leaves, arecanuts, and a measure of grain.

The barber serves almost all the okkaliga households on adade basis. Other castes like the Lingayat, Maratha and odda are also served either for adade or cash. The holeya and madiga, who are not served either for cash or kind payment, get their haircut by one of their own castefolk on an exchange basis or by going to a haircutting shop in Magadi town.

Rajapura's barber complains, indeed as most other specialists do, of increasing irregularity in grain payment by adade patrons. He is also unhappy that many young men do not take his services unlike the older men in their families. In the absence of a powerful and effective caste-panchayat, he has no way of ensuring an exclusive right to serve the patrons. Nevertheless, his service relation with most landowning okkaliga patrons is found to be continuing. The farmers who are not regular in making the annual grain payment continue to take his services by promising to settle the dues. Farmers find it inconvenient to get their hair cut in Magadi town as they have to wait for an auspicious day and time and make a visit for that specific purpose.[...]

Village and Family-oriented Services

The third category of specialists includes priests (C), washerman and the village musicians. Their duties are not only towards the village as a whole but also to individual households living in it.

Priests (C)

This category of priests serve in a village temple as well as the individual households for grain-payment. For example, the priests of Basava, and cave temples respectively, have duties to officiate in the temples, the deities of which are worshipped by all in the village. As priests of the village-temples they are compensated by a gift of land. They also serve the farmers by performing the rituals associated with annual crop-worship, purification following a birth or death in the family, and in such other occasions. In return for these services the priest is paid annually a measure of grain and straw, in addition to cash gift.

One important factor needs to be mentioned here. Over the past three decades these two temples have had many new priests replacing the old ones. Yet the villagers have entered into adade relations with each successive priest.

Washerman

Rajapura has three washerman households. Two of them are brothers, one of whom is not engaged in his caste occupation. The washerman of the village, as in the case of smiths, have had to face competition from their own caste-members. A faction of the village leaders, (the same people who had shown preference to the immigrant smith, discussed above) was unhappy with the old washerman and invited a man from a nearby village. Initially there was a protest by the old washerman. But his attempts to censure the new washerman through his caste panchayat, with its headquartors at Magadi town, did not succeed. With the support of a powerful faction of the village leadership, the new washerman was able to establish himself as an adade specialist. The hereditary washerman was, however, given the exclusive right to perform the duties towards the village as a whole. The new washerman had on an average 10 to 15 patrons at a given time. But in course of time some, of the members who were responsible for bringing the new washerman returned to the old washerman or to one of his sons who had now taken over the duties from the father.

The washerman's duties towards the village as a whole consist of carrying a torch while the procession of any of the three deities is taken out. He has to provide clean white clothes to be spread on the ground so that the carriers of the image of the deity do not walk on bare ground. He has to wash the ornamental clothes with which the images of the deities are dressed. He is also the custodian of these dresses when they are not being used.

The washerman gets paid in cash as well as in kind for his services to the village as a whole. When a procession is taken out the priest gives him money towards oil and gifts of coconut and fruits. A farmer who vows to take out a procession pays a fee in cash and kind to the washerman. During the annual festival almost every household in the village, with the exception of Lingayats, offers a sheep to the deity, the heads of which are collected by the washerman.

As regards serving the patron-households, the washernan's wife cleans menstrual clothes and post-natal clothes of women. Women in their periods and at birth are regarded as impure as also the blood-stained clothes. Every morning the washerman's wife goes round the village picking up menstrual clothes of women which are put away in a corner of the front yard.

The washernan, further, has a ritual to perform at the time of weddings in his patron's household. He provides a white cloth used for covering the vessel into which 'milk' sanctifyig a wedding is poured. Guests and relatives put money into this vessel which the washerman collects (see, for a description of this ritual, Srinivas, 1942).

In return for these services he is paid eight seers of ragi and two bundles of straw. The payment vary according to the number of married couples in a house: for each couple he is paid an extra eight seers of ragi. If the number of couples exceeds four, the oldest couple receives free service. The exemption suggests that the physiological factor of menopause is being taken into account. Further, when a member in his patron's family dies, the washerman is given the clothes in which the corpse is dressed.

In Rajapura only one of the two brothers has the office of village washerman. This is the younger brother, while the older was a bonded labourer who later became a tenant of a Lingayat landowner. The new washerman also holds the office of village washerman in a nearby village.

Like the other specialists in the village, the washerman do not serve harijans (Holeyas and Madigas). The oddas are above the untouchability line but are too poor to pay the washerman either in cash or kind.

Musicians

The team of musicians has duties to the village as a whole and to patron-households. Towards the former the musicians play at the annual festivals of the deities and on other occasions when a procession is taken out. As to the patron households, their duties consist of playing instruments for funeral procession. Formerly they played during, weddings also, but increasingly professional musicians of Magadi town are being hired for this purpose. Apart from a preference for modern music, the other reason for hiring musicians from outside is that, very often, there is more than one wedding in the village on the same day.

The team of musicians consists of four Holeyas and two Madigas. It has duties not only in Rajapura but in a few neighbouring villages also. Each musician is paid eight seers of ragi and two bundles of straw by *all* the landowning households in the village. The Priests (A) and (C), referred to earlier have an obligation, to give coconuts and fruits in the addition to money to the musicians at the end of every procession. Like all the other specialists, the musicians also complain of adade dues not being settled in time.

Concluding Remarks

From the account given till now it is evident that the institution of jajmani relations has adapted itself to suit the changing needs of the people both in the past and in recent years. Although sericulture brought an increased monetisation to the agrarian economy of Rajapura, it may be seen that it did not result in the erosion of the 'traditional' attitudes of mutual dependence and obligation between different agrarian categor;ies as argued by some. An examination of jajmani relations in the context of a new technology, namely sericulture, shows that the latter has not significantly affected one of the traditional forms of rural institutions. On the contrary it has kept some of the service-specialists relatively busy throughout the year. The description of adade relations in Rajapura can now be related to some of the other issues raised in the beginning of the paper.

First, succession to various specialist roles is not always hereditary. Over time new specialists have replaced old ones or competed with each other. Accordingly there have also been frequent shifts in patron-client composition in the network of adade relations. The principle of hereditary rights is found to be operative more often in services that are oriented towards the village as a whole (I category) than in the family-oriented services (II category). The former are usually rewarded with land which may be said to encourage inheritance of the office along with land. Division in the family is accommodated by sharing rights to serve by turns.

Second, payment of grain to the specialists ideally was not arbitrary, but was in relation to the extent of land owned, the number of tools (ploughs) used by the patrons, or the number of married couples in the patron's households. However, in recent times and increasingly the farmers are defaulting in making payments to the specialists. This is particularly so in such services where an alternative specialist serves, and is willing to have new patrons. Further, grain payment is increasingly being delinked from the extent of land or tools owned. Instead, a standard eight or 16 seers of ragi and a bundle of straw are given. Cash payment is made for all extra services. Thus although cash and kind payment coexist, adade relations have not been replaced by monetary transactions.

Why do some farmers continue to have adade relations with the specialists? Why do adade relations continue in spite of the coming of sericulture with its increased monetisation? In answering these questions one should take a look at the nature of each service, the utility value of such goods and services to the patrons, and their indispensability for the secular and religious life of the patrons. In some cases substitute services are available, as with hired musicians from Magadi or barbers in town. From the point of view of the patrons the available alternatives are not always convenient. The personal relationship involved gives confidence in the workmanship of the local specialists and ensures fulfilment of specific requirements. Moreover, adade payment also serves as a retaining fee and ensures the services at the back and call of the farmer. Yet another reason is that he need not sell the grain to make cash payment but measure them out to make the payment.

The specialists, on their part, continue to serve on adade for many reasons. Frist, most of them are found to be supplementing their income by working as agricultural labourers (two washerman, one smith, two priests 'B', as well as the thotis and musicians), or as tenants and sharecroppers (thotis, musicians, one smith, priests 'A', 'B' 'C', and one washerman). Secondly, functioning as 'village' service specialists in the adade network gives them the satisfaction of keeping up the family or caste tradition. By virtue of serving as adade specialists they enjoy a higher social status within their caste, and are often envied by their fellow caste members. Indeed, specialists of all castes keep requesting the village elders to give them the custom whenever an incumbent specialist threatens to sever adade relations.

Third important factor as to why specialists continue to take part in adade relations is the role played by the village leadership. No account of rural Indian life seems to be complete without a reference to the role of village leaders, mainly of the dominant caste. In the past the leaders in Rajapura were responsible for bringing new specialists to compete with the existing ones and accommodating them in the network of adade relations. A similar and equally powerful role is being played by the present day leaders. Whenever there is a sign of possible breakdown of adade relations the leaders intervene to settle matters. People, particularly the aggrieved ones, point out that the leaders want to maintain status quo. The specialists even now complain formally to the village leaders about non-payment of grain. After persistent protests, either the headman, or the former patel speaks to the erring farmers. If there is a stalmate, the specialists are advised to write-off the arrears and discontinue serving such farmers. The specialists also take advantage of critical moments of patrons to demand payment of grains.

In most cases both the patrons and the specialists are vulnerable to pressure from the village leaders. They need the help of the leaders, for instance, in securing loans from the cooperative credit society, grants of free building materials, or allotment of free house sites, etc.

Finally, an important observation made in the village needs to be emphasised. Not only has the 'traditional' institution of adade persisted in the wake of increased monetisation of economy, the notion of adade has been applied to certain other repetitive relations in a 'market' situation. The forest guard of the forest near Rajapura, and the visiting merchant receive a measure of grain and bundles of straw from all the farmers dealing with them. The guard receives the grain for 'permitting' the farmers to graze their cattle in the forest, and allowing the forage of firewood, wood for making ploughs, etc. Ideally the relations between the villagers and these two men are expected to be impersonal and commercial. They are not only found to be personal but also contain elements of traditionality.

Notes

1. Exception, however, is in a paper by Anthony Good (1982), although he refuses to refer to the services as part of the *jajmani* system.

2. Rajapura is a pseudonym.

3. For a detailed description of the village, see Karanth (1981) and (1984).

4. I use the word sericulture in a restricted sense to include growing mulberry and rearing of silk worm. As an agro-based industry 'sericulture' includes a third dimension, namely the reeling of silk yarn from the co-coons. For a social anthropological account of sericulture, see Charsley (1982).

5. Under the Mysore Silkworm Seed Control Act, 1951, farmers engaged in sericulture have to register themselves with the Department of Sericulture, government of Karnataka, and be supervised by its technical experts.

6. See above, note 2.

7. For a description of different operations in silkworm rearing see Krishnaswamy (1978). 8 See Srinivas (1976: 212) for another village in Karnataka.

9. Special worship, either during the annual festival or at other times, involves the cost of flowers, fruits, additional payment to the washerman, musicians, and gifts to the priests, etc. In addition, the deity has to be offered a goat, the cost of which is borne by the devotee if he is fulfilling a vow, or by the priest. There will be at least half a dozen special *pujas* of this kind every year in addition to the annual festival.

10. See Srinivas (1976: 310–12) for a description of the importance of astrology in agriculture.

11. The pocket calendars and almanacs are sold not only in bookshops and petty shops in Magadi town, but also by vendors in bus stations. A pocket calendar costs 50 paise while the price of an almanac varies from Rs 4.00 to Rs 8.00.

12. The custom is known as *Mari bali* and takes place normally during the months of October–November every year. The meat is sold so as make good the cost of the sacrificed animal.

13. The Mysore Village Offices (Abolition) Act, 1961, which came into force in 1963.

References

Aggarwal, P. C. 1975. 'Some Observations on the Changing Agrarian Relations in Ludhiana, Punjab'. In *Changing Agrarian Relations in India*, ed. V. R. K. Paramahamsa. 111–19. Hyderabad: National Institute of Community Development.

Alexander, K. C. 1975. 'Changing Labour-Cultivator Relations in South India'. In *Changing Agrarian Relations in India*, ed. V. R. K. Paramahamsa. 21–24. Hyderabad: National Institute of Community Development.

Beidelman, T. O. 1959. *A Comparative Analysis of the Jajmani System*. New York: J. J. Augustine.

Breman, Jan. 1974. *Patronage and Exploitation: Changing Agrarian Relations in South Gujarat, India*. Berkeley: University of California Press.

Brown, L. R. 1970. *Seeds of Change: The Green Revolution and Development in the 1970s*. New York: Praeger.

Charsley, S. R. 1982. *Culture and Sericulture: Social Anthropology and Development in a South Indian Livestock Industry*. London: Academic.

Dumont, Louis. 1972. *Home Hierarchieus: The Caste System and Its Implications*. London: Weidenfeld and Nicolson.

Epstein, T. A. 1962. *Economic Development and Social Change in South India*. Manchester: Manchester University Press.

Frankel, Francine R. 1971. *India's Green Revolution: Economic Gains and Political Costs*. Princeton: Princeton University Press.

Good, Anthony. 1982. 'The Actor and the Act: Categories of Prestations in South India'. *Man* 17 (1): 23–41.

Gusfield, Joseph R. 1967. 'Tradition and Modernity: Misplaced Polarities in the Study of Social Change'. *American Journal of Sociology* 72 (4): 351–62.

Harper, E. B. 1959. 'Two Systems of Economic Exchange in Village India'. *American Anthropologist* 61 (5): 760–78.

Hill, Polly. 1979. 'Comparative Agrarian Relations in Karnataka (South India) and Hausaland (Northern Nigeria)'. *Indian Economic and Social History Review* 16 (3): 243–71.

———. 1982. *Dry Grain Farming Families: Housaland (Nigeria) and Karnataka (India) Compared*. Cambridge: Cambridge University Press.

Karanth, G. K. 1981. *Rural Youth: A Sociological Study of a Karnataka Village*. New Delhi: Concept Publishing Company.

____. 1984. 'Change and Continuity in Agrarian Relations: A Case Study of Karnataka Village'. Unpublished PhD thesis. Jawaharlal Nehru University, New Delhi.

____. Forthcoming. 'Change and Continuity in Agrarian Relations in Karnataka'. In *Two Faces of India: Bihar and Karnataka*, ed. James Manor and Walter.

Krishnaswamy, S. 1978. *Reshme Hulu Sakanikaya Nutana Vaigananika Kramagalu* (in Kannada). Bangalore: Government of Karnataka.

Oommen, T. K. 1971. 'Green Revolution and Agrarian Conflict'. *Economic and Political Weekly* 6 (26): A99–A103, June.

____. 1975. 'Agrarian Legislation and Movements as Sources of Social Change: The Case of Kerala'. *Economic and Political Weekly*, 10 (40): 1571–84, 4 October.

Paramakamsa, V. R. K. (ed.). 1975. *Changing Agrarian Relations in India*. Hyderabad: National Institute of Community Development.

Pocock, D. 1962. 'Notes of Jajmani Relationships'. *Contributions to Indian Sociology* (Old Series) VU: 78–95.

Rudolf, L. I. and Rudolf, S. H. 1967. *The Modernity of Tradition: Political Development in India*. Chicago: University of Chicago Press.

Sen, B. 1979. 'Opportunities in the Green Revolution'. *Economic and Political Weekly*. 5 (13): A-33–A-40.

Srinivas, M. N. 1942. *Marriage and Family in Mysore*. Bombay: New Book Company.

____. 1976. *The Remembered Village*. Delhi: Oxford University Press.

____. 1978. 'The Social Structure of a Mysore Village'. In *India's Villages*, ed. M. N. Srinivas. Bombay: Media Promotors and Publishers.

Wilks, Mark. 1930. *Historical Sketches of the South India in Attempt to Trace the History of Mysore*, edited with notes by Murray Hammick. Mysore: Government Press.

Wiser, W. H. 1936. *The Hindu Jajmani System*. Lucknow: Lucknow Publishing House.

8

Changing Religious Practices

Their Relationship to Secular Power in a Rajasthan Village[*]

Partap C. Aggarwal

Sanskritisation, it is said, has been one of the few processes of caste mobility which have existed in the Hindu caste system and it is used by low-caste Hindus throughout the country with occasional success. But what we know of the long history of the caste system in India suggests that social mobility, if at all possible, was a rare thing until Independence. Apparently, even if Sanskritisation was recognised as a legitimate means of social mobility, it must have been neither frequently used nor always successful when it was used.

Studies of lower castes and tribal groups in post-Independence India have, however, shown that Sanskritisation has become a common phenomenon. (Cohn 1955; Orans 1965) The underprivileged castes frequently Sanskritise while the higher castes turn toward Westernisation. The case study which I present confirms this in a rather dramatic fashion. Obviously, something has happened which has, on the one hand, weakened the ability of the privileged castes to curb the ambition of the lower castes and, on the other, has stimulated the hopes and the will of the underprivileged castes to improve their status. What is it that accounts for this change? I submit that the crucial stabilising factor in the Indian caste system was unequal distribution of economic and political power among the various castes. The privileged castes normally owned most of the land and dominated the traditional village panchayat. This gave them a vested interest in the caste system and a reason to try to preserve it. Whenever members of a low caste group tried to emulate the higher castes, they were ridiculed and even subjected to coercion if they persisted. The lower castes realised that in the absence of power, emulation of the higher castes was futile. Hence Sanskritisation was rarely attempted and was even less frequently successful. As we will see in the following case study, when power was more equally

---

* This chapter has been extracted from a longer paper published by the author in the *Economic and Political Weekly* 4 (12): 547–53, 22 March 1969.

distributed, the major hurdle in the way of the lower castes was removed and the traditional hierarchy was brought into question.

The village that we are about to examine is Chavandi Kalan, situated about 100 miles south-west of Delhi in an area popularly called Mewat. The total population of the village is 640 (1964), which is slightly above average for rural settlements in the region. The major occupation of the inhabitants is agriculture, but members of specialist caste groups, such as barbers, carpenters, blacksmiths, etc. (see Table 8.1), are also represented. These specialists earn their living by serving the agriculturists under the traditional barter arrangement known as *jajmani*. The cultivated land in the village is moderately fertile, but it is especially suitable for growing mustard and wheat, which are respectively the major cash and food crops in the area. Agriculture in Chavandi Kalan is predominantly dry farming save a few small garden plots which are irrigated from nearby wells for growing tobacco and vegetables for personal consumption.

TABLE 8.1: Caste Distribution in Chavandi Kalan

Caste (listed in order of position in caste hierarchy within each group)	Number of Households	Number of Individuals	Percentage
Muslim			
Meo	66	370	57.81
Faqir	1	7	1.09
Lohar	1	4	0.63
Sakka	3	12	1.88
Mirasi	1	7	1.09
Hindu			
Brahmin	3	10	1.56
Khatri	1	1	0.16
Bania	4	25	3.90
Khati	1	5	0.78
Dakot	4	30	4.69
Bairagi	1	5	0.78
Jogi	1	5	0.78
Nai	2	9	1.4
Chamar	11	45	7.03
Bhangi	2	12	1.88
Sikh			
Sikh	18	93	14.54
Total	120	640	100.00

Chavandi Kalan is about 500 years old which, according to the villagers, is a fairly respectable age for a village by Mewati standards. During these long years of its existence the village has experienced periods of relative tranquillity as well as violent upheavals when its population was affected. The most recent disturbance was experienced following 1947 which resulted in a drastic reshuffling of its population. Several of the Muslim families migrated to Pakistan and a number of Sikh peasants from West Pakistan came to replace the emigrants. The strengths of various other Hindu and Muslim castes were reduced mainly because they had temporarily to migrate to nearby towns during the riots of 1947 and some decided not to return to the village even after peace was restored. The only caste whose numbers remained unaffected was the untouchable Chamars. They did not leave the village during communal riots, and soon afterwards were allotted land (see Table 8.2) by the state government which encouraged them to stay.

TABLE 8.2: Distribution of Land-holdings in Chavandi Kalan by Caste and Number of Households

Caste	No. of House-holds in Caste	Per cent Holding Land	No. of Households according to Size of Land-holdings						Total
			1 to 5 Bighas*	6 to 10 Bighas	11 to 20 Bighas	21 to 25 Bighas	26 to 50 Bighas	51 to 99 Bighas	
Meo	66	100	10	11	27	4	13	1	66
Faqir	1	0	0	0	0	0	0	0	0
Mirasi	1	0	0	0	0	0	0	0	0
Nai	2	100	0	0	2	0	0	0	2
Lohar	1	0	0	0	0	0	0	0	0
Khati	1	0	0	0	0	0	0	0	0
Chamar	11	90.90	1	0	9	0	0	0	10
Bhangi	2	100	1	1	0	0	0	0	2
Bania	4	100	2	2	0	0	0	0	4
Sikh	18	100	0	1	16	1	0	0	18
Dakot	4	50	0	0	1	1	0	0	2
Bairagi	1	100	0	0	0	0	1	0	1
Sakka	3	0	0	0	0	0	0	0	0
Brahmin	3	100	0	1	1	0	0	1	3
Jogi	1	0	0	0	0	0	0	0	0
Khatri	1	100	0	0	1	0	0	0	1
Total	120	90.83	14	16	57	6	14	2	109

Note: *1 acre = 1.6 bigha.

Religious Change in the Various Castes

The Meos

The largest single caste group in the village is the Moos who number 370 and constitute about 58 per cent of the total population. They claim descent from some of the most prestigious Hindu Rajput clans, but they got converted to Islam about the fourteenth century ad, However, until 1947 their adoption of Islamic customs remained only nominal and they retained most of their original Hindu religious practices. The principal reason for this was their desire to retain their high status vis-à-vis the Hindu castes, and furthermore to continue to use the latter's services according to the traditional jajmani system.

At the time of Partition the Meos were regarded as Muslims, despite their Hindu customs, and were forced to flee the village and live in a neighbouring district for about two years. During this period some Meos migrated to Pakistan while the rest returned to Chavandi Kalan and were resettled on their land. However, a number of changes became noticeable in the village. First, the Meos lost their monopoly over the ownership of land. Some Hindu villagers, particularly an energetic brahmin, who remained in the village while the Meos were gone, laid claim to a good deal of land of disputed ownership. Furthermore, the land abandoned by the emigrant Meos was allotted to the local Chamars and Sikh refugees from West Pakistan. Second, the Meos found that their political dominance was also seriously challenged by the brahmins, the Sikhs, and even the Chamars. Third, the Hindus no longer treated the Meos as high-caste Rajputs. Even the lowly Chamars now refused to accept boiled food from the Muslim Meos.

The Meos are now rapidly replacing their Hindu rituals and beliefs with those of the Muslims. For example, they are abandoning their traditional marriage rites which involved worship of Hindu deities and objects, ceremonies requiring guidance of brahmin priests, and songs praising Hindu gods and goddesses. Celebration of Hindu festivals such as Holi, Diwali, Sankranti, and Tij, is now avoided, and instead Muslim festivals, both Sunni and Shia, viz., Idd, Shabrat, Ramadan, and Muharram, are observed with enthusiasm. Occasional visits to Hindu shrines and temples which were customary among the Meos are no longer considered appropriate. Instead regular attendance at the Muslim mosque and participation in Friday prayers at the Juma Masjid are considered meritorious. Meos used to delight in studying and reciting the Hindu epics such as the Ramayana and the Mahabharata, but now they not only ignore these but also much prefer to send their children to the Muslim Madrassa where instruction is given in the reading of the Koran. The attitude of the Meos toward the cow used to be one of reverence but has changed to the extent that many younger Meos would now eat beef if available. Even dress and habits of personal conduct have undergone change to conform to the established practices of the Muslims.

To be sure, these drastic changes are not made without a certain degree of ambivalence, anxiety, and nostalgia. A doting Meo mother may, for example, insist on the performance of all the traditional rituals at the marriage of her only son lest neglect provoke the wrath of some displeased supernaturals. Also some Meo girls sing Holi songs and even sprinkle coloured water over each other during the festive season in the privacy of their homes or fields. But it is clear that Hindu practices are no longer acceptable to the Meos and the desire for learning Muslim customs is strong. One can confidently predict that in a few years the way of life of the Meos will become completely Islamised.

The Sikhs

There are 18 households of Sikhs in Chavandi Kalan, who, with 93 members, constitute about 15 per cent of the total population. All of them belong to relatively low-status gotras among the Sikhs (e.g., Labana and Warwal) and come from villages in the Lyallpur and Montgomery districts of West Punjab. There they were landless tenant farmers, but since land was fertile and canal-irrigated, they lived a relatively comfortable life by village standards. However, in that environment they were underprivileged and most of them were given to excessive drinking, fighting, and other practices associated with low social rank. When, in 1947, West Punjab became part of Pakistan most Hindus and Sikhs who lived there were forced to migrate to India, and likewise, Muslims of East Punjab had to migrate to Pakistan. The Sikhs of Chavandi Kalan were among the victims of this population exchange and they found themselves living in refugee camps in East Punjab. Since they did not have any claim to land and lacked capital, their prospects of resettlement appeared dim. About the middle of 1949 the Rajasthan state government offered land to these farmers and they eagerly accepted the offer, for nothing was more attractive to them than land. Each Sikh family that came to Chavandi Kalan received 10 acres on very attractive terms. Initially there was same friction between the Muslim Meos and the Sikhs but in a surprisingly short time (about a year) the two communities learned to get along with one another. However, the local Hindus as well as the Meos regarded the Sikhs with some degree of disapproval. The main reason for this was that the Sikhs distilled illicit liquor and consumed a good deal of it themselves. Excessive drinking not only led to frequent fist fights but also resulted in a deterioration of the economic position of the Sikhs. The land in Chavandi Kalan was much too poor to support such extravagance.

About 1958 the Sikhs of Chavandi Kalan came under the influence of a revivalist leader named Teja Singh, who has a Gurdwara in the Bhatinda district of East Punjab. Following the example of Guru Gobind Singh, Teja Singh has organised his disciples in the manner of an army. Men who take active part in the movement are given military titles, such as general, major, lieutenant, etc. The popularity of this movement is greatest in the Punjab-Rajasthan border districts and especially among refugees from West Punjab.

Teja Singh is referred to as 'Guru' by his followers. Many believe that he is an avatar (reincarnation of God) and hence possesses supernatural power. Sikhs of Chavandi Kalan often talk about the miracles performed by this "great religious leader". Many villagers visit the Gurdwara of Teja Singh once or twice a year and often contribute free labour in the hope of having a wish fulfilled. One Sikh villager of Chavandi spent an extended period of service at the Gurdwara and believes that as a result his wish for a son was granted. He therefore named his son Mehar Singh, which means one who was a gift of the Guru.

The followers of Teja Singh are required to give up tobacco, liquor, meat and eggs. These prescriptions are scrupulously obeyed by the disciples. In Chavandi Kalan the change in the behaviour of the Sikhs has been quite dramatic and, as a consequence, they have now gained the respect of all the castes in the village. In addition, they have become unified and active in the political life of the village. Their interest in economic development, too, has increased, and is reflected in their renewed interest in the community development programme.

Meticulous Care

Another distinct change in the behaviour of the Sikhs is a redoubling of their interest in religion. In their original homes in West Pakistan some of the Sikhs occasionally participated in religious activities, but because of their low social rank, they rarely took initiative in these matters. But now, in Chavandi Kalan, they organise diwan (religious meetings in which scriptures are recited and discourses are given on spiritual subjects), langar (religious feasts), satsang (devotional prayers), and other congregational activities. Furthermore, they celebrate religious festivals and observe rituals, fasts, and ceremonies with meticulous care. Occasionally, inter-village gatherings and processions are organised to which Teja Singh or some other prominent leader is invited. Once or twice a year, depending on resources, the Sikhs of Chavandi Kalan visit the main Gurdwara in the Punjab. Since literacy is still low, none of the families acquired the granth (Sikh religious scripture), but several young boys and girls are sent to the village school partly in the hope that some day they will be able to read the sacred book.

The Chamars

Shoemakers make up about 7 per cent of the population of Chavandi Kalan. Before 1947, they used to skin dead animals, cure hides, and make shoes and other leather articles. These goods were supplied to their Meo patrons who compensated the Chamars with fixed amounts of grain twice each year.

But, in 1947, all the Chamars in Chavandi Kalan were given land by the government, and as a result they abandoned their traditional occupation, although it meant considerable economic sacrifice, at least for same families. But since it is a caste injunction, everybody has had to obey it. Their caste organisation has further ruled that the Chamars will no longer accept cooked food from the Meos, nor do menial work at Meo marriages. They now treat the sweepers as untouchable, mainly because the latter still carry on their caste occupation.

The Chamars actively participate in the elections for the village panchayat as well as for the State and central legislatures. In the most recent village panchayat elections, the Chamars of Chavandi Kalan demonstrated remarkable unity and political consciousness. Consequently, the higher castes became convinced that the Chamars represented a political force of some substance, A prominent Chamar accepted the job of the village *chowkidar* merely as an entree into the political and administrative system. In order to ensure their continuous upward movement in the social hierarchy, the Chamars are sending their children to the village school. In fact, they seem eager to take advantage of everything that the new government has to offer.

Remarkable Change

The change in their religious behaviour is quite remarkable. The Chamars now celebrate Hindu religious festivals with great enthusiasm. They have begun to perform the life cycle rites of the twice-born Hindus. Recently, the local brahmin priest has begun to serve the Chamars, with the result that, together with the quantity, the quality of the ritual life of the Chamars has changed a great deal. Furthermore, the Chamars now regularly participate, on more or less equal terms, in the important rituals of the other Hindus (twice-born castes as well as clean shudras) in the village. On several religious occasions I observed the Chamars participating in the puja ceremonies of high-caste Hindus. They were allowed to join other Hindus in the performance of life cycle rites of the latter. For example, when the village carpenter's mother died, the Chamars contributed some firewood for the cremation, and later took part in the ceremonies for the deceased over which the local brahmin presided. I noticed that the Chamars have developed a great sense of belonging to the Hindu society in and outside of the village. In 1964 there were communal riots in East Pakistan and subsequently in Calcutta. The Chamars of Chavandi Kalan expressed greater concern about the fate of the Hindus in Pakistan than any other Hindu caste in the village.

The Bhangis

There are two such families in Chavandi Kalan. Both practice their traditional occupation of sweeping. Since Independence, they have taken up the job of skinning dead animals which used to be the prerogative of the Chamars, The Bhangis were given land by the government; but it was inadequate. Also, their caste membership is sparsely distributed and rather inactive. As far as I could see, there was hardly any change in their social, political, or economic position. Their ritual status and religious behaviour have not changed either. The contrast between the Chamars and the Bhangis is quite striking: the Bhangis accept untouchability without question, while the Chamars resent it vehemently.

The Brahmins

Only one out of the three brahmin families in Chavandi Kalan owned land before 1947. However, the heads of these have been religious practitioners for several generations. Land was donated to them by a Meo patron, and the brahmin family did not cultivate it. Often it was leased out to the donor family who gave part of the produce to the brahmin owner. The other two families of brahmins in the village acquired land in 1947. While the Meos were gone, the brahmins used fair and foul means to gain title to some of the village land. One of the brahmin men is presently the biggest land and cattle herd owner in the village. He is the leader of a major faction and is involved in constant strife with his rivals. He actively participates in village politics and has been a member of the village panchayat. Since his own caste group is small, he has cultivated influence among the Chamars. Being a bachelor, he recently established an alliance with a Chamar woman. The villagers know about this relationship and have come to accept it. I once asked this man whether his sexual intimacy with a Chamar woman did not affect his caste status. He replied that the Chamars were the rising caste and by establishing good relations with them he was improving his future prospects. His attitude with regard to pollution has become mild, and his interest in religious activities has weakened.

The brahmin priest has lost his Meo clientele because the latter are Islamising. He has started to serve the local Chamars and other shudra castes as their *purohit.* But his loss was far greater than his gain and he has now set up a tailoring business to augment his income. He has made two more concessions in his behaviour: (a) he accepts cooked food from the Banias, carpenters and other lower-caste Hindus; (b) he begs unprocessed plants from the farmers at harvest time.

Besides the Meos. four other Muslim castes (faqir, lohar, sakka and mirasi) are represented in the village. All of these are considered to be of a very low rank and have recently migrated to Chavandi Kalan. None of them owns land, although the Sakkas are conniving to acquire some. They practice their traditional caste occupations according to the jajmani arrangement. Due to small numbers and dependence on the Meos, they take little interest in village politics. Following the example of the Meos, these castes are trying to become better Muslims. But their zeal for Islam is much less than that of the Meos.

The behaviour of some of the Hindu castes and the Sikhs has somewhat changed toward the Sakka. One of the responsibilities of the Sakka is to supply a bucket and a rope at the village well for public use, and to keep this equipment in good repair. Only the Meos used this facility before 1947, but in recent years other castes have also begun to use it. Another and tonal task of the Sakka is to supply drinking water to the farmers in their fields, particularly at the time of harvest when men spend long hours in the sun. Because the container used by the Sakka was made of leather, the Hindus did not accept water from him, but now many have relaxed their attitude. Some of the villagers told me that they drank water supplied by the Sakka because it saved them precious time.

During the last panchayat elections in the village I noted that although all the castes were deeply concerned about the electoral contests, castes such as the Sakkas avoided overt involvement in politics. One of the Sakkas, thinking that my sympathies lay with the Muslim Meos, constantly supplied me with information about the campaigning activities going on in the village. He told me that due to his low social rank the Meos not only did not pay any attention to him, but also considered his interest in politics to be inappropriate. Therefore he could not communicate directly with them and he tried to solicit my mediation.

OTHER HINDU CASTES

Seven other Hindu castes are represented in the village in relatively small numbers. These include four families of banias, one khatri, one khati, four dakots, one balragi, one jogi, and two Nais. During the years since Independence, these castes have neither gained nor lost in political power. There has been little change in their economic or social position. Their caste and religious behaviour has not changed much either, except that they have abandoned a few of the shrines, particularly the pipal tree and the shrine of the Devi.

Traditional caste hierarchy, with the brahmin at the top and the sweeper at the bottom, obviously existed in Chavandi Kalan before 1947. There seems to be no reason to doubt that such a structure is as old as the village itself and remained strong until recently. The Meos were the dominant caste, which is indicated by the fact that they owned all the land and enjoyed unquestioned political power. It was their responsibility, in their own interest, to see that all the castes obeyed certain rules. I learned from many Meo informants that they actually prevented non-Meos from acquiring land and in this they did not hesitate to use violence if necessary. Furthermore, they obstructed the Shudras from adopting Sanskritic ritual and for this they used such means as ridicule, violence, and the threat of withdrawal of economic patronage The Meos themselves obeyed the rules of the system. This is clearly indicated by the fact that they continued to practise Hindu rituals even though they had adopted Islam. They realised that by performing the appropriate rituals they could legitimise their claim to kshatriya status and hence their dominance.

LURE OF LAND

But redistribution of land after 1947 set the stage for change, for in land ownership lies the basis for economic and political power. As soon as the Chamars received land they abandoned leather work and realised that they could now defy caste prescriptions with impunity. The lure of land was so strong that the Brahmins of the village preferred it to a flimsy ritual position which was preserved with the help of the dominant caste in the village. The Meos, on the other hand, view that their dominance was broken forever. Consequently, they saw no point in keeping up the Hindu facade and decided to become Islamised. The Sikhs, realising the implications of land ownership, tried to consolidate their gain by emulating the religious practices of the higher castes. The catalytic significance of land is further indicated by the fact that the castes which did not acquire land changed their religious behaviour the least.

In addition to land ownership, there is a second very important variable with regard to power, and that is the size of a caste group and its unity. Since the introduction of panchayati raj, the traditional power structure in the village has been revolutionised. Members of the village panchayat are now elected by popular vote and caste rank is of little importance. The Chamars, however, are slightly privileged because there is a provision in the law that proportional representation for them is guaranteed. Consequently, due to their sizeable number in the village and the legal guarantee, the Chamars of Chavandi Kalan are politically very active in the village. They have remained united in every election and have demonstrated the power of their votes. The brahmins in the village, who recently acquired land, were numerically very weak, but they established a very special relationship with the Chamars in order to gain their support. The Meos were the losers, so they emphasised their Islamic bond to remain united and to salvage their share of power. The Sikhs also became united in order to participate in the political struggle. The smaller castes, who did not make much economic progress as a result of land redistribution, found that they could not hope for political power.

Hence we find that those castes which were previously deprived of economic and political power and were now in a position to become strong, recognised the opportunity and acted with speed and determination. In order to make this gain secure, they began to emulate the religious behaviour of the higher castes. The brahmins, interestingly enough, also chose power and sacrificed ritual status. The Meos, in order to salvage what they could, completely abandoned their Hindu rituals and became Islamised. In short, the change in religious behaviour of various castes was commensurate with change in power. In other words, the greater the gain or loss in power of a caste, the more the change in the religious behaviour of its members. The result has been greater uniformity among the castes. Clearly, power and not religion maintains caste hierarchy.

I must further point out that the pollution line which separates the untouchable castes from the clean castes is, at least in Chavandi Kalan, not nearly as uncrossable as it has been claimed to be in Orissa (Bailey 1957) and in South India by other researchers. I may suggest that the reason why the pollution line was so easily crossed in Chavandi Kalan was that the amount of land and political power gained by the Chamars was significantly large.

References

Bailey, F. G. 1957. *Caste and Economic Frontier*. Manchester: Manchester University Press.

Cohn, Bernard. 1955. 'The Changing Status of a Depressed Caste'. In *Village India*, ed. McKim Marriott. Chicago: University of Chicago Press.

Harper, Edward B. (ed.). 1964. *Religion in South Asia*. Seattle: University of Seattle Press.

Marriott, McKim. 1960. *Caste Ranking and Community Structure in Five Regions of India and Pakistan*. Monograph Series 23. Poona: Deccan College.

Opler, Morris E. 1959. 'The Place of Religion in a North Indian Village'. *South-Western Journal of Anthropology* 15 (3): 219–26.

Orans, Martin. 1965. *The Santals: A Tribe in Search of a Great Tradition*. Detroit: Wayne State University.

9

Institutions and Incentives in a Garhwal Village

*Common Property Regimes in Traditional Societies**

Jishnu Das

A significant proportion of land in Himalayan settlements are non-privatised holdings in the form of forests, pastures and wastelands, commonly referred to as 'common property resources'. Several economic and environmental problems, from wide-scale deforestation to landslides and silt run-offs, have been attributed to the improper use of common resources. Hence, studies of such resources are integral for the formulation of policy in the mountainous regions of India. This chapter utilises fieldwork conducted in village Salang of the Garhwal Himalayas during 1994–95 to argue that much of the analysis of common resources in the Himalayas has been concerned with village level institutions rather than individual incentives towards the protection of common resources in the hills.[...]

Several authors (Guha 1985, 1988; Somnathan 1985 have cited the 'governance' of commons by local inhabitants during this period to argue that the pre-state village in Garhwal was characterised by sound management of common resources with well-developed access and regulatory restrictions in place. Contrary to this view, I argue that the current literature does not fully take into account the economic environment and hence, individual incentives in the pre-state Garhwali village. Doing so leads to a new interpretation of several institutions which are thought to have developed as conservationist tools. Specifically, this article points out that every

* This chapter has been extracted from a longer paper published by the author in the *Economic and Political Weekly* 35 (49): 4337–44, 2 December 2000.

I would like to thank Veena Das, R. K. Das, Carolina Sanchez and participants in the workshop on Common Property, Delhi School of Economics for helpful comments. I wish to specially acknowledge the support and guidance of Jean Dreze in the formulation and subsequent research on this project. Financial support for this project was made possible due to a generous grant from CIDA.

such institution may be regarded as a response to a chronic shortage of labour in hill economies.[...]

Once we recognise the importance of labour conservation in hill economies, a new interpretation can be provided for institutions that have been regarded as indicative of resource management techniques. As the subsequent analysis shows, restricting attention to historical institutions without analysing the economic environment may lead to erroneous conclusions; every institution that is thought of as a 'resource conserving' mechanism also has a parallel interpretation as a 'labour conserving' institution, and evidence from the village lends strong support to the latter view.

A useful framework to examine the historical relationship between the community and common resources has been developed by Baland and Platteau (1994). The classificatory scheme used by the authors is linked to the pressure on common resources at a given time, and the inter-temporal experience of the community to changes in resource availability. The authors distinguish between four types of societies using two basic criteria-regulatory and access rules.[1]

Type I societies are characterised by resource abundance and labour shortage due to low population and technological backwardness. As pressure on the resource increases, societies can move towards any of the other types depending on the resource stock and user population. In cases where the cost of extraction increases due to an increasing number of users, strict access rules tend to develop (Type III). However, if the cost of extraction increases despite the size of the user group remaining constant, regulatory criteria may be introduced (Type II). Type IV societies are those where the user group of the common resource is rigidly defined, and the patterns of usage within this group is regulated through a system of sanctions and punishments. Interestingly, the two detailed case studies that the authors discuss indicate strongly that Type IV communities develop only after a period of intense resource scarcity.

TABLE 9.1: Land Owned and Cultivated in Salang

Household Number	Total Land (Nalis)	Land used*
1	60	10 (16.5)
2	150	50 (33.0)
3	30	15 (50.0)
4	50	10 (20)
5	42	20 (46)
6	80	40 (50)
7	25	18 (72)
8	25	18 (72)
9	25	18 (72)
10	25	18 (72)
11	48	46 (94)

Contd.

Table 9.1 Contd.

Household Number	Total Land (Nalis)	Land used*
12	60	30 (50)
13	60	30 (50)
14	33	30 (90)
15	33	30 (90)
16	33	30 (90)
17	15	14 (97)
18	15	14 (97)
19	15	14 (97)
20	15	14 (97)
21	65	25 (35)

Notes: *Percentage in brackets.
The heads of families 7–10; 14–16; and 17–20 are brothers and hence their land holdings are identical. Further, since the land is tilled collectively, land use in these cases is also the same. A limitation of this data and the extent of the survey, is the non-separability of land held in Salang and in the lower settlements. Very close family ties imply that in a significant number of cases, food is exchanged between different chula groups: in this case, the producing unit should be extended to include the co-sharers.

Source: Records in the Patwari's office, Bhatwari

Most research dealing with the historical management practices of villages in the Garhwal argues that well functioning access and regulatory mechanisms had been instituted to control the use of common resources in the region, and thus the pre-state Garhwal village could be classified as a Type IV community (I refer to this as the 'conservationist view'). Subsequently, with the development of commercial forestry in the region, forests were removed from village control and monopolised by the state (Guha 1988). This commercial exploitation was accompanied by the formation of institutions that placed significant restrictions on forest use by the local population and led to the 'alienation' of the villagers from the environment around them.

Hence in the literature on the U.P. hills, the historical development of Garhwal is exemplified by a movement away from self-governance and management of commons towards a system dominated by state monopoly over forests and a hostile relationship between the state and the community. However, the perception that the local population shared a 'close relationship' with the environment and had developed complex regulatory mechanisms to conserve village level resources (Guha 1988; Sanwal 1989) is at considerable variance with local narratives and history, both in Salang and the villages around it. By placing these mechanisms within the overall economic environment of labour shortage in which they existed, we show that the incentives which gave rise to these institutions had little to do with the conservation of common resources and equating decentralised forest management with sustainability of common resources could be harmful under present day circumstances.[2]

TABLE 9.2: Classification Scheme for Common Property Resource Regimes*

	Regulatory	Restrictions
Access Rules	Absent	Present
Not Strict	Type I	Type II
Strict	Type III	Type IV

Note: *Based on Baland and Platteau (1994).

The substantial differences between the 'conservationist view' and local realities can be analysed within three distinct spheres: the availability of food; the presence of access restrictions, and the pattern of regulations governing the use of the commons. Through village interviews and data on court cases, I show that the conservationist view over romanticises the historical evidence on common resource management in Garhwal: although it might seem that regulatory and access restrictions were consciously implemented by villages, the subsequent analysis shows that in a number of cases, these were simply responses to the politico-economic situation during this period rather than institutions designed with an aim to conserve scarce resources.

FOOD AVAILABILITY

The pre-road construction period is referred to by the older men in the village as one of great food scarcity.[3] Since accessibility to food markets was extremely limited, the two main crops, cholai and mandua along with dairy products such as butter and ghee (clarified butter) were bartered with the Bhotias (traders from Tibetan regions) in exchange for wheat, salt and pepper. Further, wild vegetables and fibers (such as kundali and chullu) were used as regular supplements to the normal diet of rotis (pita-bread) and butter/ghee. The annual period of scarcity was during the winter months of November–March, when there would be a decline in milk production and availability of forest produce:

> 'In the winters we would have some tea in the morning and set off to cut grass and leaves for the cattle. During the day we would eat whatever we could find in the forest and return at night to have 2–3 rotis (pita-bread) and some buttermilk. The situation now is much better than before—at least there is a market from where we can buy food to fill our stomachs. Earlier, if food in the village ran out, there was no option but to starve' (Dilram Singh).

Proponents of the conservationist view contend that the regular use of forest produce combined with foodgrain production was more than sufficient to meet the subsistence needs of the historical community. For example Guha (1988) argues that; 'With production oriented towards subsistence needs which were comfortably met, there remained a surplus of grain for export to Tibet and southward to the plains.

Usually having six months stock of grain in hand ... hill cultivators were described as 'probably better off than any peasantry in India' (Guha 1988). Interviews with villagers in Salang seem to suggest that this idea of hill communities being able to comfortably meet subsistence needs and produce a grain surplus is erroneous. In fact, the pre-state period is described as one of great food shortage, particularly during the months of November–March, when forest products which were used as dietary supplements, were not be available. Over time, the labour requirements of meeting subsistence needs are thought to have declined and almost all villagers agree that food availability and consumption has increased with the construction of roads and markets.

The notion that Salang has moved from a situation of food scarcity to relatively greater food availability is supported by two observations: firstly, as shown in the previous section, land under cultivation has decreased over time. If one assumes that the primary constraint on production is labour availability, the emergence of excess capacity in agricultural production coupled with an increasing population, cannot be synonymous with a decline in the availability of food. Secondly, the development of food markets in Bhatwari has allowed households in Salang to divorce food consumption from production. Hence, even in lean periods it is possible to ensure (contingent on access to credit) that the availability of food does not decline in contrast to a non-market economy, where consumption and production are highly correlated.[4]

ACCESS RULES: RE-EXAMINING INCENTIVES WITHIN A LABOUR-CONSTRAINED SETTING

In the Baland-Platteau scheme, Type IV societies are characterised by strict access rules–outsiders are not permitted to use the villages' resources–as well as regulatory restrictions on common resource use within the community. Both the conservationist view and local narratives point out that strict boundaries existed around village commons and contravention of boundary restrictions was punished through monetary fines and confiscation of agricultural tools. However, if, as has been argued by the conservationist school, these access restrictions were an attempt to conserve the relevant resource, one would expect to find that the entire common land of the village would be equally well monitored to prevent indiscriminate use by outsiders. However, in Salang and the villages around it, monitoring and enforcement was strict only in the regions close to the village, while common land that lay at a distance from the village was not monitored,[5] and even today, is used by a number of outsiders (for instance, gujjars from Dehradun freely use the higher village land for firewood and pasture).

A possible framework to explain the premium on common land close to the village can be constructed through an examination of the implications of access restrictions for labour use. By combining the economic rationale of a labour-shortage community with the spatial distribution of villages and village boundaries in the region, a structure of monitoring close to that observed in Salang emerges.

Villages in this area settled close to the river, which formed one of the boundaries of the village commons (Figure 9.1). While common land between the village and the river was closely guarded, commons such as those marked 'unguarded land' were not monitored, and could be used by outsiders. Given the geographical structure of the settlements it is clear that the extraction of common resources from around the village had a far lower labour cost than those at a distance. Further, the spatial distribution of villages and village boundaries often implied that common land belonging to neighbouring villages across the river (such as that labelled 'guarded land') was physically closer than some of the land belonging to the community. This created a situation where there was high incentive to encroach upon lands belonging to villages across the river, but not necessarily upon those belonging to neighbouring villages along the same bank.

FIGURE 9.1: Guarded and Unguarded Lands in Salang: Schematic Representation

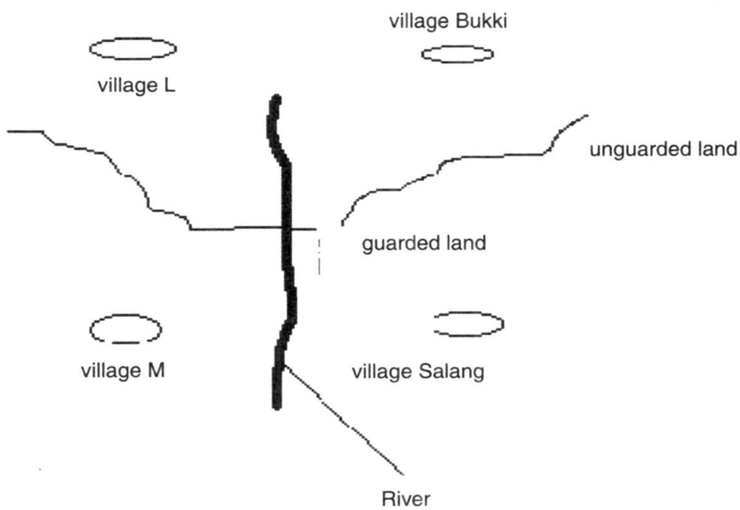

Historical records in Salang show that disputes between villages abutting each other (such as Salang and M or Bukki and L) along the river were frequent with cases referred to the kingly courts in Tehri.[6] However, disputes between neighbouring villages spread further apart were rare. Hence, disputes between Salang and M or Bukki and L occurred frequently because of the proximity of the common land of the three villages. Disputes between Bukki and Salang were however, non-existent. Even if Bukki inhabitants were to use 'unguarded land', occupants of Salang would not punish them since this resource stock did not form part of the effective resource base used by Salang.[7]

Thus, access restrictions on common resources, which existed only around the village, were a rational response to a labour-constrained economy. If the cost of labour was very low compared to the cost of the resource, it is unlikely that the pattern of disputes seen in the region would have arisen. Hence, it would be inaccurate to depict the existence of access restrictions as a solely conservationist institution, since a change in the cost of labour, would significantly affect the nature of these rules.

REGULATION RULES: RE-EXAMINING INCENTIVES WITHIN A LABOUR-CONSTRAINED SETTING

A third discrepancy between the conservationist view and local perceptions is with regard to the regulation of common resources and the existence of regulatory institutions within the village. Several authors (Guha 1988; Sanwal 1989) have argued that common land in Garhwal and Kumaon were carefully regulated through a complex system of social institutions. While it is possible that regulatory institutions did exist in isolated cases, for a number of reasons it is unlikely that these institutions were as widespread and effective as portrayed in the literature. For instance, the conservationist role of two major 'institutions' pertaining to the regulation of forests and pasturelands, which have been identified by scholars as regulatory mechanisms, is uncertain once the economic structure of the community is taken into consideration. Guha (1988) has written extensively about the existence of sacred groves and trees (deodar) as a conservationist measure adopted by hill populations. Unfortunately, the extent of these groves compared to the area of the village forests is not mentioned and the range of this measure is uncertain. In Salang for example, there are two temples and four forest deities who define an area within which trees are not cut. The total number of trees in this area does not exceed 500 as compared to the total number of trees in Salang land, which is close to 90,000 (Table 9.3). Thus, unless data is available on the ratio of the area under sacred groves to total forest area it is hard to gauge the extent of this practice, and present day analysis suggests that the range of this measure was insufficient to warrant its inclusion as a regulatory institution to control forest use.

More importantly, apart from the nature of these regulatory institutions, it is unclear whether village level regulatory institutions would have been required at all given the economic conditions of this period. Within the context of a labour

TABLE 9.3: Area Statement of Salang Land, 1986
(*in hectares*)

Compartment	2	3a	3b	3c	4a	5a
Chir	–	–	–	10.5	–	–
Rai-Morinda	225.8	9.1	70.4	–	134.8	4.5
Deodar	–	–	–	15.4	–	–
Kail	17.4	18.2	16.2	–	28.2	104.5
Broad leaf	–	–	9.3	–	16.1	–
Ban	85.8	10.2	30.8	38.2	18	50
Pasture	86	–	–	–	13.8	–

Source: Uttarkashi district, Forest Department Records.

TABLE 9.4: Tree Enumeration for Salang, 1961*

Compartment	2	3a	3b	3c	4a	5a
Chir	–	–	–	na	–	–
Rai-Morinda	16,800	625 (781)	18,600	na	26,500	400 (2,400)
Deodar	–	1,368 (3,895)	1	na	23	1
Kail	–	1,525 (1,203)	509	na	3,071	344 (866)
Miscellaneous*	Total for all compartments is approximately 1,10,000					

Notes: Numbers in brackets correspond to the tree count in 1981. Of the six compartments, only 3a and 5a surveyed in 1981, for which data is presented here.
*Includes for example, walnut, banj, maple, jamnoi and others.
Source: Uttarkashi District, Forest Department Records.

shortage economy, absence of markets and low population, the pressure on common resources would be limited to the subsistence needs of the community. It can be argued that the regenerative capacity of the village commons far exceeded the subsistence requirements of the population, and in fact was greater than the maximum possible harvest extractable by a limited labour supply–even in present day Salang, there are more than 350 trees for each inhabitant (Tables 9.3 and 9.4).

Once the issue of market access is addressed, it becomes apparent that commercial wood felling would not have been viable on an individual basis.[8] In Salang for example, the nearest market was Haridwar and roads existed only till Rishikesh. The price of chir in 1928–29 was Rs 1.05 for a sleeper measuring 18′×14″×7″ (the load carrying capacity limit of a single individual). Hence, to cut a tree, construct sleepers and carry the load to Haridwar would cost a single individual a two month labour effort. The low price of wood makes it highly unlikely that wood sales would be economically viable during this period.[9]

Similarly, with regards to pasturelands, Somanathan (1991) has argued that the practice of transhumance resulted in the differential use of pastures on a seasonal basis thus allowing them to be used in a sustainable manner. While the argument that transhumance would increase the regenerative capacity of the pasture lands is certainly true, it is more likely that the institution of transhumance was a response to a shortage of labour and not a shortage of the resource stock.[10] As I have argued previously, transhumance is less labour intensive than stall-feeding in the absence of mechanisation. Thus, the need to conserve labour would lead to the use of such cattle rearing techniques in the village. Evidence for this rationale rather than a conservationist one, comes from the experience of the local inhabitants with regards to their pasturelands.

Based on interviews, there has never been a shortage of pastureland in grazing sites above the village, and no rules have developed regarding the number of cattle each household is allowed to have, or the amount of pastureland that each family can use to graze its cattle in these sites.[11] Every year, when villagers move up to the higher pastures, three sites, with 6, 8 and 7 chaans, respectively are used. There are no rules regarding the movement of households to or within these grazing sites. When asked whether this resulted in overgrazing or overcrowding in some sites, villagers replied that the movement of families to these sites is entirely an individual decision: 'If someone thinks that they just want the buffaloes to roam and have the best grass then they go to the highest site (at least five hours from the village), but if someone needs to be close to the village, then they might go to one of the lower ones.' The choice of summer grazing sites depends on the relative importance given to migration close to the village–lower grazing sites mean more work and lower quality pasture land, but easy access to the village, while migrating to higher grazing sites which have better grass means that a trip to the village is possible only once in 5–7 days. Depending on the particular conditions faced by each household, a grazing site is chosen by the family: 'The grazing site has never been a problem. Sometimes there are as many as three families living in one chaan, and sometimes there might be an empty chaan, but all the families which have migrated to a site are always accommodated.'

When asked about the possibility of shortage of pastureland in the future, villagers pointed out that such a shortage could never arise because the size of the herds is decreasing over time. The institution of transhumance would thus retain its effectiveness as a regulatory mechanism only as long as it was the best response to the labour requirements of the population. In fact, the historical transition in Switzerland from transhumance to stall-feeding supports the argument that as mechanisation and the capital base increases, the decrease in labour requirement translates into a decline in the movement of cattle herds, independent of the state of the resource stock.

The resource conserving regulatory rules that did exist during this period were largely directives from the princely courts in Tehri rather than village level initiatives. Interviews with older people in the village show that the forests in the pre-state period, particularly trees and wildlife were controlled and regulated by the king with village areas clearly marked out and allocated. Forest produce was strictly controlled by the king; villagers were not allowed to cut trees or hunt wild animals without the permission of the kingly court. The only forest product which could be sold in the market was ringal (green bamboo), used for making baskets and floor mats. Villagers would take bundles of ringal once a year[12] to the market at Dehradun and buy oil and rice with the proceeds of the sale. To protect the forest's resources, strict monitoring and enforcement was imposed by the king's guards: 'Nobody in the village would dare to cut a tree without the court's permission. If someone did, the next day the forest guards would come to the village, and the possessions of the cutter would be confiscated (Nilam Kathur). Nowadays, forest officials are corrupt and inefficient and do not do their work properly. In the earlier days, no one dared to break the king's laws–if a forest guard came to the village, all the villagers would tremble with fear' (CR).[13]

Detailed case studies of societies with well developed regulatory and access mechanisms show that such institutions usually evolve after the community has suffered a period of intense resource shortage-regulatory and access mechanisms normally arise as pressure on the resource stock increases and efficient management rules have to be introduced to prevent significant stock depletion. Historically however, the economies of Garhwal were never subject to a shortage of resource stock, and indications that there was considerable pressure on the stock are completely absent. The absence of shortages and the evidence from cross-sectional studies show that in such societies regulatory mechanisms are rarely established—it is unlikely that local populations in this region would have instituted conservationist mechanisms to protect a non-depleting resource stock for future generations.

Conclusion: Pre-State Garhwal Economy

The differences between my portrayal of the historical Garhwal community, as a complex nexus of economic and administrative factors, and the conservationist view, centre around the overall environment within which these villages existed, and are summarised in the following observations.

Firstly, villages in Garhwal faced considerable problems in meeting subsistence food requirements, and food status has improved, rather than declined, over time. Although forest needs of the villagers were comfortably met, restricted market accessibility implied that the commercial use of such produce on a small scale was not possible. Secondly, access restrictions existed largely to the extent that they were a response to a shortage of labour in the village, and not as a conservationist strategy. Thirdly, regulatory restrictions, to the extent that they were used were not a result of the existence of village level institutions concerned with the sustainability of common resources, but a result of the power of the kingly family over forests in the Tehri-Garhwal region. In some cases, 'regulatory' institutions (transhumance) were responses to the economic setting of a binding labour-constraint in the village.

Once these institutions are recognised as responses to the labour requirements of economic activities and the political specificities of this region, it is hard to use historical precedent to show that completely decentralised forest management is optimal–the ground realities of historical Garhwal seem to present a completely different picture of common resource management practices at the village level than that which is currently advocated. In particular, with increasing possibility of production for the market and a decrease in the dependence on common resources, there has been a change in the value of labour inputs in this region. If, as I have argued, management practices in this region arose as a response to labour shortages, there is no prima facie grounds for the belief that these traditional institutions will remain optimal once the underlying parameters (such as the relative cost of labour) change.

Concluding this chapter, I would like to point out that this analysis cannot be extended without careful consideration to other regions in the hills—for example, Garhwal and Kumaon cannot be modelled as a homogeneous entity. The heterogeneous nature of the communities justifies a case-specific approach to the problem. Thus, it is entirely possible that the scenario depicted by the conservationist school is accurate for specific villages across the region. Through my discussion I have tried to argue that there is insufficient support for extending the specific cases discussed in the literature so far to a generalised portrayal of all Garhwal and Kumaon.

Any framework depicting the historical village-common resource relationship must accommodate the multiple scenarios emerging from the field.

Notes

1. Access rules refer to the restrictions on resource usage by members not belonging to the community, while regulatory rules refer to restrictions on use within the members of the community.

2. In discussing the historical institutions of Salang, it should be kept in mind that Tehri district (of which the village was a part till 1965), through a series of coincidences, never came under direct British rule or administration unlike the other districts of Garhwal.

3. The people interviewed were in the 65–90 age group, and the period of scarcity, on the basis of the interviews, can be placed between 1925 and 1955. The road to Bhatwari was constructed in 1962, and before this, the nearest food market was a 2–3 day walk from the village at Uttarkashi.

4. The introduction of markets has been beneficial because most villagers are owner-cultivators of agricultural land. Contrary to the experience of Salang, Sen (1981) has shown how the dependance on a market can prove disastrous when changes in the terms of trade lead to an entitlement failure.

5. Although rights of usage were vested in the community, and outsiders could be punished for illegal use.

6. Court orders for example, cite cases where outsiders are fined for grazing cattle in the village land.

7. Today, areas marked 'unguarded' are often used by Gujjars as pasture lands.

8. The fact that commercial felling of trees was carried out in the region as early as 1864 shows that it was possible for a large organisation to avail of the opportunities provided by the forest land. However, given the large investment requirements of such an enterprise (see for example, the historical section in the 1965 working plan, detailing the costs of timber extraction), it would not have been possible for small-scale felling enterprises to function profitably.

9. Assuming an inflation rate of 10 per cent, one rupee would be equivalent to Rs 304 today, which amounts to a daily wage of Rs 5. Since the possible activities in Salang are not very different today, it is highly improbable that the implicit wage of agriculture in the early 1900s was less than this amount.

10. For detailed discussion see Section II.

11. The management of the pasture around Udaara is discussed in the second part of this study.

12. A trip to Dehradun with a ringal load took between 15 and 20 days.

13. Guha's account and the local narratives could be assimilated if the periods to which they refer were significantly different. However, Guha's work is based on accounts written during the period 1900–40, which closely conforms to the period of the narratives—for this section interviews with villagers above 75 were used.

References

Baland, J. M. and J. P. Platteau. 1994. *Halting Degradation of Natural Resources: Is There a Role for Rural Communities*. Namur, Belgium: Facultes Universitaires Notre-Dame La Paix.

Barzel, Y. 1989. *Economic Analysis of Property Rights*. New York: Cambridge University Press.

Berkes, F. (ed.). 1989. *Common Property Resources*. London: Belhaven Press.

Census of India .1981. *Uttarkashi, Village and Town Directory*. New Delhi: Government of India.

——. 1975. *District Census Reports*. New Delhi: Government of India.

——. 1985. *District Census Reports*. New Delhi: Government of India.

Fernandes, W. (ed.). 1983. *Towards a New Forest Policy*. New Delhi: Indian Statistical Institute.

Guha, R. 1983a. 'Forestry in British and Post-British India: A Historical Analysis'. *Economic and Political Weekly* 17 (44): 1882–95, 29 October.

——. 1983b. 'Forestry in British and Post-British India: A Historical Analysis'. *Economic and Political Weekly* 17 (45–46): 1940–47, 5 and 12 November.

——. 1988. *The Unquiet Woods*. Delhi: Oxford University Press.

——. 1985. 'Scientific Forestry and Social Change in Uttarakhand'. *Economic and Political Weekly* 20 (45–47): 1939.

Guillet, D. 1983. 'Towards a Cultural Ecology of the Mountains'. *Current Anthropology* 24 (5).

Jodha, N. S. 1986. 'Common Property Resources and the Rural Poor in Dry Regions of India'. *Economic and Political Weekly* 21 (27): 1167–81, 5 July 1986.

Mahat, T. B. S., D. M. Griffin and R. Shepherd. 1986. 'Human Impact on Some Forests of the Middle Hills of Nepal, 1'. *Mountain Research and Development* 6 (3).

Maser, C. 1994. *Sustainable Forestry: Philosophy, Science and Economics*. Florida: St Lucie Press.

Ostrom, E. 1990. *Governing the Commons: The Evolution of Institutions for Collective Action*. New York: Cambridge University Press.

Sanwal. 1989. 'What We Know about Mountain Development'. *Mountain Research and Development* 9 (1).

Sen, A. K. 1981. *Poverty and Famines: An Essay on Entitlement and Deprivation*. Oxford: Clarendon Press.

Shiva, V. and J. Bandyopadhyay. 1986. *Mountain Research and Development*, 6 (2), pp. 133–42.

Shiva V. and J. Bandyopadhyay. 1988. 'Political Economy of Ecology Movements'. *Economic and Political Weekly* 23 (24): 1223–32, 11 June.

Singh, K. 1994. *Managing Common Pool Resources: Principles and Case Studies*. Delhi: Oxford University Press.

Somanathan, E. 1991. 'Deforestation, Property Rights and Incentives in Central Himalaya'. *Economic and Political Weekly* 26 (4): PE37–PE46, 26 January.

——. 1995. *Evolutionary Stability of Community Norms*. Cambridge: Harvard University.

Thomson, M. and M. Warburton. 1985. 'Uncertainty on a Himalayan Scale'. *Mountain Research and Development* 5 (2).

Section III

Social, Economic and Political Processes

Introduction

The Indian village society has been undergoing a process of churning, empirically as well as conceptually. This section has four chapters that present different dimensions of social and cultural processes of change being experienced in rural India.

Based on their field study of four villages of Meerut district of U.P., the chapter by Sudha Pai and Jagpal Singh tells us about the growing influence of Dalits and the Marginalized Backward Castes (MBCs) in the political landscape of the region. Their growing dissociation from traditional caste occupations and increasing involvement with secular economy outside the village has given them a new sense of autonomy. The democratic political process provides them with a new space for assertion and activism. The younger generation of Dalits has been mobilising themselves around the symbol of Ambedkar and framing a new assertive identity.

While in the case of western U.P. the rise of Dalits and the backward castes was facilitated by the success of the Green Revolution and the growing integration of the village into the urban economy and development. Anil Kumar Vaddiraju attributes the rise of backward castes in the rural setting of South Telengana to the lack of development in the region. The continuation of 'backwardness' in the region has pushed the traditionally dominant upper castes out of the village. As they move to the city for a better life, the political space of the village got occupied by the erstwhile backward castes. Over the years, they have emerged as politically powerful groups, both locally and at the state level.

The other two chapters in this section focus on gender. In her chapter on Gulf migrations from rural Kerala, Leela Gulati 'assesses the socio-economic impact of male migration on women of the households, who are left behind'. Through her own empirical study, she argues against the popular notion of the women being passive 'victims'. The Malyali actively participate in the process and make a variety of arrangements required for the migration of their men-folk to Gulf countries for work. The absence of men also compels them to learn skills required for engaging with the outside world. She concludes that 'women gradually take on increased responsibilities for the running of the households on their own, for the health and education of children and for the management of their funds and properties. In the process, it breaks down women's isolation, increases their mobility, and brings them into contact with a wider network of institutions that were hitherto outside their experience. This results in their gaining confidence in themselves with the length of the stay of the migrant away from home'.

The chapter by Roger Jeffery, Patricia Jeffery and Andrew Lyon also argues for a broadening of perspective on rural development by taking into account the odd jobs that women do, beyond their domestic responsibilities. One such economic activity is the 'dung-work'. In rural U.P., where they carried out their fieldwork, nearly 80 per cent of the households own cattle, and dung-work is an important part of the agricultural cycle as a productive activity, because it has 'exchange value'. It also provides support to the household economy by supplementing the fuel requirements, in 'the reproduction of the household from day to day'. However, in the conceptualisation of development or rural agrarian economy, or in calculation of income, dung-work is rarely seen as a valuable contribution because it is performed by women in the 'private space'.

10

Taking Dung-Work Seriously

*Women's Work and Rural Development in North India**

Roger Jeffery, Patricia Jeffery and Andrew Lyon

The work of transforming cow-dung into economically-valued products has not been treated as a matter of significant interest by economists and analysts of the Indian rural scene. In discussions of fuel, dung-cakes are dismissed as an inappropriate use of potential fertiliser; in discussions of fertiliser, the work of transforming dung into manure is usually ignored; and in discussions of women's work, dung-work is rarely made a central focus.... In part, this is a result of male-oriented approaches to agriculture; pace Thorner and Sau, the capitalism is male-dominated but cattle-dung and dung-work are largely matters for women. In this chapter we use cattle-dung and its place in the life of two north Indian villages to throw light on some aspects of agrarian organisation which have been unduly neglected.[...]

Our research was carried out in two villages of Bijnor district, U.P., which lies about 160 km north-east of Delhi. It has an area of 2,00,000 sq km, and a 1981 population of nearly 2 million. The two villages are called Dharmnagri, with a population of 700, and Jhakri, with a population of 350. Dharmnagri is entirely populated by caste Hindus and Harijans, Jhakri entirely by Muslims, and in the district as a whole the proportions are roughly similar. Over 40 per cent of the population is under 15, and the two villages grew by about one-third from 1975 to 1985. The sex ratio of the two villages is about 1,175 males per 1,000 females; there is little seasonal or long-term migration of men. The study villages are about 5 km from the market town of Bijnor itself, close to the river Ganga and some 50 km south of Hardwar.

---

* This chapter has been extracted from a longer paper published by the authors in the *Economic and Political Weekly* 27 (17): WS32–WS37, 1989.

Earlier versions of this paper were presented in Oxford, Edinburgh, Birmingham, Glasgow and Venice. We are grateful to colleagues for comments and encouragement to take the argument as far as we have.

In the past 25 years or so, green revolution-type changes have taken place, but not as dramatically as in Punjab and Haryana, or further west in U.P. New varieties of seed are widely used. Tractors are a common sight, although most ploughing and field preparation is still done by bullock- and buffalo-power. These changes have been made possible by assured water supplies. Under British rule, very little land in Bijnor was irrigated, despite the proximity of the Ganga: all the canals were built to the west. Since 1960, private electric and diesel tubewells have revolutionised the picture. The major staple crops have changed dramatically in the last 80 years; of the rabi crops, barley and gram have almost disappeared before the advance of wheat, largely high-yielding varieties; of the kharif crops, rice and especially sugarcane (the major cash-crop) have supplanted bajra and pulses.

At the same time as cropping patterns have changed, the cropped acreage has increased, accomplished partly by a rise in double cropping. Rice and wheat can be taken from the same land, because tube wells provide a secure water supply and new seeds mature faster. But part of this increase in grain production has also been attained by pushing back the margin of cultivable land between 1905 and 1979, irrigated land increased to 40 per cent and culturable (but uncultivated) land declined. Some swamps have been drained and protected from the Ganga flooding. Much uncultivated scrub-land has been cleared and used for crop production.

These data are somewhat suspect: cropping returns are the responsibility of low-paid village-level workers and the sugarcane acreage in particular is likely to be exaggerated, because it effects entitlements to sales to the government sugar mills at a secure price, and access to some sources of credit. But the picture is consistent with, if more extreme than, the ones provided by other sources (see for example, Byres and Crow 1985).

DUNG-WORK

Cattle-dung, known locally as gobar, plays a central part in everyday life—not something which we could sidestep, either literally or metaphorically. In the two study villages, well over 80 per cent of households own cattle, with the average being three animals. For all its ubiquity, cattledung is largely privately owned. Dung which collects in an animal's stall belongs to the owner of the animal; if an animal defecates en route to the fields, or while pulling a cart along a village track or road, someone from the household will usually try to collect it. Only if cattle-dung lies unclaimed in public space can anyone gather it up, so those without their own animals have only unreliable access to it.

Cattle ownership is not totally determined by the ownership of land.[1] Most landowners with more than half an acre own milk animals and own or have a share in draught animals. No landless people own draught animals, but some own milk cattle, though their ownership may be precarious; their cattle that die may not be immediately replaced, or cattle may be sold in an emergency.

Cattledung is largely a matter for women, though all cattle are owned by men, and women's access to animals and their dung may be complex. In the two study villages, households are sometimes members of larger production units of a man and his sons, or a set of brothers, or (rarely) of paternal cousins. Draught animals tend to be owned by production units, but a woman's work is organised through her household and her relationships with her mother- and sisters-in-law (HBW). If her household is separate, for consumption purposes, she does all the animals care and is entitled to all their products, including the dung, from all the animal owned by her household. But if she is still in a joint relationship with her mother-in-law or with a sister-in-law (HBW), she may have part shares in milk animals owned by the joint households, and these shares may continue after the households have separated for most consumption purposes. If her husband works jointly with his brothers or his father, she may have rights to a share of the dung from the draught animals they own together, whether the households are joint or separate. Thus, some women are involved in quite intricate animal care rotas, which govern which animals' dung they can collect and when.

Dung collection is work for females and it is a common sight to see young girls following herds of animals to the grazing grounds, and collecting the dung which the herd leaves in its wake. Men are reluctant even to consider handling it.[2] During interviews about the work cycle Andrew asked men whether they ever did any dung-work. His questioning was often met with great hilarity. However, he was persistent: he wanted to know what happened to dung when women were away visiting their parents. Bystanders ridiculed each man he interviewed. For example, he asked Riasat, a poor peasant farmer who lived in a nuclear household, 'What do you do about the dung when your wife is away visiting her mother?' Riasat hardly started to answer when a friend burst in, laughing,

> He collects it himself in a basket. He scoops it up with his hands, and then pops the basket on his head. Then the shit runs through the weave in the basket and down over his face!

And he slapped his knees and roared with laughter. Riasat hastily denied this account: 'No, no, brother! Dung is woman's work'.

The work associated with this resource, then, is derided by men, and relegated to women.[3] Women are hardly enthusiastic but have to comply with men's refusal to be contaminated:

> You know, our men can't even wipe a child's snotty nose. Why, if a child urinates on them they hand it over to us straight away. Just imagine what they'd do if they had to deal with baby's shit or cattle-dung!

There is evidence that some men used to be involved in dung-work: some commentaries suggest that men from the Chamar (leatherworker) or Bhangi (sweeper) castes—both of them harijan or untouchable—may have been involved in dung-work for hereditary patrons as part of the *jajmani* system.[4] More evidence exists of Chamar or other low-caste women doing dung-work for women from clean castes or the higher status groups among Muslims. This is now rare in Dharmnagri and Jhakri: even the Rajput women of the richest peasant household in Dharmnagri have to do most of their own dung-work.

The work is certainly very tiring. It involves bending and lifting heavy headloads and carrying them up to quarter of a mile on their heads; it is one of the first parts of women's work which they wish to give up when they are pregnant. A woman is only rarely let off dung-work, if she is still living jointly with an amenable mother-in-law, or if she becomes very seriously ill. For example, one had an eclamptic fit six days before delivery and became unconscious, but up to that time she had been doing all the dung-work as well as her other duties. Only in extremis will alternative workers be found, and they will always be women.

Cattledung has three main uses: as plaster and a building material; as fuel, and as fertiliser.

Dung for building and as plaster

The courtyards, grain stores and the walls of adobe houses are made with mixtures of mud, dung and chopped straw. They all require a coating to render them and help them to resist the damp and the effects of rain, and dried dung is diluted to form a thin paste, and spread by hand. House walls may be plastered a few times a season; granaries when they are repaired every year or so; but courtyards are more frequently coated as a part of everyday cleaning, or in order to show a special preparation at the time of religious rituals. Only women do this work: it probably uses relatively little dung.

Dung as cooking fuel

In this part of India, before it is used as fuel, dung is formed into 'cakes' (upla), then dried in the sun and stored. Women have separate pitches on areas of flat land on the outskirts of the two villages, and squatting on their haunches, they combine the dung with straw and water, form it into thick dinner-plate-sized cakes and set them out in rows in the sun to dry. These dung-cakes have to be turned several times before they are ready to be stored in a stack (bitaura), which line the roads or paths all over north India. Variations in style are apparent from any bus journey of more than 50 miles or so.

When the stack is complete it is sealed with a coating of dung, thatched and topped out with an inverted pot that keeps out the rain and prevents the dung-cakes turning into sludge. Women unpack dung-cakes from the stacks as they need them and take them home to use as their main cooking fuel. We did not discuss with women their views of the benefits or costs of different kinds of cooking fuels, though others have reported on the difficulties of persuading the Indian 'house-wife' (*sic*) to give up using dung-cakes, for they burn slowly and allow food to simmer well—a point which designers of 'improved' or 'smokeless' stoves seem to have had difficulty in understanding (Royal Commission on Agriculture in India 1928; Agarwal 1986a).

Making dung-cakes can occupy two hours of a woman's time every day, depending on how many animals she owns and the amount of cooking fuel required.[5] Patricia frequently found women most available for private conversations while they were making dung-cakes: these patches of land are female space, and women usually work somewhat apart from one another, so she spent a fair part of the winter months squatting on a couple of (dry) dung-cakes talking to women while they worked.

However, women make dung-cakes only for seven to eight months of the year, from about October to May. Dung-cakes are not made in the hot pre-monsoon period, because grubs destroy them, nor during the monsoon itself, when they cannot be dried.

Dung for midden fertiliser

During the hot and rainy months of May to September women and girls collect dung and tip it—along with other household waste—into the midden. Some women also reduce their burden by tipping dung into the midden in the 'wrong' season because they find making dung-cakes too heavy, for example during pregnancy or when they are ill. All the year round, the midden receives the sweepings from the courtyard and other sources of household rubbish, possibly (among Muslims and some Hindus) including the placenta of any babies born, and the excreta of small children and other domestic animals like chickens.

The rubbish is left to mulch for some ten months. Only after this do the men have anything to do with dung, but by then it is no longer regarded as 'dung' but 'midden fertiliser' (*kuri ka khad*). Midden fertiliser is a valuable agricultural input, which the men shovel out of the midden pits onto carts, and plough into the fields before sugarcane is planted in March–April. Midden fertiliser is universally regarded as an essential input for a successful crop of sugarcane.

Value of dung

Dung, dung-cakes and midden fertiliser are not usually sold. They are primarily produced for use. Placing a monetary value on them was difficult, and our informants were resistant to doing so. However, isolated instances of sales provide a way or making a rough estimate of their worth. Dung-cakes have a market in Bijnor town, and sell for about Rs 8 for 100, and a woman with the day's dung of five or six animals might be able to make 50–60 dung-cakes a day, providing a potential income of about Rs 1,000 per year, perhaps equivalent to five or six months wages as female agricultural labourer.

Midden fertiliser is sold even more rarely than dung cakes. Farmers strongly resist selling it if they can avoid it, preferring to use it on their own fields. In 1982–83 we learnt of only one cart-load of about 750 kg of compost sold for Rs 50; An average midden for a middle peasant household might produce between 40 and 50 such cart-loads each year, and a cash value of maybe Rs 2,000 to Rs 2,500, or about seven months wages for a male labourer.

Thus women's dung-work can be given a considerable cash value, either in terms of income or the opportunity cost of using dung in these ways. However, most women are not paid for their dung-work, since it is almost entirely done by family labour, nor do they obtain any informal credit for the contribution this makes.

Occasionally a woman will sell dung-cakes, and she may be able to keep control of the cash or other income she receives for this, but it represents an inadequate recompense for her hard labour.

Theoretical Analysis

How, then, should we locate dung-work theoretically, in relationship to debates on 'production' and 'reproduction'? Recent feminist discussions of this division, and the related distinction between 'public' and 'private' spheres of social life, have stressed the dangers of applying them rigidly (Beechey 1979; Young 1980). It is not useful to analyse women's position as if it depended solely on their reproductive work within the domestic or private sphere, without taking note of the contributions their work-whether private, reproductive, or in the public, productive spheres—makes to production. To maintain such dualities raises problems, because dung-work (like many other aspects of women's work) straddles the division. We prefer to look at the situation in a more integrated fashion, as one where it is seen as 'production-and-reproduction'.

Specifically, dung-work is both 'productive'—a part of agricultural activity, and what is more, specifically related to the major cash crop-and reproductive work—to do with cooking and consumption, the reproduction of the household from day to day—depending on the season. It is production for use which has an exchange value, even if it is rarely realised; it is work done in 'private space'—within the domestic courtyard and at the all-female dung-cake areas—with considerable relevance for the public spaces of the fields where subsistence and, especially, cash crops are grown. But no one locally gives women credit for the work involved.

This brings us to the second main point of paper. The invisibility of much of women's work reflects the seriously deficient ways in which 'development' is generally conceptualised. This is a point often made by feminist critics of development writing, and one we would endorse (Rogers 1980; Beneria 1982). In the case of dung-work, there are some important ecological implications of ignoring it that take us beyond narrowly 'feminist' points. However, most of these writings focus on fuel consumption, and cattle-dung or animal wastes more generally receive only passing mention, despite some estimates showing that in India, 30 per cent of rural energy consumption was provided by animal wastes; a figure for Pakistan was 80 per cent (or three examples see, Cecelski 1985; Agarwal 1986a; and Dankelman and Davidson 1988). Arnold's estimate that 400 million tonnes of cattle-dung are burned annually in Asia and Africa, leading to the loss of 20 million tonnes of potential grain output, is often quoted (see for example Eckholm 1979). Thus cattle-dung is portrayed as something which is only used as cooking fuel because of a shortage of other (presumably superior) fuels. Having lamented its misuse in this way, attention is turned to accounting for the rise in its use and why alternative sources of fuel are no longer available, rather than in looking at the meanings and uses of cattle-dung in more detail. Similarly, focus is placed on ecological balances where forests are being cut down, as in Nepal or in Madhya Pradesh, rather than in looking at the situation where change is less dramatic as in the Gangetic Plain.

Looking at dung-work highlights some ecological changes. Women's work, like men's is not timeless, and several changes have taken place recently, possibly more rapid than at any previous time. There has been a rapid growth in the output of foodgrains and cash crops—precisely the indices generally used in government circles as a sign of development. But, as has often been pointed out, these changes have had other effects (not necessarily positive) that affect women in particular (Agarwal 1986b). Looking at these changes through their effects on the role of dung helps to illuminate some of these changes.

For example, older residents of the two villages can remember when most cooking was done with wood gathered from the scrub-land, but now most of that land is under sugarcane. Although the techniques for making dung-cakes seem to have been known locally for a long time, only within living memory have women started to cook predominantly with dung-cakes. A landless Brahmin described the shift in his lifetime as follows. Previously there used to be far more animals, which grazed in the marsh and on low-lying fallow ground near the river; only young animals and those needed that day for work would be stall-fed. When he was young, cattledung was hardly used for dung-cakes: if he had said to a woman that she should cook with *upla* her reply would have been 'take it away, I can't cook with that!'. This is obviously an exaggeration: what it does seem to suggest, however, is an increase in the use of upla and a spread of its production and use to women in higher status groups.

Thus the 'jungle', which is usually classified as 'non-productive' land, had a variety of economic uses, including not only acting as a source of wood-fuel but also as a source of dung for those without animals. At today's prices, it would have provided hundreds of thousands of rupees worth of cooking fuel every year for local residents, quite apart from its use as a source of, for example, beams for roof-timbers and reeds for thatching huts. But foodgrains have been granted such a dominant sway over indicators of agricultural growth in India that the loss of jungle land goes almost unnoticed. Similarly, the work of women tends to be closely linked to the availability of such land, and as with other aspects of women's work, it is not covered by most official enquiries into land and labour use in India. The time frames are too short and the definition of work too narrow to include much of what women do, whether in fodder, fuel and water collection or the processing of crops.

Furthermore, the transformation of jungle into agricultural and has accelerated several linked processes that have reduced soil fertility and forced farmers into more intensive commercial relationships. As the jungle has declined, so has the amount of common grazing land. A rise in double-cropping, and the value of cash crops, has reduced the amount of land under fodder crops (which are also often nitrogen-fixing plants) As far as we can gauge, this is associated with a decline in the number of animals supported in the villages. A smaller absolute amount of dung is produced; proportionately more of it must be used for fuel because of the decline in sources of wood.[6] Consequently, farmers are forced to rely more on artificial fertilisers and are drawn more closely into cash relationships over which they have no control.

Furthermore, some men's and some women's work at some seasons has been intensified. Animals are stall-fed rather than grazed raising the need for fodder collection and fodder chopping. This may be done by men or women, depending on the available labour, season, and whether the chopping is mechanised. Water must also be fetched, usually by women. Women also have more work processing dung, since they have become more dependent on dung-cakes for cooking fuel and other fuels for kindling (twigs, reeds, dried grasses, etc.) have to be fetched from farther afield, by men or women. In other words, the long-standing advice to the Indian government to preserve land for grazing and fuel has had no impact on commercialisation processes in this part of India. But merely to bemoan this, declaring for example that 'the use of cow dung as a source of non-commercial fuel is virtually a crime', does not get us very far.[7]

All the efforts of the government and industry in expanding credit, fertiliser, seed and water supply, have undoubtedly commercialised important aspects of agriculture and increased the output of grain and cash crops, while equally important areas of economic activity in which women's roles are more significant have been ignored.

WOMEN'S WORK, DOWRY AND FEMALE SURVIVAL

Does the foregoing shed any light on the position of women in rural north India more generally? There is much evidence of women's poor and relatively deteriorating life-chances. For example, the sex ratio—men per 1,000 females—is high and has been rising over most of the twentieth century, with perhaps a downturn between 1971 and 1981. In rural Bijnor the sex ratio in 1981 was 1,169—not the worst in India but nearly so, whereas the sex ratio at birth is probably not much more than 1,050. Since girls are thought to be 'naturally' more robust, such an adverse sex ratio is probably a result of higher female mortality rates through the neglect of infant girls and, to a lesser extent, of women in the childbearing ages. The reported death rates in 1982 for rural U.P. for children aged 0–4 are 68 per 1,000 for females and 54 for males (Government of India 1985). At all ages up to 40, female mortality rates were above male rates.

These findings have been the cause of much recent discussion, most prominently stimulated by Barbara Miller's book, *The Endangered Sex*, but also the subject of a number of excellent articles (Miller 1981; Dyson and Moore 1983; Das Gupta 1987). Essentially, these authors conclude that the structural consequences of the north Indian kinship system leave women powerless and perceived as economic costs rather than benefits, and lead to strong son preferences and systematic (if subconscious) neglect of daughters. Furthermore, this situation is said to be getting worse. In some lower-caste groups, bride-wealth was the predominant marriage payment: some of these groups seem to have changed to a dowry system, like their upper-caste and property-owning neighbours. Furthermore, among those higher-status groups, the nature of dowry seems to have changed: as well as being seen as a heavier burden, it seems to be increasingly 'demand-led' whereas people used to 'accept what is offered' (Ahmad 1987; Srinivas 1986).

Consequently there has been a rise in the reporting of dowry deaths and harassment of young brides. Some have argued that one cause of this change is that women from poorer groups are not only finding jobs harder to get, as a result of the green revolution, but that in addition, their husbands, fathers or fathers-in-law are withdrawing them from the labour force as soon as they can afford to do so (Sharma 1980). In other words, it is argued, there is a relationship between a woman's economic contribution to the household and her 'value' as a child. Miller (1980: 127) concludes: 'One must take female roles in rural production into account, and also other factors which make sons preferable to daughters like rules of inheritance, ritual need for sons, etc.' (see also Miller 1981; Bardhan 1982; Randeria and Visaria 1984).

Here we will comment oil only part of this debate. Are women valued less as their economic contributions decline? Does this generate more demand for dowry to compensate parents of men to accept a parasite? Dung-work is one form of women's work that has changed in its nature in the memories of old women: to recapitulate, they are probably spending more of their time doing it, dung's contribution as cooking fuel is probably more significant than it was before, and its role as fertiliser of the major cash-crop is still crucial; and women from a wider range of social classes are doing the work. What are the consequences of these changes to the evaluation of men and women and their work? Do people themselves make a link between women's work and escalation of dowry?

Very simply, our data suggests that the economic contribution made by women's work is irrelevant to the question. The example of dung-work illuminates how it is possible for what seems clearly to us to be hard manual labour, with considerable financial significance, to be derided locally as women's work and treated as of no intrinsic value. Significantly, perhaps, our informants themselves do not make links between changes in women's work and, dowry levels. As one Muslim man said:

> Women's work hasn't changed at all—they do just the same work as before. Dowry's gone up because this is an era of money. We used to make lots of our own things but now we get them from the bazaar. By example wedding costs have risen.
>
> Andrew: Is that because girls are worth less now than they were before?
>
> No—girls were never worth very much!

Thus they explain rising dowry expenses with reference to the commercialisation introduced by the green revolution. (They also blame the new chemical fertilisers for making men 'hotter' and more ready to make demands.) They say that the level of competition for 'good' grooms has risen; and that people always wanted to do the best they could for their daughters, in order to make their lives with their in-laws as comfortable as possible. Because many parents can now give more, they try to do so, and levels of expectation have risen in response to this.

Of course, we do not have to accept our informants' explanations. However, we would point to one further flaw in the arguments of Miller and others. Among the Muslims in our sample, whose dowry costs are lower than those of comparable Hindus levels of excess female mortality are higher than among those same Hindus. This is counter-intuitive; but the paradox cannot be explained by differences in the work done by young married women in the two communities, for these are much the same. In other words, we would suggest that what is crucial is not the work that is done by women but its evaluation, and women's access to property and the fruits of their work; these have shown no signs of change. Certainly, attempting to improve the position of women by increasing their workloads, without attacking their lack of rights to property and income, will leave women worse off than they are at present.

CONCLUSION

This has been a limited exercise. We have not considered a number of linked issues, such as the possibility that there are too many cattle in the area; the ritual and symbolic ways in which the importance of cattle and its dung are marked; the effect on women's health of cooking by dung-cakes rather than wood; the effectiveness of social forestry as a way of remedying the situation; or the viability of biogas as an alternative source of fuel and fertiliser. Nor have we looked at the implications of current and possible alternative patterns of cattle ownership and milk marketing for the class structure; nor how dung-cakes are marketed around the major Indian towns and the role of women in that; nor how the extent of commercialisation of dung and its products affects domestic relationships. Others have studied many of these things: what we would argue is that they have not taken the dung as seriously as it warrants; and we suggest that this failure is linked to the fact that as women's work it has wrongly been felt to be beneath the contempt of development specialists.

Notes

1. We have used class categories loosely based on Patnaik (1976); for more details see P. M. Jeffery, Jeffery and Lyon (1988).

2. This is too simplistic a formulation; but in an early discussion of the division of labour by sex in agriculture, T. P. S. Chawdhari and B. M. Sharma (1961) (who place 'manuring and manures' as a 'routine agricultural activity') similarly record it as a solely female activity in Nangloi Block, near Delhi.

3. Chawdhari and Sharma make this point delicately when they note that they discovered positive awareness on the part of the younger females of the fact that certain jobs are assigned to their sex merely because these are considered degrading for male folk. The awareness is, however, not yet vocal; it was only revealed on tactful questioning of the respondents by the lady interpreter (1961: 646).

4. M. Tomar, personal communication, confirms this for Muzaffarnagar district, west of Bijnor.

5. These estimates are poor: women refused to answer repeat time-use questions, complaining of repetition and boredom, and our data cannot be analysed by season, class or household structure. Other reports suggest that two hours a day would be unusually high; T. P. S. Chawdhari and B. M. Sharma (1961) estimate 19 days-equivalent per year; D. Jain (1985), reports only 10–20 minutes per woman aged 6–44 for her Rajasthan sample, and gives no separate figure for her West Bengal sample; M. Mitra (1987), found poor peasant women spent only 15 minutes per day on dung-work, and reports no figures for other social classes.

6. Official statistics suggest that in U.P. as a whole, the number of cattle has hardly changed since 1966, whereas the number of buffalo has risen by 30 per cent in the same

period. We have no information on the balance between the two in Dharmnagri and Jhakri, nor on the consequences in terms of dung-work on any such change.

7. See for example Royal Commission on Agriculture (1928). The quote is from Government of India (1973: 73), cited by Eckholm (1975: 10); E. Cecelski (1985) also cites M. E. Khan and S. K. Ghosh Dastidar (1983), to the effect that in parts of Punjab, rights of dung-collection are now 'sold' to agricultural labourers in exchange for an extra hour's work; and R, Wade (1986), describes the auctioning of dung-collection rights in Andhra Pradesh, but he does not describe who actually does the work. We did not find such a degree of commercialisation in Bijnor.

References

Agarwal, B. 1986a. *Cold Hearths and Barren Slopes: The Woodfuel Crisis in the Third World.* London: Zed Books.

——. 1986b. 'Women, Poverty and Agricultural Growth in India'. *Journal of Peasant Studies* 13: 165–220.

Ahmad, R. 1987. 'Changing Marriage Transactions and Rise of Demand System in Bangladesh'. *Economic and Political Weekly* 22 (17): WS2–WS26, 25 April.

Bardhan, P. 1982. 'Little Girls and Death in India'. *Economic and Political Weekly* 17 (36): 1448–50, 4 September.

Beechey, V. 1979. 'On Patriarchy'. *Feminist Review* 3: 66–82.

Beneria, L. (ed.). 1982. *Women and Development: The Sexual Division of Labour in Rural Societies.* New York: Praeger.

Byres, T. J. and B. Crow. 1985. *The Green Revolution in India.* Milton Keynes: Open University Press.

Cecelski, E. 1985. *The Rural Energy Crisis, Women's Work and Basic Needs: Perspectives and Approaches to Action.* Geneva: ILO.

Chawdhari, T. P. S. and B. M. Sharma. 1961. 'Female Labour of the Farm Family in Agriculture'. *Agricultural Situation in India* 16: 643–50.

Dankelman, I. and J. Davidson. 1988. *Women and Environment in the Third World.* London: Earthscan.

Das Gupta, M. 1987. 'Selective Discrimination against Female Children in Rural Punjab, India', *Population and Development Review* 13: 77–100.

Dyson, T. and M. Moore. 1983. 'On Kinship Structure, Female Autonomy and Demographic Behaviour in India'. *Population and Development Review* 9: 35–60.

Eckholm, E. 1975. *The Other Energy Crisis: Firewood.* Washington DC: Worldwatch Institute.

——. 1979. *Planting for the Future: Forestry for Human Needs.* Washington DC: Worldwatch Institute.

Government of India. 1973. *Interim Report of the National Commission on Agriculture and Social Forestry.* New Delhi: Ministry of Agriculture.

——. 1985. *Sample Registration Scheme, 1982.* New Delhi: Office of the Resigstrar-General, India.

Jain, D. 1985. 'The Household Trap: Report on a Field Survey of Female Activity Patterns'. In *Tyranny of the Household,* ed. D. Jain and N. Banerjee. 215–48. New Delhi: Shakti.

Jeffery, P. M., R. Jeffery and A. Lyon. 1988. *Labour Pains and Labour Power: Women and Childbearing in India.* London: Zed Books.

Khan, M. E. and S. K. Ghosh Dastidar. 1983. 'A Micro-level Study on Acceptance of Community Bio-gas in Punjab'. Draft report. New Delhi: Operation Research Group.

Kipling, J. L. 1891. *Beast and Man in India*. London: Macmillan.

Miller, B. D. 1980. 'Female Neglect and the Costs of Marriage in Rural India'. *Contributions to Indian Sociology* 14: 95–129.

_____. 1981. *The Endangered Sex: Neglect of Female Children in Rural North India*. Ithaca and London: Cornell University Press.

Mitra, M. 1987. 'Women's Work: Gains Analysis of Women's Labour in Dairy Production'. In *Invisible Hands: Women in Home-Based Production*, ed. A. M. Singh and A. Kelles-Viitanen. 109–43. New Delhi: Sage.

Oakley, A. 1974. *The Sociology of Housework*. London: Martin Robertson.

Patnaik, U. 1976. 'Class Differentiation within the Peasantry'. *Economic and Political Weekly* 11 (39): A89–A101, September.

Randeria, S. and L. Visaria. 1984. 'Sociology of Bride-Price and Dowry'. *Economic and Political Weekly* 19 (15): 648–52, 14 April.

Rogers, B. 1980. *The Domestication of Women: Discrimination in Developing Societies*. London: Kogan Page.

Royal Commission on Agriculture in India. 1928. *Report*. London: HMSO.

Sau, R. 1988. 'The Green Revolution and Industrial Growth in India: A Tale of Two Paradoxes and a Half'. *Economic and Political Weekly* 23 (16): 789–96, 16 April.

Sharma, U. 1980. *Women, Work and Property in North-West India*. London: Tavistock.

Srinivas, M. N. 1986. *Dowry*. Delhi: Oxford University Press.

Wade, R. 1987. *Village Republics: Economic Conditions for Collective Action in South India*. Cambridge: Cambridge University Press.

Young, I. 1980. 'Socialist Feminism and the Limits of Dual Systems Theory'. *Socialist Review* 10 (2–3): 169–88.

11

Coping with Male Migration*

Leela Gulati

The migration of any one male member of a household to the West Asia seems to have a major impact on the members left behind. This seems to be the case irrespective of marital status, age, relation or caste of the male migrant. In all of the families studied, people staying behind had to make major adjustments in their lifestyles as a result of the migration of a male member.

The impact of migration to the West Asia begins to be felt long before the migrant actually leaves home. It starts the moment a husband or son decides to try to migrate to the west Asia and starts seriously preparing for it. He has to mobilise various social networks both at home and abroad and this he does with the support and involvement of the adult members, men and women, of his immediate family, including not only his wife and parents but also siblings, as well as other relatives; friends and neighbours too get involved.

Relatives, friends and neighbours have to be approached for: (a) contacting the right agent who will, at the minimum cost, arrange for the aspiring migrant's work permit and take care of the various formalities which need to be completed before departure; (b) collection of funds needed for the purpose and pooling of information on how additional funds could be raised from out-side the circle of various networks one has access to; (c) knowledge regarding persons already working in the west Asia, so as to approach them for recommendation regarding the most reliable agent, but also on several occasions for securing the work permit directly.

A work permit obtained without an agent's intermediation is considered the least expensive and the most dependable. But in the families we have studied, very few—2 out of 50—migrants could manage to obtain their work permits without going through an agent. Still, information with regard to the right agent can be very important. A migrant father may not be able to secure a work permit for his son, but his son certainly can benefit from the information and experience the father had of agents.

The practice of disseminating information on work opportunities, formalities to be completed, agents to be contacted, monies to be raised, etc., among relatives,

---

* This chapter has been extracted from a longer paper published by the author in the *Economic and Political Weekly* 22 (44): WS41–WS46, 31 October 1987.

friends and neighbours was quite common. Naturally, those closer to the people who had already migrated had access to greater and more reliable information.

RAISING FUNDS

When down payments of between Rs 15,000 and Rs 20,000 have to be made to obtain a work permit and meet other costs, an aspiring migrant from a low income family, with few or no assets, has necessarily to depend on relatives, friends and neighbours. Barring a few exceptions, most of the 50 migrants studied could make it only after spending substantial sums of money. Most of these migrants came from households which did not have much of either cash or assets. The major asset owned by the families studied was a piece of residential land. Then there was the gold jewellery belonging to their women.

In the case of the recently married migrants (i.e., those who get married within three to four years before migration) there was also some cash in addition to land/ or jewellery that the migrant's wife might have brought in dowry, and which the migrant or his family might have set apart to meet his migration expenses. In practically every case of a married migrant, the assets which the wife had brought as her dowry and which the family still held, were either sold or mortgaged (in most cases, the latter) to raise funds so as to meet the migration expenses. In several cases, the wife's dowry was the major source of such funding. In one particular instance, a migrant's marriage was fixed only after making sure that the bride's parents had the ability and willingness to pay for the groom's migration expenses.

TABLE 11.1: Distribution of Households by Village and Number of Migrants in Gulf

Family Members	Alakad	Bhimapally	Other Parts of Trivandrum	Total
Only one member	19	5	4	28
Two members	3	3	–	6
Three members	–	1	1	2
Four members	–	–	–	–
Five members	1	–	–	1
Total	23	9	5	37

Note: Includes only immediate family members and not extended relatives. Excepting for two migrant households all others had at least one or more extended relative(s) in the Gulf.

Here migrants were not married at the time of migration, the mother invariably contributed to the funding of her son's migration expenses by letting her jewellery be pawned for the purpose. Indeed, in several of the cases studied, mothers gave away their jewellery for the purpose even when the migrant was married and could avail of funds obtained as dowry.

Even sisters and sisters-in-law were found to contribute their jewellery. So also did aunts and cousins. Of course, the unwritten understanding in all such cases is that the migrants will pay back in cash so that each and every relative thus contributing can retrieve her jewellery fully. Does this understanding extend even to the migrant's wife? It is difficult to answer this question, although in several cases the wife did succeed in more than compensating herself for the jewellery she had given away for sale or mortgage at the time of the husband's migration. Still, it cannot be established that like other women relatives or friends contributing to the pool, the wife too has a clear claim to be reimbursed for her jewellery or for other contributions.

Women's Supportive Eole

The question remains whether women's supportive role in the matter of male migration was voluntary or not. Our evidence shows that women are more than merely passive supporters. The older a wife was, the more actively supportive she was of the decision of her husband to migrate. Even the mothers had worked actively for their sons' migration by making their personal contributions and also by raising funds from other sources. Where the migrant has worked abroad for a sufficient length of time, say more than four years, the wife possessed a great deal more jewellery than she did before the husband's migration. However, the more distant a relative was the earlier she tended to be paid back. Buying jewellery for the wife followed later.

Barring a few exceptions, almost all the migrant households had depended upon casual wage labour in one form or the other as the principal source of household income. It is a type of work where one is perennially uncertain about the job next morning. Often, there is a seasonal pattern to the availability of work opportunity. In fishing and activities related to it, for instance, the element of job seasonality can be quite high.

The Economic Calculations

Assuming a man was so engaged, he was possibly earning not more than Rs 500 per month on an average before migration. After he succeeded in migrating to the Gulf, he would start making Rs 2,000 a month in a totally unskilled job. Thus a man could make at least an income four times larger should he migrate to the Gulf. Also, it was known from the experience of those who were already working in the Middle East that men tended to save close to three-fourths of their incomes. So it seemed to make sense to the women we spoke to that their men should want to migrate. 'Yes, we have heard that conditions of work are hard, the weather is oppressive and the treatment meted out to workers feudal. Still if in four years' time one can hope to make major advances in one's economic situation it is worth one's while going through all the trouble involved. Who wants to be poor all one's life and eke out a bare hand-to-mouth existence, if there is a way out?' The women we studied perceived clearly the scope for a major improvement in their economic conditions as a consequence of the migration of their men to the west Asia, and that too within a short period. It is then a matter of no surprise that they participated actively in the preparation for their men's migration.

FAMILY NEED FOR PROTECTION

While the family the migrant leaves behind participates actively in the preparation for his migration, often separation from the migrant imposes on the family new and/ or added demands, demands that the women members, in particular, have seldom before been called upon to cope with. In meeting these demands, the family has to frequently draw upon its social network.

The belief that all women need a protective male umbrella is quite widely held. Out of 33 migrants' wives we studied, only five lived independently, i.e., they did not share the same house with any other relative or family. All these five wives had children and were in the age-group of 30 to 40. Of these five, only one had arranged with a male relative living close by, and much senior in age, to stay with her. It is necessary to bear in mind here that most of the migrant families we have studied stayed within their own groups. Thus the Alakad Muslim families, migrant or non-migrant, stayed in a cluster of their own, as did the Alakad Hindu families. This held for the other families too.

Wives 20 years or less in age and who had no children stayed with their own parents or the parents of their husbands. Four out of five stayed with the latter. Excluding those under 20, out of the migrant wives who did not stay independently, nine lived with their own parents, 17 with husbands' parents and two lived with their married sisters.

REVEALED VS DESIRED RESIDENCE PATTERN

Between living with the wife's own parents and with her parents-in-law, the revealed pattern found by us was clearly in favour of the latter. For every wife staying with her own parents, two stayed with their parents-in-law. There can be several explanations. Part of the reason could be the fact that the wife's parents stayed in a town or village different from where she had been staying before her husband's migration, so that shifting to her own parent's house would have involved a .major shift for the wife and her children. Part of the explanation lay in the wife's understanding of her husband's preference regarding where his family should stay during his absence. Whether the husband's preference was based altogether on his own independent judgment or was also influenced by his parents is an additional question to which we could not get a clear-cut response. Some of our respondent wives staying with their parents-in-law did however indicate that if their circumstances had permitted, they would have liked to live closer to their own parents.

Does the length of the migrant's stay abroad make any difference to the wife's living? Our study seems to suggest that with the passage of years as wives learn to manage things on their own, they tend more and more to take independent decisions on many matters, and in the process want to be less and less dependent on relatives. They also gain in confidence so as to live independently. Of the migrants' wives we studied, five were staying independently. Of these five, in the case of as many as four the husband had stayed abroad for a period of three years or more. In the case of the fifth household, the wife was already over 35 years old when her husband succeeded in his attempt to migrate. Also, she had six surviving children. Furthermore, the husband's parents were staying within easy walking distance. In the circumstances, while neither the wife herself nor her husband thought it necessary for the family to move in with the latter's parents, the question of moving away to where the wife's parents were living did not arise.

The situation in regard to joint living can of course change over time. We came across a few instances where a migrant's wife starts by staying with her parents or parents-in-law but moves to an independent house after a few years, or where a migrant's wife starts by staying with her parents-in-law and subsequently moves to her own parents.

Regardless of whether a migrant's wife lives separately or not, her dependence on close relatives, in the absence of her husband, goes much beyond her need for a male physical umbrella. Her need for help and guidance is the greatest in the period immediately after the migrant's first departure for the west Asia because she has to start handling matters and taking decisions she possibly never took before. Such matters range from daily shopping to investment of funds to day-to-day care of children, to taking them to doctors in the event of sickness and to the extent and type of schooling for each of the children.

Coping with Migrants' Absence

Though women are much involved in the preparation of their men to migrate, their involvement does not quite end there. It is only the beginning of an involvement which can extend to several years. Women have almost invariably to take on considerably greater responsibilities in the wake of their men's migration. The issue is how they cope with the new situation they get placed in.

Young Wives with no Children

Let us start with the young brides. These include (a) girls whose husbands migrate within a year of the marriage and who have not had time to conceive or bear a child, and (b) girls who are married off to 'gulf boys', i.e., to men already working in the west Asia, and who get married in the course of one of their home visits, usually of a short duration of four to eight weeks. These girls hardly have time to know their men before they disappear from the scene for long periods. The few weeks their men spend with them are socially very hectic but emotionally least rewarding. In one case, the girl spent just one week with her husband. She moved into a totally new social environment, where she felt as if she was under constant watch by her in-laws. Still, the girl felt she had to keep everyone in her husband's house in good humour. That is what her own parents had advised her to do. Since she hardly knew her husband, the only way she could make certain that her marriage lasted was to keep her in-laws happy. If she had known her husband longer, or had conceived a child from him, things would have been somewhat different. But now she had to rely altogether on her in-laws' goodwill.

Unlike the one-week old bride we have spoken of who came from a Muslim household, the two young Hindu (Nair) brides we studied opted to stay with their own parents, of course, with the consent of their husbands. Both these girls had got married with dowries, but that did not come in the way of their parents agreeing to their girls continuing to stay with them after marriage. Among Nairs, a matriarchal caste, it is possible for the girls to continue to stay with their own parents even after marriage. Both these girls have a decided advantage, over the Muslim girl in the sense that they are living in a familiar and friendly social environment.

Wives with Children

Women, older in age and with children, who, as we have noted above, mostly stay with their in-laws, are better equipped than the young brides to cope with the problems of separation from husbands. At least, the environment is not unfamiliar whatever their relationship with their in-laws. Also, coping with children (without the support of the father) could take up a lot of time and energy of these women so that they have less of both to feel emotionally deprived.

From amongst those who stay with the husband's parents, a distinction needs to be made, however, between relatively younger wives and those somewhat older in age. Often, where a wife is relatively young she has to submit more to the control of her mother-in-law than a wife older in age. We know of at least one such wife, married for three years yet without a child. Not having conceived so far was in itself a sort of stigma she was supposed to be under. She had to observe increasing number of fasts and other religious rituals her mother-in-law prescribed. Although she heard regularly from her husband and received a bank draft in her name, these did not seem to be enough to lift her spirits.

The position of wives with young children is decidedly better. They feel more secure and have a clear role to play within the husband's family. Given their access to funds, they feel more free to spend. Also, their movement outside the house is far less constrained.

That these young wives with children adjust with the husband's family better than wives without children goes without saying. The feeling that they fully belong to the household they live with is obviously important. Not that conflicts do not arise with the in-laws. Wives with children have been able to cope with them with greater confidence. Also, they do not have to suppress their tensions. They therefore tend to be more secure in their relationships with their husbands.

It would nonetheless be erroneous to give the impression that wives, young or old, fully overcome the feeling of insecurity once they have children. Among Muslims, divorce is permitted and quite easy. So Muslim wives have to continuously remind themselves that it could happen to them. In one of the cases studied, a wife with three children faced the threat of divorce from her migrant husband, following a dispute between him and her father over a piece of property supposed to have been given to him in dowry but not actually passed on. It must be added, however, that of the Muslim couples we studied, this was the only one instance of threatened divorce.

Women with somewhat older children, say above 10 years of age, and who were able to live independently appeared to be advantageously placed. Not only age but having relatively grown up children too gave these women a great deal of confidence. With the help of their children they could take care of several chores independently of relatives.

It is obvious from what we have said above that wives feel more secure and uninhibited in their actions when they have children than when they are without. But to want a child or two is not the same thing as wanting or having several children. The fact that the couples remain separated for long periods cannot be overlooked either. At the aggregate level, we noted some evidence of younger couples having fewer children but whether this was because husbands were away from their wives for long stretches or because of the general climate of opinion is regard to family size in the state of Kerala needs to be gone into closely. But the long absences of husbands have certainly widened the inter-birth interval.

Other Women of the Household

So far we have spoken mostly of wives of migrants. There are however other women in migrant households, mothers, unmarried sisters and, of course, daughters. They too share with the migrant's wife most, if not all, of the stresses and strains that his absence entails just as they share with her most of the gains resulting from the household's increased prosperity. All the same, it is worthwhile to examine the special implications, if any, for these other women in the households of the actual migration.

In the households of unmarried migrants, it is the mother who bears the burden of whatever strain migration, and its aftermath, entail. It is the mother's personal assets which are principally tapped for raising the amount needed to finance the cost of migration of the son. It is also the mother who usually receives the remittances from her migrant son. She has to shoulder the responsibility of managing the funds, with the support, of course, of her husband, if alive. She has also to look for a suitable bride for the migrant son and ensure that he gets suitably married.

As we have noticed, a large majority of migrant wives tend to stay with their in-laws. Given this fact, even when migrants are married, the involvement of the migrant's mother in the household has to be much more than marginal and this will be so regardless of whether the migrant sends back bank drafts in the name of his wife or his mother. In almost all cases of married migrants we studied, it is the wife in whose name the bank draft comes, not the migrant's mother, even though the two are living together. In one particular instance, where the migrant had been married for three years, the mother nonetheless retained almost total control over the management of the funds that he remitted to his wife. While this could be an extreme case, it will not be unreasonable to say that in the majority of cases where migrants' wives stay with their in-laws, the mothers enjoy considerable say in financial as well as other matters.

Migrants' wives are, it appears, less subject to pressures and interference when they live with their own mothers than when they live with their mothers-in-law. We have come across a few instances where the wife moved after a few years from her in-laws' to her own mother's house but not one instance where it was the other way round.

We found that migrants, regardless of whether they are married or not, consider it as one of their principal obligations to arrange the marriage of their unmarried sisters and the finances necessary for the purpose, including dowry. It goes without saying that the migrant feels equally responsible, if not more, with regard to arranging the marriage of his own daughters if and when they reach the age.

It was not unheard of that an unmarried migrant would defer his own marriage so that the family first attends to his sister's marriage. It has also happened that a family's search for the right household to marry the sister into and in laying by enough funds for dowry and other expenses, much time was lost. In the process, the unmarried migrant's own marriage got deferred. It must be added, however, that our overall data does not show that the age at marriage was higher in migrant households compared to non-migrant households.

We came across a number of instances where migrants helped their brothers and brothers-in-law to migrate. Indeed, the most widely prevalent belief is that the route to migration to the Gulf lies through one's wife if one does not have a brother or father working in the west Asia.

Felt Need for Literacy

Even though a migrant's family has access to support from people within the family network and even from those in the outer network comprising neighbours and friends, the ability of those left behind by the migrant—especially women—depends critically on their own capabilities.

One major determinant of these capabilities is literacy. The overwhelming majority of the migrants we studied had themselves done only 10 years of schooling or less. The literacy level of the wives of migrants was lower than that of the migrants themselves. While the median average for the migrants was nine years of schooling, for the wives it was only six years. The number of those with less than two years of schooling was twice as large for wives as for migrants.

One of the very first things a migrant does on reaching his place of work in the west Asia is to send a message back home that he has reached safely. He follows it up with letters. Usually, the migrants, we found, communicate on a regular basis. So within a fortnight to one month of a migrant's departure, the need arises to read his letters and respond to them. Before the contingency arose a woman may have hardly ever written a letter even when she may have received or read one, assuming that she could read and write. Verbal communication with their men was all that they had experienced before. Since many of the wives and mothers were only marginally literate, if not altogether illiterate, they had to depend on neighbours and friends to help them not only write but also read letters. Where their children could read and write, women did not have to depend on others. Indeed the need to be able to read and write is felt so strongly that when asked what in their view the community effort should be directed at, the overwhelming majority of wives chose adult literacy classes for women.

When a migrant's wife receives a bank draft from her husband within a month or two of his departure, the immediate thing she has to do is to go to a bank and open an account in her name. None of the migrants wives in Alakad or elsewhere in our beat had ever before even entered a bank's office. Now they operate accounts there. Those who were illiterate and could not sign their names were issued identity cards. They also had to leave a passport size photograph with the bank, something they would not have done earlier.[...]

Management of Funds

The sums flowing in the wake of migration to the west Asia of even unskilled workers are, relatively speaking, so large that their magnitude itself can be said to have create an altogether new situation for the women from the migrant households. Regardless of whether the remittance is received through banking or non-banking channels, the exposure of women to huge amounts of money would not but have posed major new challenges.

One such is the management of funds which they receive from the migrants. The remittances wives and mothers receive are usually large in relation to not only the amount needed for day to day expenses at the level of consumption which the migrant household was used to before the migrants' departure but also in relation to the amount they would require even after the household considers it prudent to raise its living standard. Two things need to be noted straight-away. Firstly, the management of day to day household expenses is never the exclusive responsibility of a woman where the household is headed by a man present on the scene. But in the absence of the husband, the woman takes on a lot more responsibility than she never shouldered before. Secondly, whatever improvement takes place in the household's consumption standard immediately following the migrant's departure, the decision where to effect such improvement and where to go slow is almost entirely the woman's. At least in the first few years following the departure of the migrant, families have tended to be cautious in regard to their daily expenses in view of the 'enormous' debt the family incurs to finance the migration expenses, the debt which, according to our study, most families have tended to repay within the first two years or thereabouts.[...]

With their men living abroad, women's awareness increases considerably regarding the range of goods and services for purchase or use. Their awareness of the alternative possibilities of placing savings too is enlarged. Earlier, not only were they not exposed to banks, but they were also generally unaware of most other forms of deposit-keeping and lending. In the past, women of the migrant households we studied had at most known of, and participated in, local 'chitties', making small contributions to a pool which one of the members of a chitty would then bid for or take in rotation. Now, when asked for the reason for not keeping their savings in bank accounts, they readily speak of the advantage of placing the savings with the local shopkeeper since he is willing to pay a much higher interest without risk. This attitude is true of most women regardless of the level of their literacy.

CHILDCARE

With improved finances, the general availability of items of daily consumption improves considerably from almost the time of the very first remittance. It was observed that in whatever upgradation in the household's living standard took place during the years following the migration, child care occupied the pride of place. Particular attention was given to food, medical care and education of children. Migrants themselves reportedly enquired of children's health and education and urged qualified medical attention in case a child fell sick and additional tutorial help in case a child would, as a result, do better in school.

Communication Between Husband and Wife

One would ordinarily assume that communication between husbands and wives suffers in consequence of the husband's migration to a distant land. The reality, strange to say, seems to be different.

The migration of men appears to have improved the understanding between husbands and wives. According to the views expressed by Alakad Muslim women from migrant households, when their men were on the scene they rarely got to see and talk to them. They left the house for the mosque early in the morning and went to work from there itself, taking their breakfast on the way. If they had time in the evening for recreation, it would be spent in the bazaar in the company of other men. Seldom would they return home to spend an hour or two in leisure with the wives and/or children.

Women seem now to be able to make a much greater impact on the husband's thinking and decision-making than before. According to one story narrated to us, it was the wife who took the initiative and suggested to her husband that their savings might be invested in an autorickshaw and that she would supervise the renting of the vehicle for hire. Wives often write to their husbands about the children's education and health. They also write about the purchase of land and the construction or repair of houses. On the whole, husbands appear to take the contents of their wives' letters sufficiently seriously and try to accommodate the views conveyed in the decisions they have to take. Probably, the long separation and distance help.

There is no question that it is a remarkable change. Given the 'temporariness' of the migration and taking into account the other factors, women, except possibly those young in age and/or with no children, seem to consider the migration of their husbands as a major gain. However, younger and newly married wives would consider no gain large enough to make up for the separation they have to undergo.

ROLE OF RELIGION

We have seen above what is involved in preparing to go to the west Asia. Things are uncertain till the very end. Even when everything works out smoothly, it takes a migrant six months to a year to make it. And this does not include the time a person spends to obtain his passport which, of course, is the least arduous and time-consuming formality to complete. It is not just the migrant himself but his whole family including close relatives who are intimately involved in the preparatory work before migration. Given the risks and uncertainties involved, it is not altogether surprising that people should turn to religion. Special prayers and offerings at every step in the migrant's preparation have become usual. Both men and women perhaps turn to propitiating the gods to ensure migration, but women appear to play the leading role here. This we found to be true in the case of both Muslim and Hindu migrant households.

Not that people turn to religion only in the initial stages when they face uncertainty about migration itself. It is true though that once a person has made it to the west Asia, the chances of his losing his job and returning are not great. At least, this is the impression we received. In fact, most migrants in our sample have been able to extend their stay beyond the period of the original contract. Even so, migrants not only suggest a substantial donation to be made to the mosque/temple and charity out of their first remittance but they continue making donations subsequently as well. Occasions for these subsequent donations are religious festivals, major property transactions such as purchase of land and starting and completion of house construction, marriages and deaths.

While the practice of making donations is widespread, it is our broad impression that Muslim men make more substantial contributions to religious institutions and charities. Everyone in and around Alakad remarks how the mosque there has prospered in recent years. The building complex has expanded and it celebrates the various Muslim festivals on a scale never witnessed before.

Whatever the level and frequency of donations to a religious institution, it is obvious that these donations are often made in the migrant's absence from the scene. Women, therefore, have a major role in such donations, particularly those made on the spot when solicited for special occasions by the mosque or temple administration.

Given the circumstances in which women from migrant households find themselves, the tension of living jointly with other relatives, difficulties over managing the children or emotional strains that overwhelm them from time to time—it is somewhat understandable that women turn to religion and at frequent intervals.

It must be said to the credit of the Alakad mosque that its management has not been unmindful of the emerging needs of the women devotees from migrant households. Ordinarily, Muslim girls do not go to the madras (school run by the mosque management for the teaching of Holy Koran) after the age of twelve. Since women from migrant households now need to read and write in the local language, the mosque management is planning to conduct literacy classes' for grown up women in a private house.

We did not hear of any similar plans sponsored on behalf of the Hindu temple. Of course, while more than half of the Muslim households in Alakad had migrants in the west Asia, the proportion for the Hindu households worked out to a mere 3 per cent. It is thus understandable that the mosque management would show greater sensitivity to the needs of the migrant households. Whether, in consequence, the influence of religion will become greater on Muslim households than on Hindu households of Alakad may be a legitimate question. At the same time, however, religion itself gets influenced by the changing demands of the devotees as is demonstrated by the fact that the Alakad mosque management has shown its readiness to undertake tasks it had shunned thus far.

CONCLUDING OBSERVATIONS

On the basis of our work done among migrant households the following major conclusions emerge with regard to the impact of the migration of any one male member to the west Asia on women left behind.

We found that migration has its impact quite some time before the migrant actually leaves the country for the west Asia. The decision to migrate is a decision in which family members including women are actively involved. Women of the migrant's immediate family play an active part in both motivating and facilitating male migration. Dependence on immediate family members, other relatives, friends and neighbours of the households is considerable in preparing for migration and after the migration actually materialises.

Dependence seems to increase all round in consequence of the migration of even one male member of a family. The kind of dependence male migration leads to is of different types. There is dependence for funds for management of funds, in terms of repayment of loans and investment in real estate, for protection of women, and for childcare. Dependence for funds to be raised for the financing of migration usually extends to a wide circle including not only immediate family members but also distant relatives, friends and neighbours. On the other hand, for the management of migrant's funds protection of women and childcare, dependence is usually confined to close relatives like parents or parents-in-law of the migrant.

Where the migrant's children are younger, the dependence for protection is generally greater on relatives than when the migrant's wife is relatively old and the children are sufficiently grown up. The latter tend to be more or less self-reliant. Also, with the passage of time, women become more self-reliant than they were immediately after the migrant's first departure for the west Asia. The kind of impact migration has on the family is closely related to the age of the wife and the stage of the family life cycle.

The migration impact on the family is a dynamic process which keeps constantly changing with the length of the migrant's stay. Women gradually take on increased responsibilities for the running of the households on their own, for the health and education of children and for the management of their funds and properties. In the process, it breaks down women's isolation, increases their mobility, and brings them into contact with a wider network of institutions that were hitherto outside their experience. This results in their gaining confidence in themselves with the length of the stay of the migrant away from home.

This is not to suggest that the process is easy or without hurdles—indeed there are many problems—but time seems to be a great resolver of difficulties for most of the women we have studied. Failures are far fewer to come by than successes in coping with the situation. This is valid regardless of whether the migrant is a Muslim or Hindu. Of course, family and other networks, including religious networks, play a generally supportive role. But the major effort is usually that of the women immediately affected in coping with the absence of male support.

Our overall impression is that women from the migrant households start with a number of handicaps, to overcome which they need considerable support from not only immediate relatives but also a whole network of relatives, friends and neighbours. Their dependence on this network certainly increases in the migrant's absence and on the whole it can be said that the networks have stood by these women. It is also remarkable how well the women have coped with the situation created by the long absence abroad of husbands and/or sons, be it in the matter of running households, management of funds, childcare and education, or their own loneliness.

12

Politicisation of Dalits and Most Backward Castes

Study of Social Conflict and Political Preferences in Four Villages of Meerut District[*]

Sudha Pai and Jagpal Singh

Since the early 1980s Uttar Pradesh (U.P.) has experienced politicisation of the Dalits and in recent years the most backward castes (MBCs).[1] The former mobilised by the BSP, and under the impact of the sociocultural process of 'Ambedkarisation' have thrown up a new generation which is politically conscious, better educated, upwardly mobile, and very aggressive towards those above them in the caste/class hierarchy (Singh 1994). This process is most marked among the Jatav/Chamars than other groups such as the Balmikis. In contrast, the MBCs—who constitute a large number among the backwards—have yet to assume a distinct and collective identity. While the OBCs like the Yadavs, Lodhs, Kurmis and Gujjars, who have been mobilised in the west U.P. plains by political parties since the 1960s, are today the most assertive among the backwards, the MBCs such as the Gadarias, Jogis, Dhiwars, Nais, Kumhars, etc., still do not have their own forum for articulation of their specific needs. These developments have led to conflict between the Dalits and the OBCs on the one hand, and sharpened identities between the Dalits and the MBCs on the other. The emergence of these numerically large underprivileged groups has contributed to the erosion of the Congress and the rise of new parties during the last one-and-a-half decades.[...]

This chapter attempts to study the politicisation and resulting conflict between the Dalits and the MBCs in Meerut district in western U.P. The conflict centres around issues of social status, distribution of governmental benefits, control over village resources, independent voting, etc., and affects the political preferences of the groups involved... The four villages selected for our study lie in the Meerut and Muzaffarnagar parliamentary constituencies within Meerut district.... The villages

* This chapter has been extracted from a longer paper published by the authors in the *Economic and Political Weekly* 32 (17): 1356–61, 1997.

are among the 20 villages selected as Ambedkar villages by the U.P. government from 1990–91 onwards. The reason for our selection of such villages is twofold. First is the high proportion of Dalits and MBCs in the population, which enabled us to analyse Dalit assertion and Dalit-MBC conflicts which characterises them. The second is the impact of developmental programmes for Dalits which has created conflicts between the various caste groups and is reflected in electoral politics.[...]

TABLE 12.1: Castewise Distribution of the Respondents

	Number
Dalits	
Balmikis	7
Jatavs	104
Weaver	1
Total (a)	112
MBCs (Hindu)	
Dhiwars (Kahar/Kashyap)	3
Gadarias	19
Gosains	1
Jogis	9
Kumhars	9
Nais	4
Sainis	1
Total (b)	46
MBCs (Muslims)	
Blacksmith/Carpenter	3
Dhunas (Sheikh Naddafs)	3
Faquir	1
Teli	1
Total (c)	9
Total (a + b + c)	167

Dalits and MBCs in Meerut district mainly belong to the rural poor, which consist of small peasants with landholdings below 3 acres who mainly depend upon selling their labour power. In the sample villages most of them are wage labourers in the non-agricultural sector employed in construction activities, etc. The proximity of Meerut city and Mawana town makes it possible for them to commute daily in search of such jobs. Traditional occupations such as scavenging, pot-making, carpentry, iron working, haircutting, etc., are still followed, but progressively by smaller number of individuals due to break down of the jajmani system. Most of the respondents of our sample do not own land and are labourers, though some own small businesses or in some cases, are involved in completing their education (Table 12.2).

TABLE 12.2: Distribution of Respondents According to Occupation

Occupation	Number
Agriculture	16
Labourers*	98
Tannery	3
Business**	8
Study	20
Teaching (schools)	7
Service	5
Others***	10
Total	167

Notes: * mainly non-agriculture
** contractors and milkmen
*** includes mechanics, tailors, shopkeepers, traditional occupations, etc.

These villages have assumed great significance in the last one-and-a-half decades in respect of Dalit assertion. Until the early 1970s, the lower castes in the villages experienced domination/harassment—ranging from prevention of casting their vote to harassment of women, etc.—by the dominant landowning classes which has been commonplace in this region. Even though the Dalits and MBCs formed the majority, and often the 'pradhan' belonged to the Jatavs, there were certain families from the Jats and Rajputs who used to prevail upon the Dalit leadership. With the emergence of a new generation among the Dalits, growing impact of the Ambedkarisation process and decline in the position of the dominant castes, there has been almost complete erosion of their power over the lower castes. Rather in recent years there have been instances in three villages of conflicts between the Jatavs and the dominant castes of Jats and Rajputs, on issues of land usurpation, installation of Ambedkar's statue over a piece of land and contention over a woman. In the 1993 assembly elections, a Jatav from Khanauda stood for election from the Sardhana assembly constituency, and no caste group other than the Jatavs could cast their votes (Singh 1994). The Pradhans in these villages today are Jatavs and the block 'pramukh' of Daurala block is a woman.

It is noteworthy that village Behzadka lies in Hastinapur assembly constituency which witnessed the RPI movement in the 1950s and 1960s and is located near village Nagla Hareru in which conversion of Dalits to Sikhism took place in 1988–89 (Deep 1989). The Jatav Mahasabha, a non-political organisation was set up in Maithana in 1982 (Singh 1994). Jatavs of Meerut also held a panchayat at Maithana regarding the Shergarhi episode of March–April 1994 which took the decision to launch an agitation against the local administration (*Dainik Jagran*, 2 April 1994).[...]

Caste Assertion, Conflict and Political Preferences

Profile of communities

The Dalits, numerically the largest group in these villages, are divided into the forward, upwardly mobile and politically conscious Jatavs, and the backward Balmikis. An earlier generation of Jatavs were affected by the formation of the RPI in the 1960s which had a brief but significant presence in this region. However far more important is the more recent process of 'Ambedkarisation' under the leadership of a younger and more assertive group of leaders which has affected to a much greater degree the younger generation of Jatavs who do not like the submissive attitude of their elders. They are politically more conscious,

Table 12.3: Distribution of Caste in Relation to Party of Choice

Caste	Parties					Doesn't Know	Goes by Trend	Total
	BJP	BSP	SP	JD	Congress (I)			
Dalits (SC)								
Balmikis	–	5	–	–	–	2	–	7
Jatavs	1	98	1	3	1	–		104
Weaver	1	–	–	–	–	0	–	1
Total (a)	2	103	1	3	1	2	–	112
MBCs (Hindu)								
Dhiwars	1	1	–	–	–	–	1	3
Gadarias	7	6	1	2	1	2	–	19
Gosains	1	–	–	–	–	–	–	1
Jagis	4	3	–	1	1	–	–	9
Kumhars	3	4	–	–	–	–	–	9
Nais	2	–	–	1	–	1	2	4
Sainis	1	–	–	–	–	–	–	1
Total (b)	19	14	1	4	2	3	–	46
MBCs (Muslims)								
Blacksmith	–	–	–	1	–	1	1	3
Dhunas (Sheikh Naddafs)	–	–	–	3	–	–	3	6
Faquir	–	1	–	–	–	–	–	1
Teli	–	1	–	–	–	–	–	1
Total (c)	–	3	–	4	–	1	1	9
Total (a + b + c)	21	120	2	11	3	6	4	167

and knowledgeable about the political orientation of parties and clearly pointed out that the BJP is a communal party. The process of Ambedkarisation refers to the tremendous growth in the consciousness among Dalits, about the ideas and life of Babasaheb Ambedkar. In many villages committees, schools, and libraries named after Ambedkar have been set up, his statues installed, and temples of their 'own', i.e., Valmiki or Ravi Das, constructed. His birthday is celebrated with great fervour and gaiety: plays exposing the discriminatory caste system/Hindu religion are staged; 'prabhat pheris' and processions to the accompaniment of songs in praise of Ambedkar are taken out. The processionists exhort Dalits to read Dalit literature, not to compromise on dignity, to greet each other with 'Jai Bhim' and not 'Ram Ram' or 'Namaste'. This has generated protest against upper caste domination at various levels: everyday forms of protest in the village; cultural protest by following Ambedkar's ideas, the extreme form being conversion to Buddhism; and political protest by supporting only Dalit parties (Singh 1994). Among our sample villages in Maithana and Khanauda villages—where Dalit households constitute 50 per cent and they are economically better off than in the other villages—this process has made its mark. In contrast, the Balmikis among the Dalits are backward and not so politically conscious. As a result in the sample villages, many of them tend not to support the Jatavs in social and political matters.

The Jatavs form the support base of the BSP in the selected villages. It is worth noting that prior to the 1994 by-elections to the Hastinapur assembly and 19 per cent Lok Sabha elections, the BSP did not make any special efforts in western U.P. Its support base was largely in the eastern districts and Bundelkhand. Since its entry into electoral politics in 1989, in all assembly elections the BSP has gained the largest number of seats from the eastern districts followed by the central districts and Bundelkhand (Pai 1996).

Several factors account for the Jatavs supporting it. The most important is of course the caste factor. The BSP is perceived as the party of the Dalits which has given them a sense of self-confidence and self-esteem. Mayawati is popular and acceptable to the Jatav villagers, because during her tenure as CM a number of welfare measures for Dalits were undertaken. Hence the party is also supported as one which undertakes programmes for uplift of Dalits. In the Ambedkar villages during the brief tenure of the Mayawati govemment, the land 'pattas' which had been allotted to Dalits during the emergency but not given, were actually distributed among them; 'pucca' roads linking the villages to the main road; construction of houses, drinking water pumps and toilets in the SC sections of the villages; pension for old persons; panchayat 'ghars'; installation of Ambedkar's statue, etc., were some of the schemes implemented. The government acted swiftly and in favour of the Jatavs in the disputes between the high/dominant castes and the former. The perception gained ground that since the BSP is a party for and led by Dalits, it could understand their problems and support them whenever they were oppressed by the upper castes. Hence, it was possible for Jatavs to identify with it and recognise it as their own. A number of women respondents held that installation of Mayawati as CM had given them confidence and motivated them to educate their daughters.

The BSP govemment also transferred officers who in the perception of the Dalits were corrupt. In fact there was a feeling that unlike other parties, the BSP fulfils its promises, and had the government survived for some more time a lot of improvement and development of the region would have taken place.

In these villages the MBCs are smaller in number, politically less conscious, and more backward in comparison to the Dalits, particularly the Jatavs. The Ayodhya movement led by the BJP has had the maximum impact on them. The lack of any cultural movement among them, unlike the Ambedkarisation process among the Dalits, and their relatively more backward educational and political level made them more susceptible to the impact of Hindu communalism. Although numerically the MBC groups together are much larger than the lower castes in U.P., none of them at present—with the exception of the Sainis—form an effective political force in electoral politics. This is not only due to geographical dispersion, but also due to lack of any strong charismatic leader with whom they can identify, and who could weld them into a cohesive force.[...]

A number of factors have helped in increasing political consciousness, awareness about happenings in the country, and assertion of identity and self-respect among all groups, most particularly the jatavs. They have moulded/sharpened their perceptions vis-à-vis their social position, potential and 'others'.

A significant development seen within all caste/class groups is the emergence of a 'new generation' whose members were born in the post-independence period, which is politically conscious, better educated and upwardly mobile. With the introduction of formal education in the rural areas in the 1950s and 1960s, they became literate and were exposed to new ideas. The development of the primary education system in the sample villages has passed through three phases of expansion/learners: a first phase up to mid-1960s; a second phase up to the mid-1970s and a third phase in the 1980s and 1990s. The members of the second phase or second generation of learners benefited most from the institutionalisation of the primary education system and now belong to the age-group of the 1920s and 1930s. Many of them are

Table 12.4: Distribution of Respondents in Relation to their Educational Backgrounded

Class	Number
Illiterate/uneducated	34
Below V	5
V–VIII	19
IX–X	23
X–XII	7
Graduation (completed or doing)	12
Postgraduation (completed or doing)	11
Total	111

Note: Most illiterates are MBCs and Balmikis and most of them belong to Behgadka.

first generation learners, and though most of them dropped-out before completing Class X, they are more articulate than their parents/grandparents (Singh 1995). In our sample about 67 per cent of respondents belong to the age groups of 18–25 and 26–40 years, and 47 per cent have not studied beyond Class X. Most of the illiterates in the sample (34/111) belong to the MBCs and sweepers, and mainly belong to village Behzadka (Table 12.4).

The members of this new generation today function as the 'intellectuals' of their caste groups and question all aspects of the social order. They play a decisive role in taking decisions and mobilising their castes, especially in political matters. While the older generation had supported the Congress, the new generation is striving hard to find alternative parties/individuals which are led by their caste/class groups. For example, the 'intellectuals' of the Saini group played an important role in their panchayat meeting held on the eve of the elections to the 1991 Sardhana assembly constituency where it was decided to support the BJP (Singh 1992: 181 and 187). Similarly, the 'intellectuals' among the Jatavs in their panchayat meeting were instrumental in the decision to support an independent candidate in the 1993 assembly elections belonging to their own caste (Singh 1994).

The new generation is also visible in terms of class or profession in Meerut. In almost all caste groups, families or individuals have emerged who have diversified into various professions. In the absence of any study or official statistics on such families, their exact number cannot be ascertained, but their number is quite conspicuous. Some rich peasant families have diversified into agribusiness—cold storage, sulphur plant, khandsari, etc.—brick kiln, contractorship, petrol pumps, milk trade, transport, etc. Income from land enables them to invest in these professions and vice versa. They generally belong to the dominant castes—Jats, Gujjars, Tyagis, Rajputs, etc. In our sample villages, a class of contractors, and milkmen has emerged among the Jatavs (Table 12.2). Earlier a landless group started investing money earned from the business in buying land from poor or small peasants of their own caste or the MBCs. We have examples of such families from three villages of our sample. The improvement in their economic circumstances has led them to play an important role in village politics.

Another important factor which has increased political knowledge and awareness is the media explosion in the rural areas in the 1980s. Up to the late 1970s and early 1980s, radio was the main source of information and those possessing radio sets rarely listened to the news, their main interest being the entertainment programmes. The advent of television sets in the 1980s led to a change. There are now TV sets in almost all localities, and all those who do not have one, watch it in the neighbouring houses. A total of 61 (36 per cent) respondents of our sample own TV sets and most of them are Jatavs. Proportion of TV owners is larger among the Jatavs than the MBCs and Balmikis.[2] There is also surprising rise in the readership of vernacular newspapers particularly *Dainik Jagran*, *Amar Ujiala* and *Maya*, among villagers in some of our sample villages.

Although caste divisions are important, people in the villages are also concerned about local developmental problems which they feel should be addressed by the authorities. The villages in our sample like many others in the district, lack basic civic amenities and facilities such as roads, transportation, schools, post office, medical facilities, veterinary hospital, etc. For most of their needs they have to depend on the nearby cities—Meerut, and Mawana in the case of Behzadka. For most individuals bicycle is the main mode of transportation as there is no public transportation system plying to these villages. As a result girls and many boys are not able to study beyond Class V or VIII. Though tempos are available, people have to walk a considerable distance to board one, as all villages do not have this facility. The Mayawati government for the first time made a special drive to link these villages with the pucca main road, though they still lack a public transport system. The action of the government won the appreciation of the Dalits for Mayawati.

Criminalisation of society and politics, corruption and liquor consumption have emerged as serious issues in the past two decades in this region. Murders, kidnapping for ransom, land-grabbing robbery and booth-capturing have become common, and there are many examples from the area of our study. There is a high level of awareness in the sample villages that funds from governmental welfare schemes are usurped by lower level bureaucrats who take their share before distributing help among the needy. Excessive liquor consumption is a problem in Meerut and the neighbouring districts of Muzaffarnagar, Ghaziabad and Saharanpur, particularly during local elections when candidates supply liquor to villagers. In recent months women in this region have been agitating for imposition of prohibition (*The Times of India*, 21, 22 and 23 August 1996). Some of the other problems agitating the villagers are lack of place for dumping garbage, adequate toilets specially in Dalit localities, unemployment, fluctuation and shortage of electricity which affects farmers who own mechanical implements, etc. Although aware of these issues, and the fact that the government has failed to provide these facilities, villagers still vote on caste lines. They agree that both distribution of tickets and voting is on caste lines, as a result of which such issues are relegated to the background.

Caste/class Conflicts and Political Divisions

The caste/class conflicts in the sample villages are closely reflected in the political divisions between various communities. Caste and class intersect as both 'social jealousies' over status, and differential economic interests play a role. Till a few years ago the dominant castes could control the Dalits and the MBCs but this is no longer possible, though even now this is more true of the former than the latter. Although MBCs and SCs do share a common perception of the dominant castes, there exists mutual apprehension between them often leading to conflicts.

The MBC respondents complained that a small section of 'forward groups' among the backwards such as the Yadavs, Kurmis, Gujjars, etc., have benefited from reservations while the rest remain uneducated and backward. Moreover, help in the form of loans, land for house-building and basic amenities such as handpumps, construction of wells and toilets, etc., by the government is provided mainly to the Dalits. In fact there is considerable anguish that special consideration is given by the government to Dalits, while poor MBC groups such as Dhiwars, Barbers, Jogis, Kumhars, etc., are the most deprived and nobody takes note of their problems. Whatever help that they may be entitled to, is misappropriated by powerful local bureaucrats and pradhans.

The MBCS while agreeing that many policies implemented by the Mayawati government, such as construction of roads, have benefited all groups, have strong reservations about their aims. They allege that Mayawati's policies were aimed at benefiting only Jatavs and no policy was made for them. In fact it was pointed out by a respondent that villages where her relatives reside, received special benefits.[3][...]

As one of the respondents, a barber, pointed out,

> In comparison to the harijans we are very poor. No government bothers about us. Only harijans benefit. Whenever we want to take loan, we are refused or given only if we pay bribes. For a loan of Rs 10,000 to get my house constructed. I had to pay a bribe of Rs 2,000.

The Jatavs, as we have seen, are politically conscious, and play an important role in local and electoral politics. Because of their numerical majority and their better economic position, they are able to harass the MBCs.[...]

Balmikis, on the other hand, standing at the lower end of the caste/class hierarchy, accuse both the MBCs and Jatavs of infringing upon their rights. While the former oppress them, the latter do not let them vote independently. They allege they do not get any help from the government and complained that their wells, and even in the case of one of the villages, their cremation site has been usurped.

As a result of these conflicts a section of the MBCs supports the BJP on a number of grounds. Firstly, due to the growing communalisation/Hinduisation in the wake of the Ram Janmabhoomi Babri Masjid issue. Many MBC respondents felt that the BJP by raising the mandir issue had made it possible to criticise Muslims, while the Congress or JD had done nothing on this score. As a barber in Maithana village explained,

BJP is the only party which can ameliorate the BCs. Since 1991 we have been voting for the BJP, because this party has raised the issue of Ram mandir which is a place of pilgrimage for Hindus. As Ram mandir belongs to Hindus, we support the BJP.

Following from this, secondly, their support to the BJP is part of their search for an alternative political party following the decline of the Congress. Unable to identify with either the BSP or the SP/JD, they have turned to the BJP which in their minds is a Hindu party.[...]

In sharp contrast, due to the impact of the process of Ambedkarisation, Jatavs are critical of the BJP and its fraternal organisations. Besides they have a party which espouses their cause and is led by a leader of their own caste—the BSP. As observed elsewhere, due to intra-Dalit rivalry, a section of the Jatavs in the district has extended support to the BJP (Singh 1994). Among the respondents many Dalits in their conversation appreciate measures taken by the BJP to curb goondaism, stop private tuitions, enact the anti-copyright act, etc., but they support the BSP due to the caste factor. As a Jatav and a BSP supporter from Maithana village remarked,

> If BJP comes to power, the poor can sleep comfortably. When BJP came to power earlier (1991), it curbed goondaism. Now I support BSP due to caste factor.

Finally, many respondents among the MBCs and Balmikis, do not have any clear political choice. They either go by the general trend, are indifferent to and/or unaware of the parties and their orientation. Some of them are still appreciative of the Congress as they feel that they earlier benefited considerably under its rule, but they do not vote for it as it is no longer a dominant force. Hence, if the party were to rebuild its organisation in west U.P., it could perform better. This view is voiced even by some of the older Jatavs who also point out that there is no other party about which this can be said. Most of the MBC and Balmiki respondents, though they vote, do not find any difference between the various parties as none of them have helped them in any way. As a dhiwar caste respondent held,

> In my opinion there is no party which cares for the BCs. I cannot tell the difference between the Congress and BJP, or any party. In our opinion, all parties are the same.

Conclusion

Our field study of four villages of Meerut district reveals an ongoing process of politicisation and resulting conflict, between the upwardly mobile, and aggressive Jatavs, and the newly emerging MBC groups. This has had a twofold impact. At the village level it has affected social relations and power equations. The emergence of the Dalits and the MBCs has further eroded the unequal caste/class hierarchy. As a result, conflict is no longer confined between the dominant and the lower castes/ classes, but has also sharpened between the underprivileged groups themselves for better social status, scarce economic benefits, and increasingly political domination. The underprivileged groups in the sample villages are aware of the economic backwardness and need to develop their region, in spite of voting along caste lines.

Secondly, this has affected their political preferences, which have had impact upon political divisions in western U.P. Both the Dalits and the MBCs were constituents of the social base of the Congress Party till the 1980s, though they deviated—specially the Jatavs—whenever they found an alternative, for example, the RPI in the 1960s and the Janata Party in the 1970s. With the decay and deinstitutionalisation of the Congress Party in U.P. in the 1980s and mobilisation by the BSP, the Jatavs have found an enduring political alternative with which they can identify themselves. An additional factor in their case is the tremendous growth of the process of Ambedkarisation, which has rendered their political identification an offshoot of their socio-cultural protest against high caste domination. The latter process as we have seen is strong in our sample villages, and in Meerut district. Due to inter-group rivalry a section of the Jatavs in this district, however, together with other Dalits groups such as the Balmikis, do support the BJP. In contrast, our study suggests the MBCs remain 'political orphans', yet to find an alternative for representation of their specific socio-economic needs. With the disintegration of the Congress, and unable to identify with the BSP because it is a Dalit party, and the SP/JD which is supported by the OBCs and more prosperous peasantry, they have been attracted by the Hindutva ideology of the BJP. The attempts in the early 1990s, to create a 'Bahujan Samaj' which would require horizontal mobilisation of all the underprivileged groups—OBCs, MBCs, SCs and the minorities—have also failed. Thus socio-economic conflicts and resulting political contradictions between the underprivileged groups, together with the decline of the Congress, have provided space for the emergence of the BJP as an important political force in west U.P. These shifts also underlie the rapidly changing and unstable political situation in the state. The process of regrouping of social and political forces following the disintegration of the base of the Congress Party in west U.P. remains incomplete.

Notes

1. The term 'dalit' in this study refers to the SCs and does not include all oppressed sections. It is used because the villagers describe themselves in this fashion.

2. The availability of TV sets was also observed by G. K. Lieten about Muzaffarnagar, see Lieten (1996).

3. The example given by a respondent was Simrauli to which Mayawati's mother belongs. Here a pucca connecting road, a water tank, police post, etc., was set up.

References

Baruah, Sanjib Kumar. 1983. 'Getting a Fair Share: Politics and Poor in Rural India', PhD thesis. University of Chicago, Chicago.

Chatterjee, Manini. 1996. 'Divided They Fall: SP-BSP Split Helps the BJP in U.P.'. *Frontline*, 28 June.

Deep, Trilok. 1989. 'Report on Conversion of Harijans to Sikhism in Nagla Hareru and Sothamali Villages'. *Dinaman* (in Hindi): 14–27, 31 July.

Election Commission of Uttar Pradesh. 1996. 'Report of the 1996 Lok Sabha Elections', Lucknow.

Lieten, G. K. 1996. 'Inclusive View of Religion: A Rural Discourse in Uttar Pradesh'. *Economic and Political Weekly* 31 (23): 1411–16, 8 June.

Pai, Sudha. 1996. 'From Harijans to Dalits: Identity Formation, Political Participation and Electoral Mobilisation of Scheduled Castes in Uttar Pradesh'. Unpublished paper.

Singh, H. D. 1996. *543 Faces in India, Guide to 543 Parliamentary Constituencies*. New Delhi: Newsman Publishers.

Singh, Jagpal. 1992. *Capitalism and Dependence: Agrarian Politics in Western Uttar Pradesh*. New Delhi: Manohar Publications.

———. 1994. 'Ambedkarisation and Assertion of Dalit Identity: Socio-Cultural Protest in Meerut District of Western Uttar Pradesh'. Paper presented at the All India Sociological Conference, School of Social Sciences, Jawaharlal Nehru University, New Delhi.

———. 1995. 'Political Economy of Unaided and Unrecognised Schools: A Study of Meerut District of Western Uttar Pradesh'. Project report. National Institute of Educational Planning and Administration, New Delhi.

Singh, K. S. 1991. *People of India: Communities, Segments, Synonyms, Surnames and Titles*. National Series. Vol. VIII. New Delhi: Oxford University Press.

13

Emergence of Backward Castes in South Telangana

*Agrarian Change and Grass Roots Politics**

Anil Kumar Vaddiraju

Ramannapet Mandal

The emergence of backward castes took place in nearly all the villages of the mandal roughly since 1970. Since then they have consolidated their position. This process was two-pronged. At the political level the backward castes challenged the authority of upper castes—mainly reddys; and succeeded to a large extent. At the economic level they challenged semi-feudal practices. Practices such as 'vetti' have completely disappeared. Now labour relations are almost entirely on the basis of free wage labour. The researcher could not find unfree labour or extra-economic coercion anywhere in the two village studies.

Commercialisation of the village political economy has also not led to the process of creation of 'capitalist landlords', who combine traditional caste power with modern economic power, for two reasons. First, there has been no drastic development of infrastructural facilities or productive forces such as irrigation canals, etc. Second, there were other pressing social reasons such as heavy dowries for upper caste endogamous marriages and division of landholdings among heirs. This led to decline of landlords economically, socially and politically.

At the political plane the periodic panchayati raj elections with reservations for OBCs and women have contributed much to the forming of caste solidarity among backward castes challenging upper castes. The emergence of backward castes was confirmed by the fact that in the June 1995 gram panchayat elections 14 out of 20 villages in the Ramannapet mandal elected backward caste sarpanches; five elected scheduled caste sarpanches (together making it 19) and only one village elected a forward caste candidate to a seat reserved for women. Thus by 1995, 19 out of 20 villages were under the political control of backward and scheduled castes.

* This chapter has been extracted from a longer paper published by the author in the *Economic and Political Weekly* 34 (7): 425–30, 13 February 1999.

This was partly due to state intervention such as enforcement of panchayati raj and reservations partly due to autonomous lower caste development. The process was partly state-induced and partly historical.

Finally, was there a proletarianisation/polarisation process in the field area? The answer is no. The process observed was deconcentration of big landholdings and strengthening of small and middle holdings and thereby the backward caste peasants.

In the village Bogaram the land passed from gampala reddy families to padmashalis, and particularly to the master weavers. Though there is substantive land concentration still in the village and another round of land reform is necessary, it is much lower that till 1970. More importantly small and middle peasants were not reduced to agricultural labourers. The export-oriented, multilayered handloom industry has absorbed some agricultural labour.

In the village Janampally, the process of deconcentration is even more clear. The brahmin landlords sold lands after family partition and later owing to unmanageability. This land was bought by backward castes: weavers, yadavas and toddy tappers. In this village the 'vatandari' power structure was already in the hands of yadavas and later they further strengthened their position.[...]

Political economists like Utsa Patnaik have argued that after the green revolution the traditional semi-feudal landlords have become capitalist landlords. But we have noted that such a phenomenon did not take place in the field area. This is owing to a combination of reasons. The historical dilemma of the semi-feudal classes is that either they modernise and compete with the emerging classes, castes (such as padmashalis and yadavas in our case), or they decline under the pressures created by the larger polity, economy and society. In our field area the semi-feudal classes started to decline because they could not modernise—by modernisation we mean modernisation of productive forces—and thereby strengthen their economic position. The state has also not strengthened the productive forces by improving the infrastructural facilities such as irrigation and canals. The physical conditions of economic production have not changed much over the last 30 years. In these conditions the semi-feudal class could neither accumulate much capital nor reinvest existing capital. This is the reason why the reddy and brahmin landlords could not become affluent capitalist landlords. This also explains why the phenomenon of capitalist landlordism is more pertinent to green revolution areas than to non-green revolution areas.[...]

The pressure to get the younger generation educated and placed in urban employment was added to this. Many landlords spoke with great anxiety about the difficulty of getting their sons and daughters educated and employed. So did the youth belonging to the landlord families for many of them have graduate or postgraduate degrees but no jobs.[...]

BOGARAM VILLAGE

The red soils Bogaram village are not richly fertile and cannot yield lucrative commercial crops. Bogaram has 1,500 acres of land, of which total irrigated land is about 400 acres. It is all well-irrigated. During droughts irrigated area goes down to 100 acres.

More importantly the area does not have any traditional irrigation system. There are no canals. The village does not even have a tank. Whatever irrigation there was, and is, depends on rains or more importantly on wells. Oral historical accounts tell us that well irrigation always played a prominent part in the village economy, and continues to do so even now.

The principal crops grown in the past, and to a large extent at present, are paddy, groundnut, castor and millets. Of these groundnut and castor are commercial crops. Paddy, which is the most important of all crops grown, is both a commercial and a subsistence crop.

Historical Background

From 1900 to 1950, the village Bogaram was the jagir of Gulam Mohammed Khan, granted by the nizam. The Gulam Mohammed Khan and his family lived in Hyderabad. But his control of the village was total. He had the right to the entire land revenue and had substantial landholdings. These lands were cultivated through the system of 'vetti' or labour service.

The ruler showed no interest whatsoever in the development of the village. He and his ancestors were primarily interested in the land revenue and the product from their personally owned lands. They left the village largely to the vicissitudes of nature. Chronic drought, at times near famine conditions, prevailed. Failure of crops, inability to remit land revenue in time, were usual features of the condition of the peasantry. This as we see below led to the evolution and shaping of the agrarian structure in the village in the succeeding period.

As the 'dora' (landlord) of the village Gulam Mohammed Khan performed three functions: (a) collection of the land revenue, (b) collection of various taxes, and (c) general village administration. This included law and order administration. As an absentee landlord and according to the administrative system of the nizam, i.e., the 'vatandari' system, Gulam Mohammed Khan appointed, on hereditary basis, three village officers. He ruled through these village officers. They were the 'patwari' (or a brahmin karnam); a 'mali patel' (Reddy); and a 'police patel' (Reddy).

It is during these 50 years that a single reddy family accumulated about 1,000 acres of land; its members acting as the village officers of Gulam Mohammed Khan. The 'patwari' or karnam (a brahmin) acting as the revenue officer accumulated about 200 acres of land. The method was often simple. Whenever a peasant could not pay the land revenue owing to drought, or some other misfortune, that land was transferred, in the records, into the account of either of the village officers. Oral accounts inform us that exorbitant taxes of the dora were often the other reason why land shifted into the hands of the patels. The reddy patels would pay the dora the taxes of those who could not pay and then take control of the land of that taxpayer. Thus one family, the gampala reddys, acting as village officers accumulated around 1,000 acres of land (which was later partitioned among five brothers).

Caste was no hindrance to this predatory process. Often fellow caste members were also victims. But it was mostly the other backward castes and untouchable castes who bore this burden. As is well known through any study of Telangana of this period the domination of the patels (and of the doras) was not just economic, but was also social and political. Landownership operated as the objective basis of socio-economic and political oppression.

The other prominent castes of Bogaram village the padmashalis (weavers), the toddy tappers, the yadavas (in that order) were prominent neither economically nor politically during this period. As is well known the system of free labour service ('*vetti*') to the local lords, i.e., the patels encompassed all. But one must take care to add here that even during this period the padmashalis (weavers) were relatively free from its effects. Numerically predominant in the village as they were, weavers retained some relative autonomy from the system of oppression. Even so they did not possess any land whatsoever. Nor could they make much out of their caste occupation during this period. Weaving became profitable much later.

The end of the dominance of the jagirdar came with one, the larger political struggle of the Telangana movement; and two, owing the abolition of zamindari by the central government. But Gulam Mohammed Khan did not relinquish his landed interests easily. Whatever was left by him was taken over by his erstwhile village officers. In the struggles that followed one patel was shot dead by the 'razaakars'. Eventually, the struggle ended in favour of the local reddy patels, particularly the gampala family of reddys. And the influence of pateldom continued. Land continued to be concentrated in the hands of five gampala reddy brothers. With the solidarity of fellow caste members they continued to dominate village affairs.

Not all reddy patels in Bogaram village were big landlords. By 1950 more than 50 per cent of the reddys owned landholding of less than 25 acres. And often the land they owned was not productive. The absolute productivities of even big landholdings were dismal. It may be remembered here that in pre-green revolution period no Borlaug-packages were available. But what is important to note is that neither class differentiation nor low level of absolute standards of living affected caste solidarity. Considerable number of reddy families were self-cultivating but when it came to social relations with the other lower caste families, they were certainly discriminatory or semi-feudal. There was a strong element of dominance at the superstructural level even when it did not exist at the economic level.

Pateldom, 1950–75

The period between 1950 and 1975 was a period of the continuance of the traditional patron-client relations. Though the dora Gulam Mohammed Khan was dispensed with, the gampala patels continued to rule the village. In this the mobilisation of caste solidarity was quite important. The first gram panchayat elections were held after the formation of Andhra Pradesh state, in 1959. In these elections Gampala Ram Reddy was elected as sarpanch of the village. He continued as village sarpanch for another term. Thus the single gampala family continued to dominate, de jure from 1959 to 1970. And de facto till roughly around 1975. In this period, and till today, the gampala reddy family was, and is, associated with the Congress Party. ...]

There was little or no state intervention to augment productive force. Electricity came to the village in 1982. State intervention even in other rural development programmes was minimal during this period. The gram panchayat sarpanches wielded political power, often backed by social domination, but they lacked public, governmental funds of any kind.

During this period the gampala reddy families, as headmen, arbitrated the village affairs and, quite importantly, the village disputes. Besides this they managed their own substantially big farms through, what appears to be semi-feudal labour relations. Vetti of the untouchable castes in particular seems to have continued, in however feeble form, till 1970.

Backward castes/classes in the village, though numerically preponderant, were not politically assertive during 1959–70. First, they were divided along caste lines. Second, the socially dominant and numerically important among them, the weavers, lacked economic power. During this period the weavers were only weaving cotton/handloom cloth for the local market which was not lucrative. The handloom industry had not yet found a world market. We will argue below how the globalisation of handloom industry led to the creation of a class structure among the weavers which in turn led to their political assertion.

But we should hasten to add here that the assertion of the backward castes took place much before the political ascendance of the weaving caste. The political assertion of the backward castes occurred basically against the gampala reddys.

Backward Castes, 1975–95

The first sarpanch Gampala Ram Reddy worked from 1959 to 1970. The de facto domination of the gampala reddy family continued till 1975. But the emergence of backward castes took place prior to 1975. In 1970 panchayati raj elections, all the backward castes worked against the vatandari gampala families. A toddy tapper was elected as sarpanch and continued in the post till 1981.

The weavers in the village were a numerous and politically important caste. But they were united against vatandari reddys. Weaving till 1980 was only meant for the local market. The raw materials yarn, chemicals, etc., used to be brought from Hyderabad and finished cloth used to be again marketed in Hyderabad. During the tenure of the toddy tapper sarpanch the most significant achievement was village electrification. This meant that even small peasants could buy pumpsets for their wells. This in turn meant that the backward class small peasants could strengthen their family farms. Interestingly during this period, from 1975 till as late as 1988, the party configurations did not change much. Both the vatandari gampala reddys and the backward caste leaders fought each other as different factions of the same Congress Party. The weaver caste which independently asserted itself in politics later was also a part of the Congress Party.

Weaving and World Market

By 1980, the occupation of weaving became a lucrative one. The local weavers started sending their cloth to metropolitan cities such as Bombay, Delhi and Madras. The premium quality cotton cloth they produced was being exported from these metropolitan cities to America, Europe and Eurasia. Some cloth was also exported to Asian markets such as Japan. Along with cotton cloth of high quality they also produced silk cloth and saris. This process of internationalisation was complex and has produced a class structure among the weavers.

This is at first reflected in the emergence of master weavers and then to a stratification among the weavers. Firstly, the enterprising among the weavers started bringing in the raw materials and distributing among the middle-working weavers. The middle-working weaver in his turn employed a worker-weaver from any labouring caste of the village. The work was divided up as follows: master weaver—distributes raw material and markets the finished cloth; middle-working weaver—applies colours, dye, etc., and hires labour; and wage-worker weaver—weaves the cloth on either daily wage basis or piece rate basis. This structure worked, and still works, in favour of the first category of master weavers. The second and third category of weavers do not get more than their daily wage. This wage fluctuates with the fluctuating prices of finished cloth in the world market. What this system produced between 1980 to roughly about 1990 is an affluent master weaver class which also started asserting its dominance over not only the weaver caste, but over all the backward castes.

The affluence of the master weavers is visible in their houses. They own modern trucks, scooters, refrigerators, air coolers, etc., and a phone is also to be found in the house of every master weaver to facilitate his communications with the local and metropolitan businessmen. None of these consumer durables are found either in reddy caste houses or in the houses of lower caste weavers. The standard of living indicated by these consumer durables is very high by local standards.

More importantly the master weavers started investing their money into buying lands, mainly from the reddys and sometimes also from other backward castes. Thus one master weaver who combines his government job with his master weaving activity has accumulated more than 100 acres of land. He is now one of the two big landlords of the village.

The deconcentration of land among the dominant reddy families appears to have taken place owing to two important reasons. First, land partition among family members; second, increasing cash dowries during marriages. Dowries in reddy caste often run into lakhs of rupees. This is one important reason for the sale of lands by reddys.

The weavers of the village are also organised into a cooperative society. Elections do take place for the society. But the entire society is dominated by master weavers. During the elections for the cooperative society money, liquor, etc., are lavishly used. The master weavers literally invest in these elections and in turn later use the cooperative society for furthering their business interests. In these elections weavers do fight among themselves on party basis. The master weavers were united under Congress Party and presently they are under the Telugu Desam Party.

Though the weavers are divided by class, when it comes to panchayati raj elections, they mobilise caste solidarity for electoral purpose. But even during the panchayat elections it is the handful of master weavers who dominate their fellow caste members. Since master weavers are engaged in the circulation of raw materials and marketing the finished product, they enter into patron-client relations with the other lower caste weavers. These patron-client relations help them in mobilising caste solidarity. Thus on its face it appears as if all the weavers belong to the same class and represent the same interests; but in reality they are divided into classes and contain inter-class exploitative relations.

In 1981 elections the master weavers asserted their political power. This time one master weaver got elected as sarpanch on Congress ticket defeating the toddy tapper candidate belonging to the rival faction of the Congress Party. It is clear that by this time though the vatandari gampala reddys in the village were supporting Congress Party they had lost their place in the political scenario of the village. Certainly, a decisive shift took place on the social basis of political power from reddys to that of backward castes; and within the backward castes in favour of the master weavers.[...]

Liberalisation and Weaving

For weaving things have changed since roughly about 1990. Prices of yarn, chemicals and other raw materials have doubled, while the price of the cloth exported has remained unchanged. The burden is transferred by the master weavers to the two lower rungs of weavers. This is done by cutting down the wage rates and/or piece rates. Thus it is the wage-workers who bear the burden of internationalisation.

Besides weaving and agriculture, the master weavers engage in moneylending. The money made out of weaving, agriculture and moneylending is now being invested in urban properties. For example, a master weaver and earlier sarpanch has properties in Hyderabad and has his son studying engineering in the US and he is himself active in district level politics. During 1970–90 the backward castes have consolidated their position economically and politically. Though a caveat is necessary here that there is a class structure within the backward castes.

Caste or Class

In this village study it is observed that a shift took place on the social basis of political power from upper castes to backward castes. But this shift took place only between the top layer of reddys to the top layer or upper class backward castes. State involvement was only by way of holding the gram panchayat elections. No decisive economic programme, such as land reforms, has been carried out by the state. The changes in the agrarian structure have come about owing to the commercialisation process on the one hand and on the other owing to the incorporation of the village political economy into the world market... .

JANAMPALLY VILLAGE

Historical Background

Janampally was a khalsa village in 1900. The nizam had three types of ruling systems: jagirdari, khalsa and sarf-e-khas systems. In the jagirdari system the jagirdar owned much or all the land of the village. In sarf-e-khas system the entire land was owned directly by the nizam's family and the land revenue went to their personal expenditure. In khalsa system, the landownership rested with the villagers. It was much like the ryatwari system of the presidency areas under the British. The significant difference with the other two land systems was that the villagers owned the land in their names and the land revenue went neither to any individual jagirdar nor to the nizam but to the treasury of the nizam government.

Village administration in all three types of land systems was run through the vatandari system. It meant a system of village officers who consisted of the vatan: these were the patwari, the mali patel and the kotval or police patel. Janampally by 1990 had vatandari system. Under the system the patwari or village revenue officer belonged to a brahmin-karanam on hereditary basis. The mali patel and police patel posts belonged to a reddy family which lived away from the village. By 1990 the mali patel and police patel vatans were transferred into the hands of local yadavas, regionally called the gollas. The yadavas' basic occupation is sheep grazing. But one family, the meda family of yadavas, accepted the vatans. While the brahmin-karanam family ran revenue matters, other matters concerning village administration were run by the meda family of yadavas. Thus in this village, backward caste leadership has existed for 95 years. Unlike in the case of Bogaram village, it cannot be said in Janampally that the backward classes, emerged in village politics at a particular time after independence.[...]

The khalsa system itself allowed less room for accumulation of land by village officers. There was less arbitrariness in the land related accounts. This meant that in the Janampally village the possibilities of accumulation of land by village officers were much less than in the village Bogaram. Another reason for this was the village productive forces. The productive forces of Janampally village are better situated than that of Bogaram village. The village has 1,200 acres of land and a big tank and four small tanks. Both tank irrigation and well irrigation played important role in somewhat stable and assured subsistence for small peasants. Thus the politically progressive nature of local elites and better productive forces worked against the concentration of land in the hands of a few village officers. Thus in this village the agricultural scenario is characterised by the preponderance of the small peasants. Another important reason for the relative absence of much feudal or semi-feudal dominance is that village did not have dominant caste dora. Though there were some reddys in the village they were not the village officers and therefore their economic power was neutralised by the political power of the backward castes and therefore whatever upper caste domination existed in the village was that of the brahmin-karanam. But the progressive and politically active nature of this village officer also diluted the semi-feudal content of the social dominance. Thus the brahmin-karanam family had about 75 acres of land. They continued to dominate the village affairs partly from 1900 to 1970.

Brahmin Dominance 1900–70

It was difficult to obtain much details about the period from 1900 to 1970 regarding social relations or political dynamics. It became clear that owing to the absence of the dora from the village scene semi-feudal practices like the vetti were not prominent. The upper caste domination was also unnoticeable because of the fact that the two village officer posts were in the hands of local yadavas.

In 1959 panchayat elections a brahmin was elected as sarpanch. Again in 1964 elections another brahmin-karanam was elected as sarpanch. Both won the panchayat elections as candidates of the Congress Party. It should be noted that it is these people who participated in Telangana armed struggle against the nizam under the Andhra Maha Sabha. So they carried the popularity of having fought against the nizam. By the same token, as the interviews with them show they were also conscious of upper caste domination—particularly of reddy domination. It would not be correct to hold that the reddy doras were alone oppressive. But the main cause which ignited the Telangana armed struggle was reddy oppression. Having been conscious of the causes and consequences of the armed struggle the brahmin-karanams of Janampally were more liberal.

Nevertheless, the brahmin patwari and other karnams continued to be the top landowners in the village; they owned more than 75 acres of land. But they cultivated this land through hired labour rather than through tenants. This land was later partitioned within both the families.

Backward Caste Peasantry

The break with brahmin dominance came in 1970. In the 1970 panchayat elections a yadava sarpanch was elected. This yadava sarpanch came from the meda family of yadavas to whom belonged the mali patel and police patel vatans. Thus it is since 1970 that the backward castes came to the forefront of village politics.

The yadavas' or gollas' main caste occupation is sheep grazing. In this village they combine it with agriculture. Most yadavas do own land and are small or middle farmers. Some yadavas own less than 10 acres and some less than five acres. The village productive forces are much better suited for the sustainability of dwarf holdings than in Bogaram. The village has four small tanks and one big tank as noted earlier. Most yadavas own their parcels of land under these tanks. (Since 1980 the four small tanks are used only as percolation tanks, i.e., the water is stored and not used directly with the idea that the stored water would percolate into the wells dug in the ayacut area of the tanks. Thus tanks are used to enhance groundwater situation.) Much like Bogaram, in Janampally also electricity came in the early 1980s. Since then almost all backward caste small peasants have acquired electric motors and pumpsets.

Yadavas are numerically the most preponderant backward caste in the village. The next most important backward caste in the village is the weaver caste or the padmashalis. Weaving in the village is qualitatively different from that in Bogaram. We turn to this aspect below.

Apart from yadavas and weavers the third most important backward caste in the village is that of toddy tappers. Together these castes form a political block in the village. They are deeply conscious of their political, economic and social backwardness and also conscious of their numerical strength.

Weavers in the Janampally village are basically subsistence weavers. They weave primarily for the home market. Cotton and silk cloth and saris are produced here. Unlike in Bogaram village there are no master weavers. Weaving is done by independent family units. The cloth is supplied to the local cooperative society. The local (village) cooperative society markets the woven cloth through Andhra Pradesh weavers cooperative (APCO). Each silk sari, for instance, sells for about Rs 1,000 to 1,500. It is precisely because there is no master weaver that there is little capital or land accumulation by weavers. In Bogaram village the master weaver system arose owing to the internationalisation of weaving. In contrast to this in Janampally village weaving is essentially for the national market.

Elections do take place for weavers' cooperative society. But the candidates do not use money, liquor, etc., for winning elections. The cooperative society chairperson is usually elected unanimously. Since liberalisation weavers have faced difficulties. As in Bogaram village, in Janampally also weavers face a rise in the prices of raw materials and stagnation in the prices of finished cloth. Besides this the weavers in Janampally also face competition from textile industry centred in and around Bombay. There is unequal competition between textile mills and handlooms. Often the market favours textile mills rather than handlooms. An inefficient system of marketing by local cooperative and APCO also aggravates the situation. The handloom weavers do not get payment promptly for the work done from APCO and consequently from the local cooperative. Padmashalis (weavers) of Janampally have not become landlords unlike those of Bogaram. There is no internationalisation of handlooms; no master weavers; no three-tier structure of weaving; and no land accumulation.

Labour in Janampally

Janampally has two kinds of labour relations: casual labour and attached labour. Casual wage labour is hired on daily basis. Wages for casual labour are around Rs 15 for women and Rs 30–40 for men. Under the attached labour or the 'jeethas' system the wage labourer is hired on annual contract basis. The rate for annual contract is Rs 6,000 to 7,000. Along with it the labourer is given a loan of about Rs 2,000 at 2 per cent per annum interest. Here the researcher could not find any debt bondage. Attached labourers never work for an employer for more than one year; the labourer usually pays off his debt at the end of the agricultural year and enters into contract for another year with another master. Usually attached labourers come from backward castes as well as from scheduled castes. Employers are either from upper castes, brahmins and reddys or from other backward castes.

Since 1980 labour is increasingly turning from work in the village to work in the nearby town. Nearly 60 labourers travel each day to the neighbouring town

Chityal to work as '*hamali*' coolies in the rice mills. There they earn more than the daily wage in the village, i.e., about Rs 70 to 80.

Landownership

In Janampally village as we have noted earlier backward castes emerged in panchayat politics from 1970 onwards. They continue to hold on to village officer post—mali patel and kotval—which were bestowed upon them as early as 1900.

Landownership is no more concentrated in the hands of upper castes. But holdings of more than 25 acres, which is above the ceiling imposed by the government, continue to exist in the hands of brahmin landlords. But the holdings have declined substantially (from about 75 acres in 1970 to about 20–25 acres now).

Weavers at first bought lands from brahmins. Later weavers sold their lands to other backward castes such as yadavas and toddy tappers. Now it is yadavas and toddy tappers who form a majority of middle and smallholders and who also run the village politics—de jure and de facto. In this village commercialisation has had considerable impact on the agrarian structure. Land values improved from about Rs 400 per acre in 1960 to Rs 25,000 to Rs 30,000 per acre in 1990. In 1995 well situated wet land sold for about Rs 45,000 to Rs 50,000. Dry land now sells from about Rs 25,000 to Rs 30,000. Landlords declined because of partitioning of holdings, unmanageability and diversification of interests. Here no particular caste/class—such as master weavers of padmashali caste in Bogaram—acquired the lands. Many backward castes benefited from the decline of big landlords. Benefited in the sense that they bought the lands of erstwhile big landlords and strengthened their small and marginal farms.

No significant phenomenon of transformation of big landlords into 'capitalist landlords' was observable in the village, primarily because no drastic change occurred in the past 30 years in the productive forces or physical infrastructure of production. The advent of electricity and electric pumpsets has benefited the small and marginal peasants as much as the big landowners. Consequently, no process of proletarianisation took place in the village.

References

Athreya, V. B. et al. 1990. *Barriers Broken: Production Relations and Agrarian Change in Tamil Nadu*. New Delhi: Sage.

Bedford, I. 1967. 'The Telengana Insurrection: A Study in the Causes and Development of a Communist Insurrection in Rural India (1946–1951)'. Unpublished PhD thesis. Australian National University, Canberra.

Beteille, A. 1996. *Caste Class and Power: Changing Patterns of Stratification in a Tanjore Village*. Delhi: Oxford University Press.

———. 1974. *Studies in Agrarian Social Structure*. Delhi: Oxford University Press.

Breman, J. 1985. 'Between Accumulation and Immiseration: The Partiality of Fieldwork in Rural India'. *Journal of Peasant Studies* 13 (1), October.

———. 1993. *Beyond Patronage and Exploitation: Changing Agrarian Relations in South Gujarat*. Delhi: Oxford University Press.

Breman, J. et al. (ed.). 1997. *The Village in Asia Revisited*. Delhi: Oxford University Press.

Byres, T. J. 1995. 'Political Economy, Agrarian Question and Comparative Method'. *Economic and Political Weekly* 30 (10): 507–13, 11 March.

Das, A. N. 1996. *Change: The Biography of a Village*. New Delhi: Penguin Books.

Frankel, F. R. and M. S. A. Rao. 1989. *Dominance and State Power in Modern India: Decline of a Social Order*. 2 vols. Delhi: Oxford University Press.

Grey, H. 1970. 'The Landed Gentry of the Telengana, Andhra Pradesh'. In *Elites in South Asia*, ed. E. Leach and S. N. Mukherjee. Cambridge: Cambridge University Press.

Patnaik, U. (ed.). 1990. *Agrarian Relations and Accumulation: The 'Mode of Production' Debate in India*. Delhi: Oxford University Press.

Rajasekhar, D. 1986. *Land Transfers and Family Partitioning*. Delhi: Oxford University Press.

———. 1992. 'Economic Mobility of Rural Households: A Study of Kurnool District in Andhra Pradesh (Circa 1860–1989)'. Unpublished PhD thesis. Centre for Development Studies, Trivandrum.

Reddy, Ram M. (n.d.). 'Agrarian Relations: A Case Study in Telengana Region'. Unpublished PhD thesis, Department of Economics, Kakatiya University, Warangal, Andhra Pradesh.

Srinivas, M. N. 1996. *Village, Caste, Gender and Method: Essays in Indian Social Anthropology*. Delhi: Oxford University Press.

Srinivasulu, K. 1988. 'Telengana Peasant Movement and Change in Agrarian Structure: A Case Study of Nalgonda District'. Unpublished PhD thesis. Jawaharlal Nehru University, New Delhi.

Yugandhar, B. N. 1996. *Land Reforms in India: Andhra Pradesh—People's Pressure and Administrative Innovations*. New Delhi: Sage.

Section IV

Perspectives on Change

Introduction

As discussed in the introduction in this volume, the popular image of the Indian village, constructed by the colonial administrators, as a stable and static system of relations, has been quite influential. However, over the years historians and social anthropologists criticised it for being superficial and impressionistic. Through evidence and analysis they showed that like any other area of social life, the village in India has always been changing. However, the processes of change and churnings have been much more speedy over the last five or six decades. The three chapters in this section offer a variety of perspectives on these processes of change.

The chapter by N. S. Jodha provides, what could be described as, an ecological perspective on change. Though inequality and deprivation have always been a feature of the Indian village life, the traditional set-up also offered some kind of security to the poor. Through an empirical study of dry agricultural regions of the country, he shows the significant role that common property resources (CPRs) played in providing supplementary income or sources of livelihood to the poor. He even quantifies the additional income they could earn by utilising the CPRs and argues that in some regions, it was more than what the official anti-poverty programme could generate. He also points to the negative side of the process of development, which has everywhere led to a decline or privatisation of CPRs.

The following chapter by John Harriss, J. Jeyaranjan and K. Nagaraj offers a historical perspective on the nature of social and economic change taking place in rural India through a longitudinal account of a village in Tamil Nadu. The village of Iruvelpattu has had the distinction of being studied by social scientists over regular intervals. The recent 're-study' by the three authors of the chapter shows that while there have been some radical changes in the social and cultural life of the village, the extent of continuity, particularly in the sphere of economic inequalities, has also been significant.

The final chapter by Dipankar Gupta provides a more radical view on the changing Indian village. The Indian village, he argues, is experiencing a process of disintegration in a very fundamental sense of the term. The traditional social and economic system of the village, viz., caste and agriculture, are both losing their value and relevance. The breakdown of the traditional jajmani relations 'has fostered greater fluidity in occupational choices' and the agricultural economy no longer seems capable of holding people back in the village. Gupta argues, that the decline of the village as an institution is bound to have long-term implications, and policymakers need to take account of this in their vision of change.

14

WHITHER THE INDIAN VILLAGE

*Culture and Agriculture in 'Rural' India**

DIPANKAR GUPTA

There is a certain resistance in accepting the fact that the Indian village is undergoing major changes, not just economically, but culturally as well. The reluctance in coming to terms with this reality arises largely from the widely prevalent belief among intellectuals that the Indian village is timeless and unchanging and that the Indian villager likes nothing more than living in a rural setting. These notions need to be revised, not just for the sake of factual accuracy, but also because of the imperatives of the planning and developmental process. If the village is really the mainstay of India's economy, then that would require a certain set of policy prescriptions that would centralise agriculture.[...]

The Indian village is not what is used to be, and is even further from what it has been for long imagined to be. There are unambiguous statistics that point to the falling rates of growth in agriculture, and to the increasing exodus from country to town. On top of this we have the phenomenon of non-farm employment whose scale has increased tremendously over the years. It is estimated today that about 24 per cent of villagers are engaged in non-agricultural occupations. This is not a small number, and in all likelihood, it is probably a conservative estimate.

While these gross statistics do suggest a whittling down of the importance of agriculture as the mainstay of Indian society, there is in addition a general undermining of values and practices that have their origins in the villages and are imbrued with the so-called 'rural ethos'. There was a time, not too long ago, when a Jat farmer in Uttar Pradesh or Punjab would proudly proclaim that farming was the noblest of all occupations. Today this swagger is missing amongst them. They want an urban foothold, and would even condescend to take up occupations in towns and cities that they would deign to perform in their own villages.

The profundity of changes in rural India is not fully captured by census figures, or by statistical surveys. Useful though they are, it is necessary to comprehend

---

* This chapter has been extracted from a longer paper published by the author in the *Economic and Political Weekly* 40 (8): 751–58, 19 February 2005.

the depth of disenchantment that prevails in the villages through in-depth field investigations. This disenchantment is on a variety of fronts. Indian agriculture has always lurched from crisis to crisis. If the monsoons are good then there are floods, if they are bad there are droughts, if the production of mangoes is excellent then there is a glut and prices fall, if the onion crops fail then that too brings tears. The artisanal nature of agriculture has always kept farmers on tenterhooks, not knowing quite how to manage their economy, except to play it by (y)ear.

Even in green revolution areas, where there has been a spectacular increase in mechanisation and chemical inputs, the dependence on the vagaries of the weather and on the insufficiency, and irregularity, of electrical supply and other infrastructural inputs can throw the best agricultural calculations out of gear. It is not surprising then that whenever the occasion arises, villagers are more than willing to desert the fields for a future outside the mud walls of their homes and in fields as distant from agriculture as industrial labour. The village is shrinking as a sociological reality, though it still exists as space. Nowhere else does one find the level of hopeless disenchantment as one does in the rural regions of India. In urban slums there is squalour, there is filth and crime, but there is hope and the excitement that tomorrow might be quite different from today.

Rarely would a villager today want to be a farmer if given an opportunity elsewhere. Indeed, there are few rural institutions that have not been mauled severely from within. The joint family is disappearing, the rural caste hierarchy is losing its tenacity, and the much romanticised harmony of village life is now exposed for the sham it perhaps always was. If anything, it is perhaps B. R. Ambedkar's analysis of the Indian village that strikes the truest of all. It was Ambedkar who said that the village was a cesspool of degradation, corruption and worse. That village India was able to carry on in spite of all this in the past was because there was little option for most people, rich or poor outside the confines of the rural space.

If rural India has lost its centrality in the minds of most villagers in contemporary India today it is not, as we mentioned earlier, only because an urban world has opened up their horizons, but also because the village economy itself has lost its sustaining power. Consequently, the country side has witnessed a kind of cultural implosion that has shaken many of the verities of the past. With the abolition of landlordism and the introduction of adult franchise (the two must necessarily go hand in hand), old social relations that dominated the country side are today in a highly emaciated form, when not actually dead. Roughly 85 per cent of landholdings are below five acres and about 63 per cent are below even three acres. What land reforms and land redistribution could not do, demography and subdivision of holdings have done to land ownership. Where are the big landlords? There are some, but they are few and far between. But does this make the village an egalitarian utopia? Far from it!

This is where the sociological dimensions need to brought in to give meaning to economic morphology. Without this exercise developmental planning will be a pure formal exercise with no ground level resonance. Medium-sized owner cultivators contend against landless labourers, both economically and socially. While the rigidities of the caste systems no longer operate in their pristine form, caste prejudices and identities die hard. The stigma of tradition sits incubus like on social relations even if the prescriptions of tradition cannot be followed with equal facility these days. Other than the lack of economic opportunities, it is the nature of social relations in rural India that drive many poorer castes and classes out of the village. Clearly, the poorer one is, the greater the temptation to up and leave the village before the sun finally sets on one.

Where landholdings are so fragmented there is little scope for agricultural regeneration. Planners would be happy if agricultural production could be sustained year after year, and elated if there is a modest increase of even 1 per cent. Last year, there was in fact a negative growth rate. In small plots there is always a preponderance of family labour and the Chayanovian logic of balancing drudgery and needs usually operates in such cases. But for that to happen without emotional philippics, the needs horizon must curve within the village perimeter. Only then is the family farm a precious gift to be harvested in perpetuity. But now needs have escalated and the family farm is no longer what it was earlier cut out to be. It cannot support the ambition to be where the bright lights are. Nor can family farms provide employment to the landless youth in the villages. Therefore, no matter which way one looks at it, as owner cultivators or as landless labourers, the village is no longer a site where futures can be planned.[...]

Traditionally, caste and village called out to each other in synergy. If the village was said to be tranquil it was argued that caste ideology was responsible for it. This is how the much vaunted jajmani system was understood. Each caste had its specific locus and all castes agreed in the hierarchy of purity where the brahman sat on top. What most scholars failed to notice was that the hierarchy on the ground was not an outcome of ideological acquiescence but an outcome of an unequal distribution of wealth and power in a closed agrarian economy. In fact, every caste values itself and its ritual practices very highly, and no caste actually believes that it is essentially impure. Origin myths of castes clearly demonstrate this. In every instance, these origin tales recall a mythic past when a supposedly 'low caste' actually held a very high status in the distant past. Loss of status took place in such cases because of chicanery, deceit, reversals in war, and sometimes also because the gods were idiosyncratic. But on no account did the members of the so-called lower caste participate willingly in their own subjugation. Nor is it that ideas of grandeur crop up once a caste has economic and political power. In fact, these ideas are always there, except that they cannot be extraverted when conditions are not propitious as in a closed village economy under the sway of a dominant caste. As this aspect of unconditional dominance is rapidly becoming a thing of the past in Indian villages, the assertion of caste identities is becoming much more strident and out in the open. This is also why caste politics has so much purchase in contemporary India (see Gupta 2000 for details).

Caste Identity and Caste System

The gradual diminution of status of the dominant castes and of the earlier village oligarchs who controlled the agrarian economy of the village have brought about a number of changes at the cultural level too. One instance is the stridency with which backward castes and scheduled castes express their political views and preferences. In U.P. the impact of the Bahujan Samaj Party has been written about quite extensively and does not need repetition here (see Jaffrelot 2003). The reason for the rise of scheduled caste political assertion in recent times is primarily because the propertied classes in rural India can no longer exercise economic domination over the landless peasants. As they cannot employ the landless any more because of the shrinking size of their own landholdings, the power of landowners as patrons and as political leaders has also diminished over time.

Apart from the political side of scheduled caste mobilisation in recent years what needs also to be mentioned is the symbolic defiance of the hitherto subaltern castes towards those who, till less than a generation ago, were their unchallenged social superiors. In Punjab, the once low caste chamars now identify themselves as adi-dharmis (Jodhka 2002: 1816). Without formally rejecting Sikhism they have established their own gurudwaras and do not go to those that are controlled by jat Sikhs. In order to mark their distance further from Jats, the adi-dharmis display a portrait or statue of Guru Ravi Das in their gurudwaras.... The Jat Sikhs do not approve of the ascendance of the adi-dharmis but there is little they can do about it. In fact, in Talhan every third adi-dharmi household has a family member living abroad. I found three beauty salons in the adi-dharmi hamlet of Talhan village. All these are signs of prosperity and a clear indication that the adi-dharmis can do without jat patronage. Even in districts where the adi-dharmis are not as assertive as in Jallandhar, such as in Taran Taran, they, nevertheless, refuse to do menial work, nor will they work in fields owned by jats as agricultural labourers. The mazhabi Sikhs, who were traditionally scavengers, have now begun to be employed as agricultural labourers, when the occasion presents itself, but the adi-dharmis refuse to be engaged in that kind of work anymore as they consider it humiliating to bow before Jat landowners. The mazhabi Sikhs still do not have the economic capabilities to oppose Jats frontally. Though many of them have their own gurudwaras, as they feel slighted in those run by Jats, yet they have not made a defiant, symbolic break with Jat culture and orthodoxy as the adi-dharmis have. Yet, the dominant trend everywhere is to seek jobs that are non-agrarian even as they live in what are still called 'villages'. In several instances, both adi-dharmis and mazhabis would not work in a landowner's field if they are able to get a job elsewhere even if the wages are slightly lower. They would rather work as coolies and rickshaw-pullers for, as a mazhabi Sikh said: 'At the end of the day I know how much I am taking home as a mazdoor. If I work in the fields of Jat landowners I am not sure how much I will be paid and when. This way as a construction labourer or as a rickshaw-puller I am more secure.'

This story is a familiar one and is played out in different parts of India by different castes. In Uttar Pradesh the jatavs refuse to be agricultural labourers so the valmikis have taken their place. Even so, the valmikis are not supine either any longer. During my visit to Behrichi village in Saharanpur district of U.P., I found that a large number of valmikis had left the village in search of jobs outside to the utter disapproval of the landowning tyagis of that region. The tyagis, like the Jat Sikhs of Punjab, cannot complain enough against what they consider the upstart effrontery of those whom they consider to be of low caste. The tyagis never let scheduled castes enter their Shiv temple, and this is an age old phenomenon. In recent years, however, the scheduled castes have built their own temple dedicated to Ravidas and play recorded hymns (bhajans) which are often lifted from popular Hindi films. In Maharashtra, the literate and culturally advanced mahars have for a long time now given up their traditional occupation and have moved over to cities and towns where they are employed in a variety of services. This process has a much longer history in Tamil Nadu, with the chakaliyar (arunthodiar), the pariyar (adi-dravida), and the pallar (devendrakula vellala) showing scant respect today to local dominant castes. In recent years the arunthodiars have raised their levels of defiance by setting up Ambedkar statues which the landed Gouders find objectionable. The arunthodiars are also very mobile and clearly prefer non-farming jobs to working on Gouder fields.

Caste identity has resurfaced at every level now. It is no longer the case that the property less castes in the village could only speak of their origin tales in hushed tones. Now every caste proudly digs into deep pockets of heritage in order to claim an elevated status, frontally denying the station that tradition had accorded to them. Thus while the caste system has collapsed, caste identities are to be seen everywhere in a highly exaggerated form. This has given rise to the optical illusion that the caste system is enjoying a fresh lease of life. In fact, because caste as a system is dying in rural India that caste identities can now afford to come up. In the reign of the closed village economy ruled by the oligarchs of the dominant caste there was little scope for poorer castes to express their sense of self-worth through origin myths without being subjected to persecution from the superior communities. Now that the pressure of the upper class, landed castes has been lifted in the economic domain, the ex-untouchable castes have the space and the opportunity to proudly extravert their origin myths and their sense of identity without fearing reprisals. There are still some pockets where landed castes can be quite domineering, but the writing is already on the wall and the trend is irrevocably set against them.

Farmers' Movement

Rural agitations today are no longer between agricultural labourer and landlord as used to be the case as late as the 1970s. During this period there were a large number of organisations with political allegiance to left wing national parties that were active in rural India campaigning for the landless labourer and poor sharecropper. Such mobilisations have become historical anecdotes in most rural regions of contemporary India. Except for certain pockets in Bihar and Andhra Pradesh, the concerns of the agricultural worker do not get political expression anywhere else. Even in these areas, such as Bihar, it is not clear to what extent the Naxalite brigades are actually Maoist in their orientation and to what extent they are now extortionate groups feeding off a poorly organised state machinery. The simple reason why such organisations have lost their initial focus is because agricultural labour is no longer a critical issue that involves masses of rural Indians. As most holdings are family farms, the need for wage labour is intermittent during peak seasons. This has reduced the scope for left wing organisations to be active on their own terms.

By the 1980s it was clear that landless labourers had no viable future in the economy of the village. The increasing incidence of family farms made hired labour less critical for agricultural production than before. Where there was substantial agricultural prosperity in the years following the green revolution, such as Punjab and Haryana, labour could be hired from among migrants who came from east India in search of employment. Agricultural prosperity among capitalist farmers almost always meant a scarcity of local labour. This is primarily because even in large farms the amount of labour required per acre decreased substantially owing to mechanisation. Increased prosperity of the region also meant greater opportunities outside the farm which is where the local labour set off for in search of employment. This left the field open for migrants from east India who were happy to get some employment even though they were far from home.

In this context it must also be kept in mind that in many parts of India, particularly in Punjab and west U.P., those who worked earlier as agrestic labour are no longer willing to work in the same capacity. As we mentioned earlier, harijans and adi-dharmis of U.P. and Punjab respectively have more or less set their minds against labouring on others' fields. Cumulatively, this led to the diminution of the agricultural labourer's presence in rural India. By the time the 1980s came around agricultural labourer movements that involved huge rural unions and supra-local organisers became more or less a thing of the past. Now was the turn of Mahendra Singh Tikait and Nanjudaswamy to lead agitations espousing the interests of owner cultivators. In these mobilisations it was clearly stated that anyone who did not own land was not really a farmer. There was no room now for agricultural labourers in these movements which the Bharatiya Kisan Union of Uttar Pradesh and Haryana articulated most cogently.

Even as the owner cultivators were getting restive, a new configuration was taking place in rural politics. In the past when agricultural labourers mattered most in rural uprisings the target was always the local landlord, jotedar, or thanedar. With the shift to owner-cultivator brand of agitation the enemy was no longer local, but supra-local, even the government of India. Not surprisingly, BKU and Kshetkari Sangathan were constantly moving into cities to impress upon the public, and upon recalcitrant politicians, the authenticity of their demands. Thus while they were still agriculturalists, in the main, already the link between town and country was being strongly established (see Gupta 1997). Concurrently there was the demand among the same category of owner-cultivators for reservations in urban jobs and in educational institutions. The Mandal recommendations of 1990 were timed just right to coincide with the urban aspirations of cultivating castes such as yadavas, gujars, and jats. An urban job was clearly a prize catch for communities that for generations prided themselves in being farmers first and last. There is a play on a famous couplet in west U.P. that captures this sentiment rather nicely. The famous

Urdu poet, Ghagh, had once eulogised rural life when he wrote: 'Uttam kheti, madhyam baan; nishidh chakri, bhikh nidam.' Translated it means that agriculture is the best, followed by business, salaried jobs and beggary. Today, the villagers have recast the ditty along the following lines: 'Uttam chakri, madhyma baan; nikrisht krishi, bhik mahan.' In this case a politician who begs for vote is on top, followed by a salaried job, and at the bottom of the heap is the agriculturist.

Marginalised World of the Owner-Cultivator

Though it is difficult to say where the process of cultural alienation from the village began, it can nevertheless be maintained that the relative stagnation of the rural economy has contributed significantly to it. This can be gauged not just from the growth rates between industry and agriculture, but also in terms of the quite remarkable shift that is taking place in the number of agricultural workers of all descriptions.

The belief that India is overwhelmingly an agricultural society obviously is in need of further finessing. The sectoral distribution of rural net domestic product for agriculture is down to 54.41 per cent down from 72.37 per cent in 1970–71 (Chadha 2003: 58). As G Parthasarathy et al. argue, workforce changes in India did not match the production structure of its economy (Parthasarathy et al. 1998: 140). The National Sample Survey points out that the number of rural people working in urban India has doubled between 1987–88 and 1993–94. Also the annual GDP growth in agriculture in value added terms has declined from 3.5 per cent in the 1980s to 2.8 per cent in the 1990s. Thereafter, the figure dipped even more dismally to 1.3 per cent in 1999–2000 and unbelievably to a negative growth rate of minus 2 per cent in 2000–2001 (Mujumdar 2002: 3983). Further, trends show that urban households earn more than their counterparts in villages and that the disparity is growing. In a 1975–76 survey urban households earned on an average 1.82 times more than rural households, but today the figure stands closer to 2.1 (Pradhan et al. 2000: 2531). Though there is a noticeable increase in inequality in urban India, poverty levels are on the whole much lower than in the countryside (Vaidyanathan 2001: 1814).

Just because a majority of Indians live in villages, it would be rather hasty to conclude from this that India's national culture is determined by the village. Most of the political debates in the country do not have a rural character at all. This is rather surprising given the fact that a large number of politicians in the parliament and legislatures have rural origins. Occasionally a Mahender Singh Tikait or a Nanjudaswamy will stir things up in the villages, but in the main, political ideologies that inform most of the national parties do not have a strong rural component. The usual concessions are made in terms of subsidies or minimum price for agricultural produce, but the kernel of political ideologies do not reflect any major pre-occupation with the village. Even Laloo Yadav and Mulayam Singh Yadav demonstrate little by way of rural concerns. Playing the arithmetic of caste does not necessarily mean committing oneself to the chemistry of the village.

Yet, because it is also a question of arithmetic, politicians often vie against each other in appearing as champions of the beleaguered owner-cultivators. Current political discourse shows little concern towards the interests of agricultural labourers. But even here there is a strong element of political gamesmanship at work. In the name of protecting the poor farmer, political parties have in general opposed the institution of tax on agricultural incomes. Yet, as many owner-cultivators have told me repeatedly, this tax concession makes no difference to them as their incomes would be below the taxable amount anyway. These farmers argue that the exemption on agricultural tax is to help the rich entrepreneurial farmers and those in cities who want to escape the burden of taxation by diversifying into agricultural production, or in animal husbandry, or poultry farming, and so forth. At the same time, politicians are alive to the fact that the opening up of agricultural imports would ruin the owner-cultivators who are in substantial numbers. As this would lead to political and economic instability, they are obviously cautious about it. Even so there are peasant activists like Sharad Joshi of Shetkari Sangathan who welcomes an open market for he believes that the peasants in Maharashtra would do very well if they could take their produce abroad. Sharad Joshi's calculations need to be looked at closely, for he is obviously not keeping his books very carefully. To imagine that the Indian farmer could compete against the west where agriculture is industry is quite difficult to conceive. Indeed this is precisely the reason why India constantly opposes moves in international forums to let market dynamics control Indian agriculture.

While the owner-cultivators are protected politically, their futures are left unplanned. In 2000, the National Agricultural Policy formally recognised that agriculture has become 'a relatively unrewarding profession,' and that efforts to revive it had to be multi-pronged in character. Horticulture, floriculture, the cultivation of aromatic and medicinal plants, over and above animal husbandry and fisheries are some of the alternatives they have presented to improve agriculture. While these recommendations sound good on paper, there are vast infrastructural deficits that have to be overcome. To begin with, the conditions of owner-cultivators do not in general favour heavy investments in chancy cash crops. The suicide rate of farmers in Andhra Pradesh and Punjab is most alarming. In search for a better economic future they had taken loans to upgrade their agricultural production which they could not repay. According to reports, the overwhelming number of suicides among farmers is on account of their inability to pay back loans. Further, this happens with those agriculturists who are ambitious and want to move on, but are suddenly pulled up because the empirical structures are far too unyielding which makes their attempts to take off lack drive and thrust. Further, the village lacks other kinds of basic facilities like transportation systems, cold storages, modern silos, and a sound marketing framework.

Without this kind of infrastructural back up, the hope that the production of non-food crops will revive the village is not very realistic. Regardless of how feasible this strategy will eventually be, there is no gainsaying the fact that agricultural production of food is far from being either romanticised or valorised for its own sake any longer. Though the majority of Indians live in villages, the village leaves little impress upon the national culture today.

Rural Non-Farm Employment

Perhaps the most telling aspect of the transformations being wrought on rural culture can be gauged from the extent of rural non-farm employment. Till 1983, there were 12 states where the Rural Non-Farm Employment (RNFE) was below 20 per cent. These states included Punjab, Maharashtra and Gujarat. This left only five states where the RNFE was more than 20 per cent. In 1999–2000, roughly 20 years later the situation has changed dramatically. Now 12 states have RNFE figures above 20 per cent and only five are below 20 per cent. In the 50th round of the NSS held in 1993–94, the data suggest that about 32.9 per cent of rural households were outside agriculture. By the 57th round in 2000–02 the percentage has gone up to 35.2 per cent. In fact in Kerala, Haryana and Punjab over 50 per cent of rural households are non-agricultural in the 57th round of the NSS. Further, in Jammu and Kashmir, West Bengal, Himachal Pradesh, and Bihar (yes, Bihar), about 40 per cent of households are non-agricultural.[1] These figures are indeed staggering.

It is however difficult to see any pattern beyond this except to say that RNFE is widely prevalent across the country and is not exactly in proportion to rural prosperity, or the lack of it. This is because Maharashtra and Gujarat have RNFE below 20 per cent in the 1999–2000 survey. These states rank below even Orissa, Rajasthan and Uttar Pradesh. But in Punjab the RNFE climbed from a modest 17.4 per cent in 1983 to 27.1 per cent in 1999–2000. In Haryana, likewise, the figure went up from 22.3 per cent in 1983 to over 30 per cent in 1999–2000. Himachal Pradesh showed a dramatic increase for the figure doubled in these years from 12.4 to 25.2 per cent (Chadha 2003: 55). We can approach the same scenario from another angle of vision. If one takes into account the number of male workers engaged in agriculture one again finds a significant drop in numbers from 77.5 per cent in 1983 to 71.4 per cent in 1999–2000. In other words about 30 per cent of male workers in rural India are not working in the primary sector any more (ibid.: 12; Simmons and Supri 1995: 136). Chadha estimates that the services sector attracts a majority of those who are engaged in RNFE. According to him in 12 of the 17 states in the country, the service sector plays a much 'weightier' role than manufacturing when it comes to RNFE (Chadha 2003: 16). At any rate the rural non-farm sector contributes as much 45.59 per cent of Rural Net Domestic Product (ibid.: 58).

But what accounts for the growing incidence of RNFE? True, as we mentioned earlier, the scope for agricultural employment has fallen rapidly, but along side that there has been are focusing of aspirations as well. It is argued that the growth in agricultural production creates many types of post-harvesting activities that relate to trade where a high degree of non-farm employment takes place. Though this argument can be sustained up to a point by demonstrating the extent of RNFE in Punjab and Haryana, it is difficult to explain how the figure is so low in this regard in Maharashtra and rather high in Assam (ibid.: 55).

It has also been argued that RNFE is an instance of 'distress employment'. Unlike many other historical instances when the fall in rural employment is accompanied by high rate of agricultural growth, RNFE has continuously increased in India in spite of stagnant rates of agricultural growth. Thus, the rural unemployed go out searching for jobs and are willing to do whatever comes their way (Parthasarathy et al. 1998: 141). Simmons and Supri show from their research an inverse relationship between land ownership and RNFE (Simmons and Supri 1995: 145). Eighty eight per cent of their sample who were engaged in RNFE had less than 10 acres of land and hence the deduction that there is a distress aspect in RNFE (ibid.: 149). There is little doubt that the poorer one is, the greater the pressure to seek off-farm employment. Yet, it must also be mentioned that owning around 10 acres of land in India does not really signify a poor farmer who is in distress.

Our field studies indicate that in Punjab and west U.P. villages, all castes are active in rural non-farm employment. Adi-dharmis and Jats in Jalandhar own stores, run STD booths, sell grocery, sweets and snacks and stitch footballs for multinational companies. Surprisingly, in village Khara in Taran Taran district, we also found Jats who work as tailors (Abbi and Singh 1997). But it also needs to be mentioned that in U.P. villages the non-landowning caste is more active in RNFE than the landowning communities. In Behirchi in Saharnapur district and Baijalpur in Ballia district, both in U.P., the tyagis and thakurs respectively are not as active in non-farm occupations as the other poorer castes are. In fact, in Baijalpur in Ballia, very few thakurs were involved in non-farm occupations, other than joining the army or buying truck and taxis for commercial purposes.

Thus while there are indications that villages in east India are less dynamic than those in north-west India in shedding some of their values and prejudices, what is common in all instances is the general disenchantment with village life. The ambition to leave the village for a better life outside it, or to stay in the village but not to work on land, is too pronounced to be overlooked. It is also true that while RNFE attracts people from diverse castes, their location in the structure of employment outside the farm depends a lot on where they come from, and to the kinds of household they belong. What is also common is that the SCs are not without ambition, and in terms of RNFE they show a much greater degree of aggression. In every village SCs resent the treatment of the hitherto dominant castes, and have in many instances given up performing the menial tasks that they traditionally performed and which they believed, rightly so, to be humiliating in character.

Quite clearly, at an all-India level there is no pattern as such, though traditional and landowning castes in regions such as Uttar Pradesh are less prone to step out of agriculture than their counterparts in places like Punjab. But these are caste specific predispositions, and they cannot be generalised across the country. Nevertheless, what our findings show is that the recourse to non-farm employment varies, not just with respect to one's economic position, but also with caste related attitudes and prejudices.

In an interesting case study by Ruthven and Kumar (2002) it is the availability of off-farm employment that drives the local villagers to seek jobs outside the village. This exodus of locals from the village obviously draws in a sizable number of migrants who are willing to work for less. And yet, because wages outside agriculture are better, it is those who live in the vicinity who can take advantage of it first. Yet, the study conducted by Parthasarathy et al. suggests that the degree of urbanisation in a district has little impact on RNFE (Parthasarathy et al. 1998: 149). Certainly, if agricultural income had been plentiful perhaps such labouring jobs in urban areas would have less attractive, but the jury is still out on whether or not it is distress employment, or pure urbanisation, that drives up the figures of RNFE (see Basu and Kashyap 2002: A180–A181).

The availability of jobs outside agriculture is certainly an important factor for RNFE, almost axiomatically so. What one would really like to know is the nature of these jobs and their provenance. Pravin Visaria details the contribution of public utilities investments that have spurred RNFE (Visaria 1995: 404). Indeed, Ruthven and Kumar's study of a U.P. village provides empirical micro-level data that substantiates this position (Ruthven and Kumar 2002). Men are the main takers of jobs that arise from investments in public utilities and construction. In addition, as Visaria pointed out, villages which have gas, electricity and water are places where there is a greater incidence of RNFE (Visaria 1995: 404). Statistically, where land productivity is high, RNFE is also high (Basu and Kashyap 1992: A181), but this cannot be posited as a general condition either. In some cases it is distress RNFE, in other cases, the incidence of RNFE is driven up by better wages (ibid.: A187). When this happens it helps to increase the bargaining power of farm labourers. What, however, remains incontrovertible is that there is a growing increase in the number of those who work in non-agricultural operations in the village.

Finally, it is, not as if all the non-farm employment is in the villages. Indeed, the number of people working in off-farm jobs outside the village must not be ignored. This is a factor that the census enumerators have not quite grasped and hence the census figures are probably not very reliable. In an earlier work I had pointed out, with data from west U.P., that a large number of landless villagers work in towns and cities in the day, but return at night—or even during the weekend (Gupta 1997). It is, therefore, safe to conclude that RNFE can well be a local phenomenon that is often encouraged by supra-local factors. Further, RNFE is also an indicator of other changes that are occurring in the culture of the village, some of which we have already mentioned.

The Vanishing Indian Village?

In terms of the many diacritics of village life a lot seems to be changing in rural culture. Old taboos against holding certain kinds of jobs are disappearing. The caste system does not operate though, there is a strong assertion of caste pride and caste identity. Untouchability is not practiced widely, though there are pockets of upper caste intransigence. On the economic front, even prosperous landowners seek a future outside the village or in non-farm enterprises. We did not find too many instances of satisfied farmers. Most of them have grievances against the government for not providing them better amenities.

Predictably, wealthy landed people often have considerable political leverage in villages and form a vested interest group. While many of them draw their wealth and esteem from the village, they either live in cities, or hope to recreate an affluent urban ambience in their rural setting. In stark contrast to the poorer villagers with urban aspirations, when the rural rich engage with the outside world they do so from a position of relative strength. Yet, they too see their future outside the village, or in interacting with the town in enterprises that require rural and urban inputs.

It is against this background that the culture surrounding agriculture must be understood. This culture is not a stable one. History has not left behind a consistent legacy, nor does rural culture have a temporal overhang that is safely cantilevered on present commitments. Agriculture is an economic residue that generously accommodates non-achievers resigned to a life of sad satisfaction. The villager is as bloodless as the rural economy is lifeless. From rich to poor, the trend is to leave the village, and, if that entails going abroad, then so be it.

All this may sound a trifle alarming, but this is what India's villages are telling us whether or not we are inclined to listen to these rustic murmurs.

Note

1. I am grateful to Omkar Goswami for sharing his data on this subject with me.

References

Abbi, B. L. and Kesar Singh. 1997. *Post Green Revolution Rural Punjab: A Profile of Economic and Socio-Cultural Change*. Chandigarh: Centre for Research in Rural and Industrial Development.

Bandopadhayay, Suraj and Donald von Eschen. 1991. 'Agricultural Failure: Caste, Class and Power in Rural West Bengal'. In *Social Stratification*, ed. Dipankar Gupta. Delhi: Oxford University Press.

Basu, D. N. and S. P. Kashyap. 1992. 'Rural Non-Agricultural Employment in India: Role of Development Process and Rural-Urban Employment Linkages'. *Economic and Political Weekly* 27 (51–52): A178–A189, 19 December.

Beidelman, T. O. 1959. *A Comparative Study of the Jajmani System*. New York: Locust Valley.

Béteille, André. 1980. 'The Indian Village: Past and Present'. In *Peasants In History: Essays in Honour of Daniel Thorner*, ed. E. J. Hobsbawm et al. Kolkata: Oxford University Press.

Bose, Pradip K. 1991. 'Mobility and Conflict: Social Roots of Caste Violence in Bihar'. In *Social Stratification*, ed. Dipankar Gupta. Delhi: Oxford University Press.

Chadha, G. K. 2003. 'Rural Non-Farm Sector in Indian Economy: Growth, Challenges and Future Direction'. Paper presented in the joint JNU-IFPRI Workshop on The Dragon and the Elephant: A Comparative Study of Economic and Agricultural Reforms in China and India, India Habitat Centre, New Delhi, 25–26 March.

Chakravarti, Anand. 2001. *Social Power and Everyday Class Relations: Agrarian Transformation in North Bihar*. New Delhi: Sage.

Cohn, Bernard. 1987. *An Anthropologist among the Historians*. Delhi: Oxford University Press.

Djurfeldt, Goran and Staffan Lindberg. 1975. *Behind Poverty: The Social Formation of a Tamil Village*. London: Curzon Press.

Dumont, Louis. 1970. *Homo Hierarchicus: The Caste System and Its Implications*. George, London: Weidenfeld and Nicolson.

Dwyer, Rachel and Divia Patel. 2002. *Cinema India: The Visual Culture of Hindi Film*. Delhi: Oxford University Press.

Epstein, Scarlett. 1973. *South India: Yesterday, Today and Tomorrow*. London: Macmillan.

Fertiliser Association of India (FAI). 1988. *Report of the High Powered Committee on Fertiliser Consumer Prices*. New Delhi: FAI.

Gupta, Dipankar. 1997. *Rivalry and Brotherhood: Politics in the Life of Farmers of North India*. Delhi: Oxford University Press.

____. 2000. *Interrogating Caste: Understanding Hierarchy and Difference in Indian Society*. New Delhi: Penguin.

Harriss, John. 1982. *Capitalism and Peasant Farming: Agrarian Structure and Ideology in North Tamil Nadu*. Delhi: Oxford University Press.

Inden, Ronald. 1991. *Imagining India*. Oxford: Basil Blackwell.

Jaffrelot, Christophe. 2003. *The Silent Revolution: The Rise of the Low Castes in North Indian Politics*. Delhi: Permanent Black.

Jodhka, Surinder. 2002. 'Caste and Untouchability in Rural Punjab'. *Economic and Political Weekly* 37 (19): 1813–23, 11 May.

Marriot, McKim. 1955. *Village India: Studies in the Little Community*. Chicago: Chicago University Press.

Mujumdar, N. A. 2002. 'Rural Development: New Perspectives'. *Economic and Political Weekly* 37 (39): 3983–87, 28 September.

Parthasarathy, G. et al. 1998. 'Determinants of Rural Non-Agricultural Employment: The Indian Case'. *Indian Journal of Agricultural Economics* 53: 139–54.

Pradhan, Basanta K. et al. 2000. 'Rural-Urban Disparities: Income Distribution, Expenditure Pattern and Social Sector'. *Economic and Political Weekly* 35 (28–29): 2527–39, 8 July.

Rasul, M. A. 1974. *A History of the All India Kisan Sabha*. Kolkata: National Book Agency.

Ruthven, Orlanda and Sushil Kumar. 2002. 'Moving Mud, Shifting Soil: Change and Development in Wage Labour Livelihoods in Uttar Pradesh, India'. Mimeograph. Working Paper no. 176. London: Overseas Development Institute.

Sahay, Gaurang Ranjan. 2001. *Village Studies in India: A Case of Bihar*. Jaipur and New Delhi: Rawat Publications.

Simmons, Colin and Salinder Supri. 1995. 'Participation in Rural Non-Farm Activity in India: A Case Study of Cultivating Households in Jalandhar District, Punjab'. *International Journal of Punjab Studies* 2: 133–53.

Srinivas, M. N. 1987. *The Dominant Caste and Other Essays*. Delhi: Oxford University Press.

Vaidyanathan, A. 2001. 'Poverty and Development Policy'. *Economic and Political Weekly* 36 (21): 1807–14, 26 May.

Visaria, Pravin. 1995. 'Rural Non-Farm Employment in India: Trends and Issues for Research'. *Indian Journal of Agricultural Economics* 50: 398–409.

Wiser, W. H. 1969. *The Hindu Jajmani System: A Socio-Economic System Interrelating Members of Hindu Community*. Lucknow: Lucknow Publishing House.

15

Land, Labour and Caste Politics in Rural Tamil Nadu in the Twentieth Century

Iruvelpattu 1916–2008[*]

John Harriss, J. Jeyaranjan and K. Nagaraj

'Village studies', once an important mode of research, have largely been neglected in India in recent years—perhaps for good reason, having come to be conducted, often, very casually. More generally, research on agrarian change has languished latterly, alongside the neglect of the agricultural economy in public policy in the years of economic liberalisation. But there are signs now of some revival of research interest in rural economy and society,[1] as well as of policy attention (notably with the introduction of the National Rural Employment Guarantee), as seems wholly appropriate in the context of a country in which it is still the case that a substantial majority of the people live and work in the countryside. Our paper is a contribution to this renewed interest, based on a village study, which we believe continues to represent a potentially valuable way of approaching the study of rural social and economic change. In this case our study

---

* This chapter has been extracted from a longer paper published by the authors in the *Economic and Political Weekly* 45 (31): 47–61, 31 July 2010.

The paper is based on a revisit by the authors to a village in Tamil Nadu first studied by Gilbert Slater, an economist with the University of Madras during the second decade of the twentieth century', and subsequently restudied by other scholars with periodic gaps: by P. J. Thomas and K. C. Ramakrishnan (1936–37), Margaret Haswell (1961), and by S.Guhan and Joan Mencher (1981). Our research has been funded from a President's Research Grant awarded to John Harriss by Simon Fraser University. We are grateful to SFU for these resources; and John Harriss is also grateful to the Institute of South Asian Studies at the National University of Singapore for the opportunity of working on this paper during his tenure of a Visiting Research Professorship in 2010. We thank Barbara Harriss-White and Judith Heyer for their helpful comments.

has an unusual historical depth because we have taken up for research one of the 'Slater villages' of Tamil Nadu.

Gilbert Slater was appointed in 1915 to head a new Department of Economics in the University of Madras, and he believed that, for his students, both that understanding 'the causes and remedies of Indian poverty' was essential, and that they stood to learn a great deal about it from studies of village economies. As a way to achieving his objective he set them about studying their native villages, which were spread across the Madras Presidency—five of them lying in what is now the state of Tamil Nadu—and he published their studies in his book *Some South Indian Villages* in 1918. Resurveys were then completed in all the villages in 1936–37 under the direction of P. J. Thomas and K. C. Ramakrishnan, also from the Department of Economics in the University of Madras (1940), and the comparison of the Slater and the Thomas and Ramakrishnan studies has been drawn upon by the leading historians of the Madras Presidency in the 1920s and 1930s, Christopher Baker (1975) and K. A. Manikumar (2003) as a means of assessing trends of change in the rural economy. More recently, some of the 'Slater villages', as we may now describe them, were studied in 1961 by the Oxford economist Margaret Haswell (1967), and some by the Agro-Economic Research Centre of the University of Madras at about the same time. Most recently, the five Tamil villages in the Slater set were studied by S Guhan and colleagues of his associated with the Madras Institute of Development Studies early in the 1980s. Guhan himself, together with the anthropologist Joan Mencher, and with the assistance of three young research assistants, pioneered the 1980s studies in much the way that Slater himself had done more than 60 years earlier, with work in the village of Iruvelpattu, in the former South Arcot District of Tamil Nadu. He and Mencher published their study of 'Iruvelpattu Revisited' in the *Economic and Political Weekly* in 1983. Together the 'Slater village' studies constitute what is probably a unique set of village surveys, without comparators anywhere else in India, and—for all their limitations[2]—they provide a valuable means for studying rural economic and social change in Tamil Nadu over the last century.

We have taken up fresh studies of the Slater villages, now almost thirty years on from the time of Guhan's studies and almost a century from that of the first round. Our initial study has also been one of Iruvelpattu.[3] Here we focus upon what have seemed to us to be the most significant findings from comparison of the successive studies of the village, which concern trends in the control over land and labour, and caste politics, through the twentieth century. We tell a story of the continuity of landlord power, even if it has been chipped away through the century, and of the continuing dependence of a majority of households on agriculture in spite of the significant diversification of employment that has taken place, and of apparent stagnation in the agricultural economy after the relative success of the 'green revolution' in the 1970s. And while it is too much to speak of a 'social revolution' as having taken place, we do record some empowerment of dalits. Some tightening in the labour market and dalit political mobilisation has brought about an historic shift in agricultural wage rates.

THE VILLAGE ITS SETTING

Iruvelpattu is now in Villupuram district and lies twelve kilometers south of the district headquarters along the Grand Southern Trunk Road … It is in the broad region of the Tamil country described by historians as the 'plains' … outside the 'valleys'—the centre of high Tamil culture of the major river valleys—and for long forested and used more for grazing than for agriculture. Baker argues that 'The mobilisation of the plains was achieved partly by the immigration and settlement of Telugu warrior chiefs and clans …' (Baker 1980: 40). Much of the agricultural settlement of the area of Villupuram was led, in this way, by Telugu-speaking warriors in the Vijayanagara era, amongst them, Reddiars like those who have historically been dominant in Iruvelpattu, and who were the hereditary village headmen (or 'munsiffs'). E.V.Sundaram Reddi, Slater's student, who assisted in the first study in 1916, came from the family described by Haswell as that of the 'plutocrat' of the village, and by Guhan and Mencher as that of the 'Big Landlord' or 'BL'. They concluded their study in 1981 by summarising the ways in which BL exerted control over the village and they said 'developments ten to twenty years from now vis-à-vis BL will be interesting to watch'. As we shall explain, one of the more striking findings of this re-study of the village is that BL has continued to dominate the village, even if his power is less extensive than it was.[…]

Iruvelpattu, like most villages in the Tamil country, includes a caste settlement (the *uur*), occupied now very largely by Vanniyars with the few remaining Reddiar families—and a separate *cheri*, or 'colony', occupied by dalits—here Paraiyars. The colony is on the eastern side of the main road, which today—given the heavy traffic along it—constitutes a more significant barrier between the 'two civilisations' (of caste Hindus and of dalits) of which Slater spoke (1918: 11), than it would have done in 1916.[…]

In 1916 Slater could claim that 'To a great extent the village is self-supporting', because of its reliance on local materials for building and for implements, the proximity of a weaving village, and the presence in the village community of all the principal specialists from artisan and service castes to supply the goods and services commonly required. As it has ceased to be 'self-supporting', however, so members of the specialist service castes have moved away … and the village has become more homogeneous in terms of its caste composition.

POPULATION

A striking feature of Iruvelpattu through the 20th century is that its population has grown very little, the annual compound growth rate being a very low half a per cent, which is certainly lower than the natural rate of growth of the population. In net terms the village has lost a considerable part of its population, and there seems only to have been one decade, that of the 1970s, when there was some inward migration.[…]

While in overall terms the village has seen steady net out-migration, the picture is more complex if we consider different social groups.

If we look at the two major caste groups, dalits and 'caste Hindus', it appears that for the period 1937–2008 as a whole there has been net out-migration from both populations: the annual compound growth rate of population for dalits for this period as a whole is 0.72 and it is even lower at 0.62 for the caste Hindus. Since these rates are likely to be lower than the natural rate of growth of population both the communities have seen net out-migration. But a closer look reveals that there are distinct periods when people from the two communities either migrated out of the village or migrated into it. The period up to around 1981 may have seen in-migration of caste Hindus whilst dalits moved out. Guhan and Mencher found evidence from interviews that a number of dalit families had moved out for work on coffee plantations in Chikmagalur in Karnataka, while young men were going out for work as coolies in Chennai or in Bangalore. 'On the other hand', they said, 'there was little evidence of any migration from the caste village', and they concluded that 'the middle castes [meaning, essentially, the Vanniyars] have constituted a non-migrant and growing element', probably linked with the relative success of the agricultural economy in the 1970s. The period after 1981 has seen the reversal of these trends, with the dalit population of the village having grown whilst the caste Hindu population has declined. The Vanniyar streets, with numbers of houses that are shut up, and others that have fallen into ruin, provide visual evidence of this. Agricultural work in Iruvelpattu, and labouring occupations generally, have become more distinctly the sphere of the dalits.

Amongst caste Hindus there has been especially sharp decline in population belonging to castes other than Vanniyars. This is true of Reddiars, the socially and economically dominant group in the village, whose number declined from 57 in 1937 to 46 in 1981, and to a mere 18 by 2008; and of artisanal and service castes like the Vannan (from 15 in 1937 to 2 in 2008); barber (7 to nil); and Achari (19 to 15). The village today has essentially become a two-caste village with Vanniyars numerically predominant (their 1003 members accounting for 56 per cent of the population) and dalits the other numerically significant community (with 697 members accounting for nearly 39 per cent of the population). The rest, who accounted for 16.2 per cent of the population in 1937, account for just about 5 per cent of the population today. The relative increase in the numbers of the dalits may be a factor contributing to their assertion in the village in recent times.

Education

An important trend of the recent past has been the distinct improvement in literacy, especially amongst dalits. There was already a village school with three teachers, in 1916 (and '67 boys and 7 girls on the rolls'). ...The total numbers of pupils in the village school are now rather low, partly because of the opening of the new school but also because so many parents choose to send their children out to private convent schools to which they travel in school vans.

The overall literacy rate in the village was calculated by Guhan and Mencher in 1981 to have been only 32.5 per cent, lower than in the district, and very much lower than in the state as a whole; and at that time the literacy rate amongst dalit women was only 6.7 per cent and amongst men 13.7 per cent. Guhan and Mencher observed that 'The disparity between the caste Hindus and the *Harijans* (dalits), and the still abysmally low level of schooling in the case of the Harijan women are striking'. The data for 2008 show that great strides have been made in levels of literacy (as given by the proportion of those over the age of 7 who have received some schooling), and that gaps both between men and women, and between dalits and others are nothing like as great as they were. The improvement in the literacy of dalit women from 6.7 per cent to 54.6 per cent is considerable. We observed the pride of dalit women, especially in their girl children's school uniforms and their school books. This, for some women with whom we spoke, was for them the big change of the last twenty five years. Yet even now, in spite of the progress has been made, one-third of the village population remains illiterate, and 40 per cent of the dalits.[…]

Whereas there was still in 1981 a significant gap between caste Hindus and Dalits, after the primary level, it had virtually disappeared by 2008 and while Guhan and Mencher found no graduates in the colony, in 2008 there were 23 with tertiary qualifications, one of them a PhD, seven of them women. This is a big and important change that has taken place over the last quarter-century, though clearly inequalities do remain between dalits and others in the sphere of education.

The Village Habitat and Public Services

It is still possible in Iruvelpattu today to recognise Slater's description of the built environment.… Living space remains severely constrained.[…]

Not long before the 1981 study BL had opposed moves by government to grant house sites to dalits, and he had even succeeded in persuading some of the dalits to sign a petition to the effect that they were not in need of house sites! This situation has changed since 1981, as a result of the dalit political mobilisation that we analyse below, that was eventually successful in securing house site *pattas* for the dalit households in 1996. Security of tenure of their house sites is an extremely important advance for them.

There have been improvements for dalits, too, in regard both to drinking water supply, and electricity. Historically people in the village depended for drinking water especially on spring channels from the Malattar river, and there was one drinking water well in the cheri. By 1981, however, the caste village was being supplied with piped water from an overhead tank—while there was still only one well in the cheri, and that was dry for six months in the year of the study. In these circumstances the dalits had to bring water from irrigation wells, travelling up to two kilometres for this, and making as many as five trips in a day. Another important change over the last 25 years for the dalits of Iruvelpattu, therefore, has been provision of a piped water supply for them too, from two overhead tanks—again, as a result of their political mobilisation.[…]

In spite of the continuing lack of progress with regard to sanitation, there certainly have been improvements in the village infrastructure and public services in the Twentieth Century, and especially over the last quarter century—and and these improvements have spread, with an appreciable lag, to the dalits.[...]

The Village Economy: Land Holding and Other Assets

There has historically been a high level of concentration of land ownership in Iruvelpattu, and given that the Reddiar landowner described as 'Big Landlord' (BL) by Guhan and Mencher is still there, nearly thirty years later, it seems appropriate to start with him—the grandson and heir to the landlord whom Slater met in 1916. According to Slater's estimates the family at that time owned about 400 acres in Iruvelpattu,[4] about two-thirds of all the village lands, and another 200 acres in adjoining villages. The landlord cultivated some 200 acres himself and leased the remainder of the land out. At the time, Slater reckoned, the average holding of all the others in the village was no more than four acres.[...]

By the 1960s it appears from Haswell's account that BL still held around 300 acres in Iruvelpattu alone... and in 2008... he himself spoke of having 150 acres in the village, though there was also no doubt that he had divested land. But it is still the case that there is a sharp polarisation between his very large holding on the one hand, which still accounts for almost one-third of all the land owned by people of Iruvelpattu, and the very large numbers of small and marginal land holdings on the other. The seven holdings of ten acres and more in extent, including BL's, account for about 43 per cent of the total area owned. On the other hand there are 186 holdings of less than 4.00 acres in extent (what Slater thought was the average size of holding in 1916), accounting for 41.8 per cent of the total area (comparable with Guhan and Mencher's findings from patta statistics in 1981), and there are just 22, apart from BL's, that are larger than this, accounting for 28.9 per cent of the area. The numbers of those who might be described as having 'substantial family farms', or as those potentially of 'rich peasants', are small, and small and marginal holdings persist, now in the context of part-time farming in households in which—as we explain below—some members carry on other occupations. There is now very little tenancy of agricultural land at all, and the number of landless households has apparently doubled since 1981 (Guhan and Mencher say there were 95 such households in 1981–50 of them dalit—and there are 197 now)—which might be taken as striking evidence of 'proletarianisation' (in 2008 49 per cent of households owned no land compared with 29 per cent reported in 1981). Though the dalits still have a higher incidence of landlessness than the others in the village they do make up a somewhat smaller share of all the landless than they did in 1981. Many more of them, clearly, own some land than was the case earlier (72 households as opposed to 40, owning about 58 acres instead of 18) but the majority (41) are holdings of less than one acre. Just one man owns as much as five acres.

Apart from land, historically the most important assets in a village like Iruvelpattu, were cattle. A major change, therefore, between 1981 and 2008 has been the general replacement of draught cattle, first by tractors and more recently by power tillers, together with the introduction of combined harvesters. By 2008, amongst the people of Iruvelpattu 13 owned tractors (including one dalit), 11 owned power tillers (also including one dalit), and there were four combined harvesters (all owned by people in the caste village, one of them by BL), while the numbers of draught cattle are now down to just four or five teams. Electric pumpsets were introduced for irrigation, replacing the traditional water-lifting devices, following the arrival of electricity in 1958. By 2008, given the general fall in the water table from 40 feet to 100, groundwater irrigation was by means of submersible pumps operating in borewells, and there were 68 of them in all (14 of them owned still by BL). The ownership of agricultural assets, as well as land, therefore, remains concentrated.

THE VILLAGE ECONOMY: AGRICULTURE

There has been very little change either in the pattern of land use in Iruvelpattu over the century, or in the cropping pattern. Paddy has always occupied more than three-quarters of the gross cropped area, but the extent of double-cropping and even of triple-cropping has increased as a result of the developments of groundwater irrigation. By 1981 higher-yielding, 'green revolution' varieties had been widely adopted. The same varieties (notably 'Ponni' and 'TKM9') are still cultivated, which suggests that the wave of innovation of paddy varieties of the 1970s and 1980s in Tamil Nadu has passed. Reported yields, too, show little if any increase over 1981.[...]

Production Organisation

The big change that has come about in the agricultural system of Iruvelpattu and the surrounding area over the last quarter century has been its extensive mechanisation. There were tractors by 1981, and around that time, or a little later, mechanical threshing was introduced. But ploughing was done, as it always had been, by bullock or buffalo teams, commonly still drawing an old 'country' plough; and harvesting and most threshing was still done manually. By 2008, however, it was said by the Reddiars in the village that 'In a couple of years' time they [referring to dalit labour] won't know the sickle', because of the taking over of harvesting and threshing by combined harvesters. Ploughing, too, as we mentioned, is now done almost entirely by tractors and increasingly by power tillers which are more handy in small fields, and in the normal course of events the few remaining bullock teams in the village appear on the scene only at the stage of levelling the ploughed fields to get them ready for planting. The old bullock carts, used for generations as the principal means of transport of goods in the Tamil countryside, have mostly gone, too. Some have been adapted with wheels with rubber tyres, but most have been replaced by carts of a different construction—so that village carpenters and blacksmiths no longer have the roles that they once had—and much carriage of goods has been taken over by tractor-trailers.[...]

Occupations, Employment and Migration

The earlier studies of Iruvelpattu provide little information on employment outside agriculture, referring only to traditional village specialists without offering any

TABLE 15.1: Occupational Pattern of Households (1981 and 2008)

Household type	Caste Hindu		Dalit		Total		Percentage change in number of households between 1981 and 2008		Dalit households as a percent of total households	
	1981	2008	1981	2008	1981	2008	Caste Hindus	Dalit	1981	2008
Cultivator households	130 (55.8)	109 (42.7)	6 (6.7)	21 (14.9)	136 (42.1)	130 (32.8)	–16.2	+250.0	4.4	16.2
Agricultural labour households	35 (15.0)	33 (12.9)	74 (82.2)	70 (49.6)	109 (33.7)	103 (26.0)	–5.7	–5.4	67.9	68.0
Non-agricultural labour households	68 (29.2)	113 (44.3)	10 (11.1)	50 (35.5)	78 (24.1)	163 (41.2)	+66.2	+400.0	12.8	30.7
Total	233 (100.0)	255 (100.0)	90 (100.0)	141 (100.0)	323 (100.0)	396 (100.0)	–	–	27.9	35.6

numbers. There were carpenters, blacksmiths, potters, goldsmiths and oil—pressers present in the village in 1916 and 1937, as well as washermen, at least one barber, temple priests and perhaps one or more school teachers. By 1981 the goldsmiths, oil pressers and barbers had gone, and the numbers of the artisans was declining. This is a process that has continued. The fact that the authors of the first two studies mention no other non-agricultural occupations is probably significant, and one of the most striking changes to have taken place in the village over the last half-century, but especially over the last twenty years or so, has of course been the considerable diversification of occupations. Guhan and Mencher found that 78 (24 per cent) of the 323 households in Iruvelpattu in 1981 could be described as 'non-agricultural'. By 2008 this number had doubled and those households depending primarily on non-agricultural occupations had come to make up, we estimate, more than 40 per cent of all village households (see Table 15.1), while the numbers both of cultivator and of agricultural labour households had declined. The numbers of agricultural labourers in Iruvelpattu now—229—are only a few more than the 210 reported by Veeraraghavan in 1937, though the population of the village has increased by about 60 per cent over this time. In 2008, though cultivation still remained the most important single activity of Iruvelpattu, and employed two-thirds of the village labour force, it was no longer so essentially an 'agricultural village'.

In 1981, while 85 per cent of caste Hindu families were either cultivating households or dependent on non-agricultural occupations, amongst dalits 82 per cent were dependent upon agricultural labour. It is still the case that more than 80 per cent of cultivator households are Caste Hindu, and that nearly 70 per cent of all agricultural labour households are dalit. But a notable change since 1981 is the reduced dependence of the dalits on agricultural wage work. Now 'only' 50 per cent of their households are so dependent. There were only ten dalit households amongst the 78 non-agricultural households of 1981 (13 per cent of the total), and they are described as having been in 'the poorer occupations, such as duck keepers, washermen and toddy tappers'. Now the dalit households account for about a third (31 per cent) of all the households engaged in non-agricultural occupations. There still are toddy-tappers amongst them, but they also include drivers and others in 'technical' occupations, and a small number of professionals and salaried people.

Slater's view in 1916 was that emigration, then to plantations in Ceylon, seemed to be the principal means whereby it was possible for the people of Iruvelpattu to relieve their 'population problem'; and in 1937 Veeraraghavan noted that though 'for the last 20 years none has left the village as coolie for overseas plantations', there was seasonal migration. He mentioned 20–30 families, from both cheri and village, as going out for work seasonally, some as far as Salem (130 km away), picking groundnuts, and reported that a few of Vanniyars were going out for work in Chennai. In 1981, as we noted, evidence was found of emigration from the village by dalits, especially in the 1960s, but it was said that 'there was little evidence of any recent migration from the caste village', and only passing references are made to circular, seasonal migration. In these respects things have definitely changed.

By 2008 it was clear that Vanniyars and other caste Hindus have been moving out of agricultural occupations and some of them out of the village altogether, and that while the dalits too are involved in these shifts, the numbers of them moving into other activities and out of the village are fewer. Both agricultural work and the village community are becoming more significantly 'dalit' than was the case before. These findings would no doubt be reinforced if we were able to determine the numbers of households from the different caste communities that have left the village altogether since 1981.

Not only have Vanniyars moved away in greater numbers but they—and people from other caste Hindu families—have moved especially into non-agricultural, non-labouring employment. The dalits, however, are more commonly employed in labouring occupations, particularly in Chennai (as construction coolies on a temporary basis) and Bangalore, though there are a few in professional positions. In general the dalits of Iruvelpattu work outside the village in large numbers, in activities such as sugar-cane cutting, as well as in construction work and brickfields (though there were also four brick kilns in the village itself in 2007–08). There are reported to be as many as 'five or six sugar cane cutting teams each with about 20 members', or as many as 'two hundred people' according to another account, from the dalit colony, who travel widely, south to Thanjavur, and north into Andhra. They are outside for long periods but come back to the village for festivals, and it seems possible that our census of the village missed some of these people. The numbers involved in some of the reports we heard seem exaggerated, but it does appear likely that there are larger numbers of people from Iruvelpattu who are working outside than we have been able to trace through our census and household listing.[...]

Wages, Conditions of Employment and Levels of Living

Gilbert Slater was much exercised by the conditions of the labourers of Iruvelpattu as he observed them in 1916. He described the conditions of employment of padials—labourers attached to a particular landowner/cultivator by long-term debt bondage—of whom BL's grandfather alone employed around 40:

> A 'padial' is a sort of serf, who has fallen into hereditary dependence on a landowner by debt.... Quite recently a lad of 18 borrowed Rs 25 in cash and grain to celebrate his wedding with due festivity and became a padial. Such a loan never is repaid, but descends from one generation to another; and the padials themselves are transferred with the creditor's lend when he sells it or dies.

According to Slater's calculations such labourers were paid the equivalent of about a pound and a half of raw rice each day (around three-quarters of one kilo), and their working days lasted usually for at least twelve hours. He was appalled by their conditions of work, and found that the padials of Iruvelpattu probably received rather less than 'the *gaol* allowance for a man doing hard labour'. But he also thought that the efficiency and productivity of labour were low, and one of his principal conclusions was that 'the Indian worker earns very low wages, has a very low standard of expenditure, and attains a very low level of efficiency, and these three characteristics of Indian life are so inter-connected that it is impossible to say which is cause rather than effect'. Though he did not say so, he described the idea of a 'poverty trap'.

In 1937, Veeraraghavan described daily-paid wage labour as well, but emphasised that 'A semi-servile system of labour survives in the padiyal' and provided a comparable though even more detailed description than had Slater. There were then '85 padiyals in this village', he said. In 1981, almost half a century later, Guhan and Mencher identified a total of 36 padials, 22 of them being in the employ of the BL. These men were mostly older, wanting somewhat lighter work, and they were engaged in the operation of pumpsets, in 'watch and ward' and such duties as feeding cattle and cleaning cattle sheds. The researchers could find no evidence on the existence of debt bondage (an observation reflecting the apparent weakening of the padial system, that was in accordance with others made at around the same time in Tamil Nadu, as Guhan and Mencher noted. See also Harriss 1982). Padials were then being paid 30 Madras measures (mm) of paddy per month, with seven and a half measures of ragi, plus an annual payment of two bags of paddy—somewhat higher rates than those recorded by both Slater and Veeraraghavan. By 2008 the 'semi-servile system of labour' had declined still further and only five padials were still employed, all of them by BL. He himself says that he employs only pump watchmen, who may be paid in cash at the rate of Rs 35–40 per day + one quarter measure of ragi, or cash of Rs 900–1,000 per month plus a meal, or in kind at a rate of one bag of paddy per month, plus one meal per day *and* three bags of paddy at the time of harvest. These rates were confirmed by a woman in the colony who told us that her husband, working as a pump watchman for BL, was being paid 2mm/day (which is equivalent to one 75 kg bag of paddy per month). Wage levels for these permanent labourers do seem to have been increased since 1981, but it is very striking that they still work out to be equivalent only to about the 3kg of cereals per day that it is suggested has been the historical level of payment to day labourers in agricultural economies across different continents (according to sources cited by Guhan and Mencher).

The authors of the 1981 study attempted to compare wage rates for agricultural operations as these could be deduced from the 1937 study with those then prevalent in Iruvelpattu. They concluded that wage rates for transplanting and weeding of paddy had declined or at best stagnated, though it was possible that those for harvesting (the most important source of income during the year for many agricultural labourers) had increased slightly. This, even though Veeraraghavan had noted in 1937 that 'wage rates here are very low'. In 1981 the general wage level worked out as being equivalent to 3.4kg of rice for men and half that for women. In other words wage levels seemed to have remained at the historic mean.

It is now quite difficult to compare agricultural wage levels with those obtaining in the past, because of the changes that have taken place with the extensive mechanisation of cultivation, including harvesting and threshing by combine harvester, as well as tractor ploughing. The best single comparator is the general daily rate for 'coolie' labour which in 1981 stood at Rs 5 for men and Rs 2.5 for women. These rates, we saw, were equivalent to about 3.4kg and 1.75kg of paddy, respectively. The rates for this kind of work (and plucking seedlings from nurseries for men, and bunding, and for transplanting paddy and weeding for women) in 2008 stood at Rs 60 plus a meal, valued at Rs 5, for men, and Rs 35 for women—probably for a shorter working day.[5] These are equivalent to 6–7 kg of paddy for men and 3–3.5 kg for women.[6] Those now few labourers who are employed in harvesting operations—reaping corners of the fields that are beyond the reach of the combine harvesters, bagging and carrying—are paid 5mm per day (= about 6kg) in place of the 3mm or 4mm (for a longer day, in this case) that were paid in the past. These rates have increased, therefore, though not by as much as the general coolie rate. In real terms agricultural wage rates have roughly doubled, moving well beyond the long run historic mean—and the complaints of the Reddiars and others in the caste village about the costs of labour and 'labour problems' are understandable. It is reasonable to suppose that wage levels in agriculture have been driven up by the general tightening of labour markets with the increased availability of non-farm employment. The average daily rates that we have recorded in other labouring occupations are all higher than the daily rate in agriculture in the village: sugar-cane cutting, about Rs100 per day; construction labourers, Rs 80–100 (this is the rate for 'helpers'; the rate for masons was Rs 250); brick kiln labour, Rs 150 per day for a husband and wife team; work in the Koyambedu market in Chennai, Rs 200 per day over 20 days in a month; even for women from the colony employed as day labourers for cleaning beer bottles in a nearby government store the daily rate was Rs 50 plus the cost of their bus fares. The basic agricultural wage rates increased again to Rs 70 for men and Rs 40 for women in January 2009, apparently reflecting labour shortages. Given wage levels outside village agriculture, and given, too, that employment under the National Rural Employment Guarantee Scheme[7] has been available in the village at rates of Rs 65 per day (on average; Rs 80 was sometimes paid to some people, depending upon the amount of work that they did) for both men and women, it might even be found surprising that agricultural wage rates have not been increased by more than has been the case.

What, however, of the duration and continuity of employment? Guhan and Mencher report that they were only able to obtain 'broad orders of magnitude', and their estimations, based on a careful consideration of seasonal variations, suggested that average employment for men and women taken together, could be placed at 180 days per year. They thought that it was possible that the availability of employment had increased as a result of the introduction of the green revolution technology, though there were also off-setting trends due to mechanisation, even at that time. Our own enquiries—again about 'broad orders of magnitude', taking seasonal variation into account—suggested that the average number of days of employment available in village agriculture has definitely declined, unsurprisingly given the extent of mechanisation of operations. If the average was 180 days in 1981, it is of the order of 100–120 days now, so that even though daily real wages have improved, average real incomes from agriculture cannot have improved by very much. According to Guhan and Mencher's calculations the annual income for an agricultural labouring couple would have been of the order of 900 kg paddy [180 days × (3.5+1.7 kg)] in 1981. The equivalent at present is of the order of 1000–1100 kg (100/110 days × (7+3.4 kg)). This will supply the minimum staple food requirements of an average household of 4.7 members, which is equivalent to about 4 standard consumption units. Those depending solely on agricultural labour, therefore, are still living at or below the poverty line.[8] [...]

VILLAGE SOCIETY AND THE VILLAGE POLITY

As Slater described it, as we mentioned earlier, the village seemed to be 'self-supporting' and quite self-contained, with a sufficient range of artisans and specialists as to meet most essential functions from its own resources. He might have been influenced by the notion of the 'village republic' invented by earlier generations of colonial administrators, but his account suggests that this was not an entirely inappropriate idea. By 1937 Veeraraghavan's account gives less of an impression of self-containment, but it also supplies details about the customary payments made to carpenter and blacksmith, potter, washerman and barber, for their services. There are definite hints here of the relationships between service castes and landowners that anthropologists used to describe as 'the jajmani system', or what was observed in practice in a village in North Arcot in the early 1970s where the system of customary relationships was known as talaimurai (the word murai meaning order). At that time (see Harriss 1982) carpenter and blacksmith, washerman, barber, village temple priest, and the 'untouchable' (Dalit) village servants, were all still paid customary amounts on the cultivators' threshing floors, as well as being paid for their particular functions or specialist roles in life-cycle rituals, while the washerman, at least, would take food from cultivators' houses each day. The idea of talaimurai was familiar to some of our informants in Iruvelpattu in 2008, but it was evident that the system had broken down. Not least the shift to mechanised harvesting meant that most cultivators no longer threshed out their grain on a threshing floor, and—so one of the Reddiars said—servants didn't like to come to cultivators' houses for payment. The blacksmith now makes locks, the carpenter has a furniture polishing business, both of them outside; the washerman will still do pressing for payment but not laundry. These former village service providers do still undertake their specialist ritual roles, for payment, but the more generalised system of relationships of dependent service has ceased to operate.

In a number of other ways, too, the hierarchical organisation of village society that lent a certain kind of 'village solidarity', has ceased to be. In the past it seems that it was the case in Iruvelpattu, as was observed in the North Arcot village Harriss studied in the early 1970s, that the members of the cheri participated in the main village festival, which takes place in the Tamil month of *aadi*, as well as celebrating their own comparable festival centred on the goddess Mariyamman (Harriss 1982). In the case that Harriss observed the organisation and the events of the festival clearly reflected the social hierarchy of the village as a whole. But in Iruvelpattu by 2008 the dalits were no longer participants in the festival of the caste village,[9] and celebrated only their own Mariyamman festival.

Another aspect of the old village hierarchy according to some of the accounts of ethnographers, was the existence of a traditional political institution, the panchayat, sometimes labelled as the *uur panchayat*, which functioned as a decision-making body and acted to resolve disputes. There has been some debate amongst anthropologists about these bodies, and one view was that they were more an expression of the power of the dominant caste than being in any, even very restricted sense, a representative institution. Such traditional panchayats have been observed in operation in villages in Karnataka by Kripa Ananthpur (Ananthpur and Moore 2007). Of Iruvelpattu, however, Veeraraghavan wrote in 1937 that there was no panchayat; and in 2008, though the idea of the *uur panchayat* was clearly familiar to people, it was said that the voice of the Reddiar landlord, BL, had always been decisive. These days serious disputes are more likely to be referred to the police. Amongst the dalits there is said still to be a panchayat, however, constituted by the *naattaanmai*, or elders, of each of the major lineages, who meet together to settle disputes and to run the affairs of the Mariyamman temple.

Another traditional village institution had some vitality in Iruvelpattu. This was the common fund, described as follows by Slater in 1916:

> In spite of the social and religious severance between pariah and caste-man, and the economic severance between land-owner and padial, the general impression made on my mind during my four days in Eruvellipet, was that of a spirit of local solidarity. I heard no mention of what is so frequent, the division of the village into two hostile factions. It was said that the munsiff (the Reddiar landlord, we understand) was able to deal with such disputes as occurred. There seemed to be no trouble about the administration of the common fund of the village, the very existence of which is a testimony to the existence of this village solidarity. It is derived partly from the sale of an exclusive right to catch fish in the tank to one villager, and of that to cut reeds, which grow extensively in the tank, and which are valued for thatching, to another. (Slater 1918: 14)

The more important source of money for the common fund was, however, the auctioning of rights to the produce of the tamarind and palmyra trees from the roadside, the profit from which amounted to about Rs 200 per year, quite a sum in those days. The fund was used 'to promote the economic well-being of the village, by religious ceremonies which secure favourable seasons, and by presents bestowed where the giving of presents is deemed a profitable investment'.[...]

What were once common resources have, however, through the Twentieth century (as we see from Veeraraghavan's and then from Guhan and Mencher's accounts) been first partially privatised and then substantially taken over by the state.

Landlord Power

Even if, as seems possible, Slater had a somewhat rosy-tinted view of 'village solidarity' in 1916, there is clear evidence of the existence of elements of a village community ordered by the caste hierarchy, under the dominance of the Reddiars. There was an overlap between the authority that the Reddiars held by virtue of their economic dominance, and that deriving from the state for the Reddiars also supplied the village headman (the munsiff). BL himself was the munsiff from some time in the early 1950s until 1967, when he had to resign on becoming an MLA, and the position passed to another of the Reddiars. The authority of the Reddiars is reflected in the title given locally to the family of BL, that of the 'Kambattan Reddiar'. The meaning of 'kambattan' is obscure. It may mean something like 'the one on a pedestal', but it was also said to mean 'the one who pays taxes'. The big house that BL still occupies when he is in the village, rather than in his house in one of older, once very fashionable parts of the city of Chennai, is known as 'the Collector's House'. This might perhaps be a reference to the fact that District Collectors stayed in the house on their tours (it was originally a guest house, constructed in 1901, when the main house was on the other side of the road), but it could also be a reference to the role of the Reddiar landlords in the collection of the land revenue.

The account given by Guhan and Mencher shows just how extensive was the power of BL in 1981, in spite of land reform legislation and the years of DMK government. He owned at least a third, and perhaps more, of the village lands, and about a third of the private irrigation assets of the village so that he alone had succeeded in privatising an important share of the groundwater resources of Iruvelpattu. He employed a large number of the agricultural labourers of the village, a good number of them still as padials. BL also accounted for about 70 per cent of the land that was then still held on lease, much of it given out to people who worked for him; he owned the land sites of about half of the dalit colony and had succeeded in resisting efforts to grant the rights to their house sites to these people, while he had also blocked efforts to secure milch cattle loans for the dalits under the Integrated Rural Development Scheme of the time; as we have seen he owned what had once been common resources—the fish and the reeds in the tank. Thanks to his influence wage rates were lower in Iruvelpattu than in surrounding villages. He owned 35 or so houses, and was the landlord for the salaried people temporarily resident in the village. Important visitors to the area were always his guests. The official panchayat of the village that functioned between 1957 and 1977 had had only one president during all this time, a man who worked for BL, and all the other members of the panchayat were his nominees, including the two Harijan members. The village accountant, the karnam, was an old client of his. He himself was a strong supporter of Congress, and had served as the Congress MLA for the constituency between 1967 and 1971, and as the District Congress President between 1974 and 1980. For a long time he was able to forbid the flying of the flags of any of the other parties, and to ban the wearing of a dhoti with a red and black border, the colours of the DMK, though this had changed a little by 1981, by which time the Congress party in the state had to ally with others.

On the other side of this picture of extensive, almost absolute authority, there is the evidence of BL's patronage of the village in Guhan and Mencher's account. He always contributed substantially to the costs of temple renovation and of the running of village festivals, even in the dalit colony. He had secured the Primary Health Care centre for the village, and a veterinary sub-centre during the time in which he was the MLA; he had been instrumental in getting a new school building, and the piped water supply for the caste village. Unsurprisingly, given the extent of his authority, he was also turned to for help on different occasions, including for the resolution of personal disputes. It was customary for him to give half a bag of paddy on the occasions of weddings and funerals in the caste village. Much of this benevolence—paternalistic patronage—of course, did not extend to the cheri, but he clearly 'looked after' his people there, ensuring compliance, whilst still enforcing rigid caste discrimination. Still in 1981 dalits were not permitted to wear chappals in the village street or to enter the teashop if a caste Hindu was present, or to receive water in a cup.

As Guhan and Mencher suggested would be the case, it is very interesting to reflect on what has changed over the last quarter of the 20th century. BL is still there, of course, and we've seen that he still owns a large share of the village lands, though he himself admits to having sold off land gradually. He no longer leases out land and he employs few padials, describing them only as irrigation watchmen (which may be fair). He still owns houses but lets most of them out on a grace and favour basis, and he has had to surrender his control over house sites in the dalit colony. Dalits are no longer forbidden from entering the village wearing chappals, though it is likely that few of them venture across the main road unless they absolutely have to—the separation between the two worlds of the *uur* and the *cheri* described by Slater remains. BL no longer controls the formerly common resources of fish and reeds from the tank (which have passed into state control). His authority is no longer absolute and he can no longer command labour as he once did. This substantially accounts for his decisions to cut out sugar cane cultivation and to switch over large areas of his lands to casuarina production. Yet, it is still the case that he is able to pay lower wages than anyone else, or to secure an extra hour of work for the same rate as that paid by others. And he still exercises significant influence in village politics. If he had succeeded by 1981 in replacing village solidarity by hegemony, BL had lost his hegemonic position by 2008, yet still held considerable power. With the apparently final loss of power by the Congress in government in Tamil Nadu, he no longer, nor for a long time, had had such good contacts with the administration as once was the case. And yet on one morning when we were talking with him and the panchayat union chairman arrived to pay his respects, BL kept the man waiting outside until such time as our discussion had come to an end.

The Village Panchayat and the Gram Sabha

The panchayati raj system of local self-government has been revived in Tamil Nadu following the passage of the 73rd Amendment to the Constitution of India in 1993. The village panchayat, with six members and a president, is now reserved as one to be headed by a member of the Scheduled Castes, and the last elections were held in 2006. There are now four Vanniyar members and two dalits, and the President is a dalit widow (whose husband worked in the office of the Agricultural Extension Officer at the block headquarters—his position now having been taken over by his eldest son). According to her own account and that of others, there were large numbers of candidates put up for the position of president in the 2006 elections (some said 16, others 13), with different ones from amongst them being supported by different people from the caste village. There seems to have been a deliberate policy of proliferation in order to divide and rule. The president—supported covertly, or perhaps not, by BL—spoke of having sold land in order to finance her campaign for election, of having given Rs 100 per vote, and of having spent one lakh on liquor. By 2008 the dalit colony was rife with stories of her corruption (though in supposedly 'face-to-face' village society, such accusations appear always to be common).

The upshot of the elections and of subsequent events is that the village as a whole is divided into what are effectively two factions. There are supporters of the panchayat president, in both the colony and the caste village, and they are opposed by those of the vice-president, a Vanniyar. We saw this division in a meeting of the gram sabha, called by the president, following the instruction of the District Collector and the Panchayat Union, in October 2008. The meeting began at about 10 in the morning in the open space beside the village school and it was attended by about 150 people, including some Vanniyars and more dalits, perhaps because the latter had been encouraged to attend by the promise of Rs 50 from the president on the previous day. Several panchayat union officials were in attendance, and four policeman. The meeting became noisy and contentious right from the start when demands were made to have the agenda for the meeting announced. Then the vice-president, a Vanniyar, demanded to know from the president what had happened to the house taxes that she had collected. He claimed that she had collected Rs 16,000 but—brandishing papers in support of his point—he claimed that she had deposited only Rs 5,000. At this point the meeting degenerated into a shouting match between the supporters of the president and those of the vice-president, with dalits on both sides. Efforts by the panchayat officials and by the police to restore order failed, and eventually the crowd dispersed. Later in the day the president went into Villupuram to file a case with the police against the vice-president and his supporters.[10]

It may have been true at the time of Slater's visit to Iruvelpattu that the village was perhaps unusual in not being divided into factions, but it is now. The division of the panchayat allows space in which BL can continue to exercise power.

Dalit Politics and a 'Social Revolution' in Iruvelpattu?

Slater noted the very clear distinction between the 'pariah village' and the caste village of Iruvelpattu, and we have seen that it is a division that has persisted through into the new century. Guhan and Mencher in concluding their study in 1981, summarised the disparities between the 'caste Hindus' and those they referred to as the 'Harijans' of Iruvelpattu, disparities that are the more striking for the fact that the 'caste Hindus' in this case are mostly Vanniyars, who are classified as a 'Most Backward Class', and whose political party the Pattali Makkal Katchi regularly proclaims the poverty and the disabilities that are suffered by the members of this numerous caste community of northern Tamil Nadu. At that time the Dalits/Harijans owned as little as three per cent of the village lands, as little of other agricultural assets and very few of them were cultivators; hardly any of them owned even the sites on which they had their poor houses; and while the literacy rates across the village as a whole were poor they were 'abysmal' amongst the Harijans, and especially amongst the women … the facts that we have recounted in this paper. But we have also shown that over the past quarter century some very major changes have taken place. To speak of a 'social revolution' as having taken place is certainly to overstate the case, but some historically profound changes have come about. The dalits of Iruvelpattu now do own a little more land than before, and one or two of them have been able to acquire significant productive assets; they own their house sites now; fewer of them are dependent upon agricultural wage work, or upon the grace and favour of BL; their literacy levels have risen very significantly, and the gap between them and the caste Hindus with respect to literacy has been greatly improved; they no longer tolerate the kind of day-to-day discrimination to which they were subject (though this is of course not to say that discrimination has disappeared or that they are not still subject to all manner of abuse). Times have changed, though conditions in the cheri of Iruvelpattu still make a mockery of the notion of 'India shining'.

Change has been driven significantly by the tightening of rural labour markets that has come about, with greater physical mobility, better information and more education, and the opening up of some new employment opportunities. The changes are expressed most clearly in what we consider to be the most striking of all, which is the increase in real agricultural wages, in spite of the relative stagnation of the agricultural economy. At last wages have broken through the historic ceiling on agricultural wages of around the equivalent of three kg of raw foodgrains per day, that showed the power of the dominant controllers of agricultural surplus to depress real wages (Tomlinson 1988). That power has at last been broken. We should not neglect the role that government policy has played in this, not by any direct intervention in the labour market but through welfare provision, especially through maintaining a public distribution system with more or less universal access, and now through the introduction of the National Rural Employment Guarantee scheme (about which landowners complain bitterly, arguing that this scheme, in combination with the availability of ration rice at very low prices reduces all incentives for people to work).

But the changes that have come about have to do not only with the consequences of the tightening of the rural labour market. There is also politics. Guhan and Mencher explain that soon after the completion of their fieldwork, early in 1982, there came about an unprecedented mobilisation of the dalits of Iruvelpattu. This was as the result of the return to the village of a young man whom they describe as 'One of the Harijan boys, an unemployed SSLC …' who, with the support of his educated brothers, organised an Ambedkar Sangam, and succeeded—against the opposition of BL—in taking out a padyatra to the office of the District Collector in Cuddalore, and presenting a petition with a set of demands. These were the long-standing demands of the dalits, going back even to Slater's time—for their own school, for house sites, for a proper drinking water supply, for repairs to the road to the colony and to their few street lights, for repairs to their temple, for a balwadi—a crèche where the many working dalit women could leave their children, and for adult education. After this it seemed that BL had at least partially acquiesced in the existence of the sangam and promised—and in fact gave—funds for the repair of the temple. It remained to be seen, said the researchers, whether this dose of 'opium to the people' would work.

Has it? Or has the political mobilisation of the dalits continued and deepened? The answer to both these questions is perhaps the vague one of 'a bit'. This is to say that the dalits have continued to assert themselves much more than in the past but that those who led the Ambedkar Sangam—who are members of the Republican Party of India—have not succeeded in realising all their aims. They pursued a case against the Reddiar over house sites from 1985 through to 1995 before they finally won, and as we have said, secured the allocation of, in the end 250 pattas. In 1984 they put up a candidate in the elections of that year to the Legislative Assembly, which was an action that in the end provoked an open confrontation with Vanniyars. If Guhan and Mencher were right about the absence of any major conflict between the two communities this situation changed in 1984. A clash came about over the removal of an RPI pandal and flag. In the upshot the cheri was attacked by Vanniyars, but the latter were then encircled by the dalits, with reinforcement from Villupuram. Ever since then the dalit activists have kept up their opposition to the Reddiar and to the Vanniyars whom he has supported in successive elections. But they have not been able to maintain a united front, as is shown up all too clearly in the story of the division of the panchayat and of the factionalism that extends into the cheri. So the dalit political mobilisation has been compromised. Yet we should not underestimate the significance of the change in attitudes amongst the cheri people that have been encouraged by this political activism, and have contributed in some measure to what the larger Reddiar and Vanniyar landowners describe as 'the labour problem', and the breaking of that historic ceiling on real agricultural wages.

CONCLUSION

This short account of the history of one village in Tamil Nadu through the Twentieth Century presents a kind of kaleidoscope. Viewed from one angle little seems to have changed: the built environment of the village in 2009 is not radically different from that observed by Slater in 1916; Iruvelpattu remains an agricultural village centred on paddy cultivation; the highway still marks a boundary between the two different worlds of the caste village and the cheri, and caste identities remain a powerful factor in daily life and in politics; the dalits are still heavily dependent upon agricultural labour for their livelihoods, and may be subjected still, to all manner of abuse; poverty may not be as acute as it was but levels of living are still very low; and the village remains subject to the dominance of the same Reddiar family that owns less of the village lands than it used to, no doubt, but still a very major share of them. Viewed from another side, however, it appears a very different world: access to services has been transformed by state investments in schools, in health services, in drinking water supply and in electricity; there has been an extraordinary diversification of employment, linked with the mobility of the population in India's most urbanised state; and these changes have provided some of the conditions for the empowerment of the dalits. Another way of looking at the recent history of the village is to say that it reflects all the contradictions of present-day Tamil Nadu: a state with a comparatively high level of public provisioning (save in regard to sanitation), and relatively high levels of 'human development', but one in which old power structures remain deeply entrenched, and the disabilities of 'untouchability' remarkably persistent, in spite of many years of government by political parties that descend from a leader, Periyar, who espoused an agenda of social reform. No great social transformation is in evidence.

Iruvelpattu is of course not a 'representative' village, though it does fairly represent the general failure of the implementation of land reform in Tamil Nadu. But here too, as was generally the case in the state in the Twentieth Century, the agricultural economy was penetrated by capitalist relations of production, and these relations were internalised in the organisation of small-scale farming. 'Landlordism' in the classic sense—with the dominant controller of land appropriating surplus from tenant cultivators—persisted in Iruvelpattu perhaps longer than elsewhere, but it had passed well before the end of the century, even if the landlord remained powerful. Guhan and Mencher's account of it from more or less the height of the 'green revolution' years, shows that the village saw trends that were observed very widely, as a small class of rich peasants developed, here amongst the Vanniyars.

At the time that Guhan and Mencher undertook their study, CT Kurien published a major analysis of the dynamics of rural transformation in Tamil Nadu, in which he argued that the state had experienced significant growth in the agricultural economy 'without major structural changes'. He went on, however, to say that 'in another sense a quiet structural transformation has been going on in rural Tamil Nadu. The main feature of this transformation is the tendency of small farmers to leave land and farming to join the ranks of the rural proletariat' (1980: 389). In other words he thought that a process of proletarianisation was taking place, and associated it with a tendency for mass poverty to persist and even increase, partly because of the decline in the real wages of agricultural labourers. These trends have only partly been observed in Iruvelpattu over the last quarter century. 'Proletarianisation' is perhaps reflected in the increased numbers of landless households, but small scale farming has continued to reproduce itself, and there are indications as we have shown, of an historic shift in agricultural wage rates. What has rather gone on in the village, as has been the case very widely indeed across the world, is what Bernstein refers to as 'the *fragmentation* of labour' (2004: 204). As he puts it: 'Classes of labour in the conditions of today's 'South' have to pursue their reproduction through insecure and oppressive—and typically increasingly scarce—wage employment and/or a range of likewise precarious small-scale and insecure 'informal sector' ('survival') activity, including farming; in effect, various and complex *combinations* of employment and self-employment' (2010, mss)—'spread across different sites of the social division of labour: urban and rural, agricultural and non-agricultural' (2004: 205). This describes rather well the increasingly complex, highly diversified ways in which the very mobile people of Iruvelpattu secure their livelihoods across a geographically wide range of locations—reflected in the fact that, walking round the village on most days, one sees large numbers of houses locked up with no-one there. The village is just one, possibly quite minor site, in the livelihood spaces of village people these days.

What may distinguish Iruvelpattu and rural Tamil Nadu generally from other parts of 'today's 'South'', including much of the rest of India, is the level of state intervention in the interests of social security—through primary health care provision, and schools in which teachers are actually present, and through the maintenance of a universal public distribution system, as well now as the operation of the National Rural Employment Guarantee. These have made for some improvement in well-being in the last quarter century (as Djurfeldt et al. also find 2008) and for such political change as has occurred—and that has played a part, in turn, in ensuring the delivery of welfare provisioning.

Notes

1. We note some renewal of interest in the pages of the *Economic and Political Weekly*, with the publication of articles such as that, with particular reference to Tamil Nadu, by Djurfeldt et al. (2008)—with the findings of which we find many similarities in Iruvelpattu. With regard especially to village studies, the Foundation for Agrarian Studies (www.agrarianstudies.org), is carrying out an ambitious programme of work in all the major states.

2. Their limitations include the lack, in some cases, of comparability of data across survey points, and in general the fact that the five villages in the set—unsurprisingly, given that the initial selection was based on students studying economics in Madras in 1916—are all relatively well connected, with significant higher caste communities: Brahmins in two of the villages, Brahmins and Naidus in another, Nayakars in one other, and Reddiars in Iruvelpattu.

3. The study, including a complete listing of households and a sample survey of the economics of cultivation, was carried out in 2008 and in the earlier part of 2009 with the assistance of a team including G Jothi, who was one of those who worked with Guhan and Mencher in 1981, Kumar, Lenin and Anbu Pakyaraj. We are very grateful to them all. We ourselves visited the village for several days at a time on three occasions in 2007–8.

4. Guhan and Mencher present convincing reasons for thinking this figure was somewhat exaggerated, and suggest that it is more likely to have been around 350 acres.

5. The rate of Rs 60 + meal was for work from 9-12 for men, and that of Rs 35 for work for women from 9-1. The wage rate for a full working day (9-5) for men was Rs 150 with a meal.

6. These conversions are based on the prices of Rs 5-600 per bag of paddy that obtained in 2008 for paddy of middling quality. For a finer variety like Ponni the rates were much higher.

7. Known locally as the 'One Hundred Days Work Scheme', NREGA was introduced into Iruvelpattu in July 2008, when we saw work going on in the de-silting of the village tank. Reportedly in this first phase the project went on for 18 days and generated 3000 person days of employment at Rs 65 per day (and so cost about Rs 2 lakhs). Both the caste Hindus of the village (most of whom—the Vanniyars—are scheduled as Most Backward Class) and Dalits participated. Eighty per cent of the participants were women (the rate of Rs 65 per day being unattractive for men). A further, more substantial project, for clearing the channel supplying the tank, was started in September 2008.

8. Our calculations here are as follows. Following Guhan and Mencher we take it that the daily calorie requirements of a working adult (one 'consumption unit') can be supplied by 400 gm of rice. We assume, like them, that the average household includes members who are not full consumption units, being young or old, non-working members, and so we take

it that the household includes four consumption units, therefore requiring 1.6 kg of rice per day. The 1,050 kg of paddy that we think is the likely average annual income equivalent of the combined wages of an agricultural labouring household will produce about 700 kg of rice, which means that the household will have available 1.9-2.00 kg of rice per day, about 20 per cent more than the requirement of cereals. This is pretty much the poverty line according to most ways of thinking about these measures.

9. Apart from the main festival the other principal festivals of the caste village of Iruvelpattu are, now as in 1916, Vinayaka Chatturti, celebrated in the month of *aavani*, dedicated to Vinayaka, and *panguni uttram*, dedicated to Murugan.

10. We are grateful to G. Jothi for this description.

References

Ananthpur, K. and M. Moore. 2007. *Ambiguous Institutions: Traditional Governance and Local Democracy in Rural India*. Working Paper No 282. Brighton: Institute of Development Studies.

Baker, C. J. 1975. *The Politics of South India, 1920–1937*. Cambridge: Cambridge University Press.

Baker, C. J. 1984. *An Indian Rural Economy, 1880–1955: The Tamilnad Countryside*. Oxford: Clarendon Press.

Bernstein, H. 2004. '"Changing Before Our Very Eyes": Agrarian Questions and the Politics of Land in Capitalism Today'. *Journal of Agrarian Change* 4 (1–2): 190–225.

———. 2010. 'Rural Livelihood and Agrarian Change: Bringing Class Back'. In *Rural Transformations and Development*, ed. N. Long, Y. Jungzhong and W. Yihu. Cheltenham: Edward Elgar.

Djurfeldt, G. et al. 2008. 'Agrarian Change and Social Mobility in Tamil Nadu'. *Economic and Political Weekly* 43 (45): 50–61, 8 November.

Guhan, S. and J. Mencher. 1983. 'Iruvelpattu Revisited'. *Economic and Political Weekly* 18 (23–24).

Harriss, J. 1982. *Capitalism and Peasant Farming: Agrarian Structure and Ideology in Northern Tamil Nadu*. Bombay: Oxford University Press.

Haswell, M. 1967. *Economics of Development in Village India*. London: Routledge and Kegan Paul.

Kurien, C. T. 1980. 'Dynamics of Rural Transformation: A Case Study of Tamil Nadu'. *Economic and Political Weekly* 15 (5–7): 365–90.

Manikumar, K. A. 2003. *Colonial Economy in the Great Depression: Madras (1929–37)*. Hyderabad: Orient Longman.

Slater, G. 1918. *Some South Indian Villages*. Oxford: Oxford University Press.

Thomas, P. J. and K. C. Ramakrishnan. 1940. *Some South Indian Villages: A Resurvey*. Madras Economics Series No 4. Madras: University of Madras.

Tomlinson, B. 1988. 'The Historical Roots of Indian Poverty: Issues in the Economic and Social History of Modern South Asia'. *Modern Asian Studies* 22: 123–40.

16

Common Property Resources and Rural Poor in Dry Regions of India*

N. S. Jodha

Introduction

An important factor completely disregarded by development policies and programmes in India is the role of common property resources in the economy of rural people, particularly of the rural poor. Common property resources (CPRs), broadly speaking are the resources accessible to the whole community of a village and to which no individual has exclusive property rights. In the dry regions of India, they include village pastures, community forests, waste lands, common threshing grounds, waste dumping places, watershed drainages, village ponds, tanks, rivers/rivulets, and riverbeds, etc.[1] Despite their significant contributions to the economy of rural people, these resources have seldom received enough attention of planners. The important reasons are: (a) Rural development planning has largely emphasised private property resource (PPR) centred activities, be it the promotion of high-yielding crop varieties, or distribution of cross-bred cattle, or supply of electricity for groundwater lifting devices;[2] (b) Inadequate understanding of the survival mechanisms used by the poor as well as the complementarities between CPRs and PPR-based activities in rural areas; (c) The contributions of CPRs are not only numerous and varied but they are often available as a matter of routine. Consequently, they often go unnoticed by rural researchers as well as by development planners. This paper, based on household and village data from 21 dry tropical districts in seven states in India, attempts to quantify some of the contributions of CPRs with special reference to the rural poor whose dependence on CPRs (excluding water-based CPRs used through irrigation) is greater than that of the well-to-do villagers. The paper also examines the changing status of CPRs, especially its impact on the rural poor. After commenting on the methods used

* This chapter has been extracted from a longer paper published by the author in the *Economic and Political Weekly* 21 (27): 1167–81, 5 July 1986.

for selection of areas and collection of field data in Section II, the paper briefly describes in Section III general benefits accruing to the rural people from CPRs. Section IV presents evidence on rural households' dependence on CPRs, as well as on employment and income generated by CPRs. Section V deals with the changes in the status of CPRs, particularly the decline in the areas of selected CPRs, and how it has affected the rural poor.[...]

CPRs and Their Contributions to Rural Economy

To understand the significant role played by CPRs in the life and economy of rural people, we briefly highlight the general benefits offered by CPRs. The way in which these benefits and contributions emanate from different CPRs, is elaborated by Jodha (1985a) and are briefly indicated below (Table 16.1).

(1) Through supply of fodder and grazing space some CPRs help individuals in saving their land for crops. Put differently, these CPRs help in sustaining a number of animals for draft and livestock production which would not have been permitted by individuals' owned land, especially for small farmers.
(2) CPRs like dry beds of rivers/tanks used for off season cropping and rivulets, tanks used to collect irrigation water, play an important resource-augmenting role in the PPR-based farming system.
(3) The traditional farming systems in dry areas partly derive their stability and viability through an integrated production strategy involving crops, livestock, trees/bushes, the latter being less sensitive to temporal variability of rains. Village forests, grazing lands, rivulets, and watershed drainages play a significant role in this strategy.
(4) CPRs, as sources of both physical supplies as well as employment and income, cushion dryland farmers' welfare during crisis periods, e.g., droughts.
(5) Rural inequalities generated by the PPR-based farming system are partly reduced by CPRs as the resource-poor households (unlike the rich), significantly supplement their income from CPRs. CPRs also greatly contribute to the poor man's nutrition by facilitating his food gathering from forests, ponds, and other sources and strengthening his self-provisioning system.
(6) Management of CPRs should be an integral component of resource-centred prospective technologies and development strategies directed at conservation and better use of waste lands and the environment in the dry regions.[...]

Rural Poor's Dependence on CPRs

Dependence of a community on CPRs can be indicated in several ways. They include the proportion of households making use of CPRs, per household average number and type of benefits derived from CPRs, or actual extent of benefits in cash or kind received from CPRs.

Table 16.1 summarises some details that indicate the dependence of rural households on CPRs in the study villages.[3] Between 84 per cent and 100 per cent of the poor households gathered food, fuel, fodder, and fibre items from CPRs. In contrast, just 10–28 per cent of large farmers depended on CPRs for these items. However, a greater proportion of large farmers collected items like silt from CPRs, eg, ponds to enrich soils of their fields, and timber (mature trees from the village forest that are not legally allowed to be cut) for their private use. Though not indicated in the table, the households who freely used water from rivulets for irrigating their land did not include 'poor' households.

The number of CPR-based activities as well as the number of CPR products collected[4] by respondents, as reported and physically verified in most cases, were also higher for poor households compared to the rich households (Table 16.1).[...]

Firstly, the poor households have high man-to-land ratios and in most cases high animal-to-land ratios, and CPRs indirectly provide an important means for adjusting factor proportions in farming systems. CPRs, through grazing space and cut fodder/fuel, help the poor households to devote all of their land area to food or cash crops rather than sparing part of it for fodder/fuel supplies. Similarly, the CPRs' role as a cushion during the crisis situation, non-crop season or drought period, is greater for the poor households, as unlike the rich, they do not have many other adjustment mechanisms (Jodha 1985a).

Secondly and more importantly, poor households' dependence on CPRs is reinforced by some degree of match between the characteristics of CPR-based activities and features of the labour endowment of the poor. For instance, the extraction cost or cost of using CPRs, except the lifting of water from rivulets or wells, is quite low and the main input required in the process is human labour. This matches very well with the labour surplus resource position of the poor. Furthermore, because of over use and degradation, the returns from CPRs to individual users, in most cases, are not very high and are unattractive for the rich. However, poor households, with surplus labour and low opportunity cost, readily accept the low pay-off activities possible through CPRs.[...]

Additionally, most of the CPR-based activities, except collection of seasonal fruits and spices, are neither time bound nor full-time jobs and workers can engage in them without sacrificing alternative employment opportunities. Specific skills for harvesting CPRs are not required, except in the case of collection of honey, fish from ponds, and game from forests, and even unemployable members of the family such as young children and old people can help. Thus, a self-selection process of CPR users, governed by low pay off from CPR use and still lower opportunity cost of labour of the users, initiates and perpetuates the poor's dependence on these resources.

The oral histories revealed that in the past, until CPRs became very 'unproductive', large farmers' dependence on CPRs was also greater. Even today in areas like Madhya Pradesh, where CPRs continue to be more productive, proportionately more of large farmers depend on CPRs than in many other regions.

Table 16.1 also reveals considerable inter-regional differences in households' dependence on CPRs in terms of the number of CPR items collected and CPR-based activities followed. Without information on volume or value of these entities, they are at best crude indicators of relative dependence of households on CPRs

TABLE 16.1: The Location and Agro-climanc Features of the Areas Covered by the CPR Study in the Dry Regions of India[1]

State/District	Taluka/Tehsil	No. of Villages	Rainfall[2] mm	Soil Type[3]	Proportion of CPRs to Total Area of Villages (Per cent)	Density of Rural Population[4]		
						Persons/Km[2] of Total Area in		Person/10 ha of CPRs Area in the Village
						Taluka	Villages	
Andhra Pradesh								
Anantapur	Anantapur	2	563	A-L, G	15	90	106	71
Mahbubnagar	Athmakur, Kalvakurthi, Mahabubnagar	5	721	A-D, A-L	9	124	162	186
Medak	Medak	3	834	A-D, V-D	11	177	158	145
Gujarat								
Banaskantha	Kankrej, Vadgam	5	655	S	10	210	201	205
Mehsana	Sidhpur, Vijapur	5	633	S	11	340	332	301
Sabarkantha	Prantij	5	739	S, V-M	12	238	253	208
Karnataka								
Bidar	Balki, Bidar, Humnabad	3	907	A-M, A-D	12	162	137	113
Dharwar	Kalghatagi	3	691	A-M	10	134	156	154
Gulbarga	Gulbarga	3	702	V-M, A-D	9	106	129	146
Mysore	Gundulupet	3	680	A-M	18	106	103	55
Madhya Pradesh								
Mandsaur	Mandsaur	4	847	V-M	22	142	116	51
Raisen	Gairatgunj	6	1181	V-M	23	82	91	41
Vidisha	Vidisha	4	1134	V-M, V-I	28	91	98	38

Contd.

Table 16.1 Contd.

State/District	Taluka/Tehsil	No. of Villages	Rainfall[2] mm	Soil Type[3]	Proportion of CPRs to Total Area of Villages (Per cent)	Density of Rural Population[4]		
						Persons/Km² of Total Area in		Person/10 ha of CPRs Area in the Village
						Taluka	Villages	
Maharashtra								
Alola	Mangrulpir, Murtizapur	5	840	V-M	11	116	145	130
Aurangabad	Aurangabad	4	727	V-M, G	15	128	114	76
Sholapur	Akkalkot, Mohol, Sholapur (N)	4	667	V-D, V-M	19	122	111	59
Rajasthan								
Jalore	Sanchor, Bhinmal	5	421	S	18	67	98	54
Jodhpur	Jodhpur	3	319	S	16	68	81	50
Nagaur	Jayal	3	389	S, G	15	71	73	48
Tamil Nadu								
Coimbatore	Coimbatore, Palladam	4	718	A-L, S	9	250	361	402
Dharmapuri	Dharmapuri, Pennagaram	3	844	A-L, S	12	286	210	169

Notes: (1) Based on district, taluka and village records and field work in the villages during 1982–85.
(2) Average annual rainfall of the nearest rain gauge stations of the study villages.
(3) *Soil types*: S = Sandy and/or sandy loam, G = Gravelly, A = Alfisol (red soils), V = Vertisol (black soils), D = Deep, M = Medium deep, L = Shallow.
(4) Population and area data relate to 1981.

in different regions. Yet, they do indicate considerable interregional variation, e.g., Madhya Pradesh or Rajasthan compared with Maharashtra or Tamil Nadu. Several factors individually or jointly help explain the above differences. Factors operating on the supply side of CPR products include

(1) overall greater size of CPRs (as in the case of Madhya Pradesh and Rajasthan);
(2) higher productivity of CPRs, in terms of type and quantity of produce, as in the case of Madhya Pradesh where village forests and waste lands offer good supplies;
(3) availability of high value products like honey, gum, spices, soapnuts, and fish as in some villages of Madhya Pradesh, Maharashtra, and Karnataka; and
(4) coinciding of CPR-product availability with the labour surplus period, e.g., in Rajasthan when a number of wild fruits like *ker* and *sangari* become available in the summer.

The factors operating on the demand side of CPR products include the general inadequacy of the household's own resources to sustain the family, as seen in many poor families of Madhya Pradesh, Tamil Nadu and Andhra Pradesh in particular; greater profitability of PPR-based activities that are supported by CPRs, e.g., poor man's dairying in Gujarat and sheep/goat rearing in Rajasthan; easy marketability of CPR products, like minor forest products, fuel, fodder, etc., in Tamil Nadu, Karnataka and Maharashtra; distress caused by drought or crop failure which compelled people to depend on CPRs to a greater extent as in some villages of Rajasthan, Tamil Nadu and Karnataka.[5][...]

CPRs as Source of Fuel

Table 16.1 gave broad indications of poor people's significant dependence on CPRs for collection of fuel and other supplies. Information about fuel requirements met from CPRs and other sources is presented in Table 16.2. Actual fuel consumption (kg of dry weight) by a limited number of households was monitored for one week during each of the three seasons in VLS villages. Though family size was more or less the same, the average quantity of fuel consumption by large farm households was substantially higher, ranging from 185 to 219 kg for 3 weeks compared to poor households, ranging from 104 to 185 kg for 3 weeks.[6]

The results in Table 16.2 further show that poor households met 66–84 per cent of their fuel requirements from CPRs. The corresponding figure for large farmers ranged between 8 per cent and 13 per cent except in Raisen in Madhya Pradesh, where large farmers also gathered and used considerable amount of fuel from CPRs. The poor households collected fuel material (including dung) from CPRs in small quantities almost throughout the year. Large farmers cut and collected bushes from CPRs at the end of the monsoon, initially for purpose of fencing and using them as fuel subsequently. Of course, unlike the rural poor the large farm households have relatively self-sustaining fuel supply system where crop by-products and animal dung playa n important role (Table 16.2).

Table 16.2: Benefits From Village Common Property Resources[1]

Benefits	Contributions to Farming Systems[2]	CPRs[3]						
		A	B	C	D	E	F	G
Physical products:								
Food	e, c	✓		✓				
Fodder	a, c, d, c	✓	✓			✓		
Fuel/timber, etc.	a, e	✓	✓	✓		✓	✓	
Water	b, c, d				✓	✓		✓
Manure/silt/space	b, c	✓	✓	✓			✓	
Supplement income/ employment:								
Off-season activities	e, d	✓				✓	✓	
Drought period sustenance	d	✓	✓				✓	
Additional crop activities	b, d			✓	✓		✓	✓
Additional cattle	b, d	✓	✓					
Petty trading/ handicrafts	d, c	✓					✓	
Social gains:								
Resource conversion	f	✓	✓					
Drainage/recharge of G W	f, d, b			✓	✓	✓		
Sustenance of poor	e							
Stability of farming systems		✓	✓	✓				✓
Renewable resource supply	a, b	✓	✓	✓				✓
Better micro-climate/environment	d	✓	✓		✓			

Notes: (1) Table adopted from Jodha (1985a).

(2) The benefits can be regarded as contributions to private property resource (PPR) based farming systems and can be classified under categories (a) Resource saving for PPR based farming systems, (b) Resource augmentation for farming systems, (c) Fuller use of environment, (d) Seasonal buffer and stability of farming systems, (e) Rural equities and nutrition, and (f) Importance in resource-centred technology.

(3) CPRs A = Community forest, B = Pasture/waste land, C = Pond/tank, D = River/rivulet, E = Watershed drainage/river banks, F = River/tank beds, G = Ground-water.

Dependence for Animal Grazing

After fuel, fodder is the major item for which practically every poor household depends on CPRs. However, the extent of dependence on CPRs for fodder will be far greater if animal grazing, along with the collection of odder, is also considered.

Accurate recording of information on the extent of grazing is a complex and difficult task. Nevertheless, monitoring of animal grazing for a small number of households was attempted in the selected villages for one week in each season. That information is summarised in Table 16.3. The procedure used for monitoring animal grazing days and their conversion into animal unit grazing days is described in footnote 1 of Table 16.3.

Except in Jalore and Nagaur districts of Rajasthan, where livestock raising was a major occupation, poor households had fewer animal unit grazing days than the large farm households. However, the proportion of animal unit grazing days provided through CPRs for poor households was two to three times higher compared to the large farmers in all districts except Raisen. Jalore, Nagaur and Raisen are the only areas where CPRs were used to meet more than 35 per cent of the grazing requirements of large farmers. Availability of better grazing material or larger grazing space besides the limited extent of stall feeding practised in the areas, determined these interregional differences in grazing on CPRs by large farmers (Jodha 1985b). Mehsana and Sabarkantha were at the other extreme, where large farmers' dependence on CPRs for grazing only reached 15 per cent. In these areas, dairying was well developed and livestock management, involving higher extent of stall feeding, was also improved. Consequently, dependence on degraded common grazing lands had significantly declined. Moreover, in Gujarat, as in some other areas, privatised CPR lands received by large farmers were used for grazing only.

The poor households' greater dependence on CPRs for grazing is mainly because they do not own grazing land. Furthermore, they owned, a larger proportion of currently unproductive animals, including those through the salvage system,[7] such as young stock, dry milch stock, which were sustained through free grazing on degraded pastures. Moreover, poor people also owned more sheep and goats which were able to survive on degraded pastures, on which cattle could barely subsist.[...]

Employment Generation

CPRs are not only a source of physical supplies for the rural people. CPRs also greatly contribute to employment and income of the rural people. Depending on the type of worker, the CPR-based activity, and the season, employment through CPRs may be both a continuous or an irregular activity.[...]

Income Generation by CPRs

It is quite difficult to translate all the supplies and services offered by CPRs into income flows. Furthermore, since most of the CPR-based activities have a low pay-off, their contribution to monetary income may not be high. However, the importance of income received from the use of CPRs should be evaluated more in terms of its temporal and situational contexts, rather than in terms of its magnitude alone. Only two components of CPR-based income are discussed here. They are income from CPR product collection'[8] and proportion of income from animal husbandry that

TABLE 16.3: Indicators or Rural Households Dependence on CPRs in the Study Villages in Dry Areas or Seven States of India[1]

Details	States (Study Districts, Villages)													
	Andhra Pradesh (2,5)		Gujarat (3,6)		Karnataka (3,7)		Madhya Pradesh (3,7)		Maharashtra (3,6)		Rajasthan (3,7)		Tamil Nadu (2,4)	
Category of households	Poor[2]	Others[2]	Poor	Others	Poor	Others	Poor	Others	Poor	Others	Poor	Others	Poor	Others
Number of households	65	41	84	62	64	33	98	72	102	64	72	64	48	23
Per cent households collecting CPR products:														
Food items	95	10	96	16	84	14	100	18	98	13	100	23	93	12
Fuel, fodder, fibre	99	15	100	19	100	18	100	11	100	16	100	28	100	17
Timber, silt, etc.	37	59	29	83	41	78	21	84	19	90	31	89	92	42
Per household average number of:														
CPR based activities[3]	4	2	5	2	5	3	6	3	3	2	5	2	4	3
CPR items collected[4]	7	4	8	3	7	4	12	5	7	3	10	5	6	3

Notes: (1) Based on field surveys during 1983–85.

(2) 'Poor' households include agricultural labourers and small farm (<2 ha of dry land equivalent) households. 'Others' include large farm households only.

(3) Activities included product collection, grazing, processing and handicrafts based on CPR products and marketing of CPR products.

(4) Items included fuel, fodder, various wild fruits and flower, roots, leaves and skin of plants and trees, honey, gum, fish, small game, silt and clay, etc., for more details (including prices of these items) see Jodha (1985a).

TABLE 16.4: Average Annual Household Income from CPRs in the Study Villages of Selected Districts in the Dry Regions of India[1]

District[2]	Per Household Annual Average Income in the Case of[3]							
	Poor				Others			
	Households (Number)	Value of CPR-Products Collected (Rupees)	CPR-Share in Livestock Income (Rupees)	Total (Rupees)	Households (Rupees)	Value of CPR-Products Collected (Rupees)	CPR-Share in Livestock Income (Rupees)	Total (Rupees)
Mahbubnagar	15	382	153	534 (17)[4]	10	109	62	171 (1)
Mehsana	26	421	309	730 (16)	24	88	74	162 (1)
Sabarkantha	35	432	336	818 (21)	19	111	97	208 (1)
Mysore	26	534	115	649 (20)	11	112	58	170 (3)
Mandsaur	23	400	285	685 (18)	18	113	190	303 (1)
Raisen	37	568	212	780 (26)	15	283	185	468 (4)
Akola	16	342	105	447 (9)	9	85	49	134 (1)
Aurangabad	22	405	179	584 (13)	21	110	53	163 (1)
Sholapur	17	443	198	641 (20)	9	143	92	235 (2)

Contd.

Table 16.4 Contd.

District[2]	Per Household Annual Average Income in the Case of[3]							
	Poor				Others			
	Households (Number)	Value of CPR-Products Collected (Rupees)	CPR-Share in Livestock Income (Rupees)	Total (Rupees)	Households (Rupees)	Value of CPR-Products Collected (Rupees)	CPR-Share in Livestock Income (Rupees)	Total (Rupees)
Jalore	24	447	262	709 (21)	27	170	217	387 (2)
Nagaur	32	473	358	831 (23)	25	143	295	438 (3)
Dharmapuri	30	530	208	738 (22)	11	112	54	164 (2)

Notes: (1) Based on field work during 1982–85.
(2) Number of villages covered in Mahbubnagar, Akola, and Sholapur was one each. In other districts it was two.
(3) CPR income was estimated by valuation of CPR-products collected by the households on the basis of village level prices of those products.
Livestock income attributed to CPRs was estimated on the basis of contribution of CPR grazing to total livestock maintenance. The procedures used, briefly mentioned in the text, tended to underestimate the contribution of CPR grazing to livestock income. In the ease of villages in Mahbubnagar, Akola, Sholapur, Sabarkantha, and Raisen, all incomes were estimated on the basis of cost accounting method, while in others they were based on recalls during three seasonal rounds of field work.
(4) Figures in the parentheses indicate total CPR-based income as per cent to total income from other sources.

is attributable to grazing on CPRs.[9] CPRs' contribution to household income and its stability, through their support to PPR-based crop farming, and processing and marketing of CPR products, are not considered. The income data in Table 16.4, therefore, considerably under-estimate the total income contribution of CPRs.

Average annual income of poor households from CPRs ranged from Rs 445–830 during the reference period. CPR income of large farmers did not exceed Rs 300, except in the Rajasthan and Madhya Pradesh villages. A substantial share of this income originated from CPR product collection in most regions. The exceptions were large farm households in Nagaur, Jalore, and Mandsaur districts where livestock production is important. Except in the Akola and the Aurangabad villages, the CPR-income accounted for 15–23 per cent of total income from all other sources, for the poor households. The corresponding proportions for large farm households were 1–3 per cent only.

In 6 of the 12 study areas, average annual income from CPRs per poor household exceeded Rs 700. CPR income constituted more than a fifth of poor households' income from all other sources in these districts (except Mehsana). In the case of two districts at the bottom, this figure was less than Rs 550. The regional differences in the income from CPRs can be explained in terms of the extent and productivity of CPRs and major activities supported by them. For instance, high CPR income areas like Raisen, Jalore and, to an extent, Nagaur are endowed with larger extent of CPRs (Table 16.1). Similarly, availability of high-value CPR products such as gum, honey, fruits, and game, contributed to higher CPR income in Raisen and Dharmapuri. Poor man's animal husbandry, sustained mainly through CPRs, was responsible for higher CPR income of the poor in households of Nagaur, Mehsana, Sabarkantha and Jalore. Limited area of CPRs and limited number of CPR products on the one hand and greater availability of agricultural employment opportunities due to cotton and paddy dominated cropping patterns on the other, may explain the lower CPR incomes of the poor in the Akola and the Mahbubnagar villages.[10]

Reduction in Income Inequalities

The pattern of inter-class differences in CPR income suggests that CPRs help reduce the rural inequalities. The inequalities of the VLS-household incomes, measured with the Gini coefficient, are reduced when CPR incomes are included in household income (Table 16.5). The values of the Gini coefficient varied from 0.37 to 0.50 in different areas when income from all sources excluding the CPRs was considered. However, once CPR-based income was included in household income, the value of the Gini coefficient declined and ranged between 0.32 and 0.41 in different areas.

In view of the fact that CPRs contribute more than a fifth of the incomes from other sources for the poor, they should be recognised as an integral part of programmes directed towards reduction in rural poverty and inequality. In fact, the CPR-based income works out to Rs 112 per worker in an area like Akola and Rs 243 per worker in Nagaur, even when not all components CPR-related income have been quantified here. If the unaccounted income components are added,

TABLE 16.5: Impact of CPRs on Inequality or Household Incomes in the Study Villages of Selected Districts in the Dry Regions of India'

District and Number of Villages		Mean and Gini Coefficient of Household Income from			
		All Sources		All Sources Excluding CPRs	
		Mean (Rupees)	Gini Coefficient (Per Cent)	Mean (Rupees)	Gini Coefficient (Per Cent)
Mahbubnagar	(1)	7443	0.41	6777	0.50
Akola	(1)	9549	0.40	8928	0.48
Sholapur	(1)	6989	0.32	6008	0.37
Sabarkantha	(2)	9249	0.33	8205	0.45
Raisen	(2)	5186	0.34	4150	0.44

Note: * Based on data (for 1983-84) from panel household covered by the 'VI S. The panel of 40 households from each village included 10 households from each category namely landless labourers, smalt farmers, medium farmers, and larger farmers.

CPR-based income could be much higher in many areas than the per household income generated by a number of anti-poverty programmes.[11]

Changing Status of CPRs

Investigation into the village-level records and oral accounts of the recent past in the study areas indicated that the contribution of CPRs towards the income of the rural poor as well as rural equity was probably much higher in the past than it is at present. Both the area and physical productivity of CPRs, in terms of quantity and quality of products, have declined. We tried to document this change by comparing total CPR output in the early 1980s with the early 1950s, when following the independence, the land reforms were introduced.[12] For, both periods physical productivity of CPRs and their area were recorded. The CPRs covered are: village pastures, village forests, waste lands,[13] unoccupied catchments of ponds, tanks, river banks, watershed drainages, and community threshing grounds.[...]

DECLINE OF CPRS

Decline of CPRs can take three forms:

(1) Physical loss of resources, such as the submersion of grazing land in the newly constructed irrigation dam or area of CPR covered by roads and buildings.

(2) Deterioration of physical productivity of resources, as revealed by degradation of pastures, forest lands.

(3) Re-assignment of usage and property rights as indicated by transfer of CPR lands to private ownership.

As mentioned earlier, the following discussion is confined to the last category of the decline of CPRs.

In the dry areas we studied, CPRs mostly occupy sub-marginal land with undependable water supply. With increased resource scarcity, it can however be expected, that common property rights will be infringed or substituted by de jure or de facto private property rights. In the areas covered by this study, the above substitution of property rights has taken place on a large scale. For instance, during 1982–84, the extent of CPR lands in the study villages ranged from 9–28 per cent of total area (Table 16.6). These proportions ranged between 15 per cent and 42 per cent in 1950–52. The area of CPRs during the last three decades has thus declined by 26–52 per cent.

Details of technological, institutional, and demographic circumstances causing decline in the area of CPRs, and also their physical productivity, have been discussed elsewhere (Jodha 1985a, 1985b). Here we will confine our discussion to those aspects of the decline of CPRs that affect particularly the rural poor. The main form of decline is the privatisation of CPRs.[14] Under various welfare programmes CPR lands had been distributed to people for private use. CPR lands had also been illegally appropriated often with subsequent legalisation. The stated intention of privatisation of CPRs was to give land to the poor who were landless or who had very little land. Hence, from the days of land reforms in early 1950s to the present day, programmes such as the 20-Point Programme, allotment of land titles to the poor of CPR lands, already used collectively by the poor, was an important measure. The consequent decline in the area of CPRs, and the resultant overcrowding and degradation of CPRs have led to a considerable reduction in the overall quantity of CPR benefits for the poor. However, it is quite possible that the losses the poor suffered collectively, might have been compensated by the individual gains from possessing more private land. This balance could be examined by comparing the magnitude of the decline in CPR-based income of the past with the returns from privatised CPR lands owned by the poor. A few case studies investigating the losses and gains have been initiated and await completion.

Alternatively, one may analyse the changes in the land resources base of the poor following the privatisation of CPRs.[...]

Disentitlement of the Poor

The complete process of privatisation of CPRs as it affected the rural poor involved three stages: (a) they were deprived of their right to collectively use the CPRs, (b) they were given individual title to small parts of privatised CPRs, and (c) the circumstances disentitled them of the newly received lands.[...]

To sum up, our analysis shows that privatisation of CPRs as a strategy to help the rural poor yielded a negative result. The collective loss of the poor from a decline of CPRs has not been compensated by acquisition and retention by the poor of privatised CPRs. Alternative strategies to help the poor are needed. One strategy could be to develop CPRs and improve their use through technological and institutional interventions. However, it may be pointed out that growth in the CPR productivity alone may prove counterproductive. At present the process of self-selection of CPR users, tend to induce mainly the poor to depend on these

TABLE 16.6: Extent and Decline of CPR Land in the Study Villages of Selected Districts in the Dry Regions of India[1]

State and District	Number of Villages	Area of CPR-Lands (ha)[2]	CPRs as Proportion (Per Cent) of Total Village Area		Decline in the Area of CPRs since 1950–52 (Per Cent)
			1982–84	1950–52	
Andhra Pradesh					
Anantapur	2	221	15	24	36
Mahbubnagar	5	408	9	16	43
Medak	3	198	11	20	45
Gujarat					
Banaskantha	5	167	9	19	49
Mehsana	5	224	11	17	37
Sabarkantha	5	198	12	22	46
Karnataka					
Bidar	3	297	12	20	41
Dharwad	3	242	10	18	44
Gulbarga	3	291	9	15	43
Mysore	3	335	18	27	32
Madhya Pradesh					
Mandsaur	4	327	22	34	34
Raisen	6	770	23[3]	42	47
Vidisha	4	338	28[3]	38	32
Maharashtra					
Akota	5	192	11	19	42
Aurangabad	4	304	15	21	30
Sholapur	4	422	19	25	26
Rajasthan					
Jalore	5	639	18	29	37
Jodhpur	3	591	16	38	58
Nagaur	3	619	15	41	63
Tamil Nadu					
Coimbatore	4	187	9	17	47
Dharmapuri	3	225	12	26	52

Notes: (1) Based on village-level records and field work during 1982–85.

(2) CPRs included are village pastures,, village forests, waste lands, unoccupied catchments of ponds/tanks, river/rivulet banks, watershed drainages, and community threshing grounds, etc., which are used for free animal grazing and collection of fuel, fodder, and other items.

(3) In Raisen and Vidisha villages large area of CPRs initially taken over by forest department but now available for use by the villagers is included with CPRs.

resources. CPR activities are low pay-off options. The poor chooses them as the opportunity cost of their labour is lower than the returns from CPR activities. An increase in CPR productivity will induce greater demand on CPRs through (a) increased number of users, (b) pressure for privatisation including through illegal appropriation, and (c) encroachment by government in the form of handing over of more paying CPRs to contractors as has happened in the past. The consequence in all cases would be reduced benefits to the rural poor. Hence, the management or regulated use of CPRs is as important as any measure directed to raise their productivity. Identification and evaluation of intervention measures to meet these objectives, form a part of our ongoing work on the subject.[...]

Notes

1. Groundwater is also often regarded as a CPR, although it may not (unlike other CPRs considered by us) belong to any identifiable community.

2. The neglect of CPRs in the process of rural development has been so great that even when some programmes are directed to these resources, they are adopted more as physical measures and have little concern for their CPR context. For instance, efforts in terms of research and development activities relating to forests and grasslands or measures to harness runoff and groundwater, are seldom adopted in the framework of CPRs. Even in the programmes connoting group orientation, e.g., rural cooperatives or community development projects, the 'community' is usually by-passed due to the PPR orientation of development activities (Jodha 1973).

3. Details about rural households, dependence on CPRs, and their employment and income gains from CPRs for Raisen and Nagaur districts as reported in this paper may slightly differ from the preliminary results about the same districts reported earlier (Jodha 1985a). This is due to the availability of additional information and exclusion of medium farm households from this paper. This also applies to employment and income details reported in the paper.

4. The highest number of CPR items recorded from a small farm household in a village in Raisen district of Madhya Pradesh was 22. For a similar account of product collection and dependence of the rural poor on CPRs in the irrigated areas of Uttar Pradesh and tribal areas of Andhra Pradesh, see, Dasgupta (1985) and AERC (1985) respectively.

5. In view of the situation-specific relative role of these factors in different villages, it is difficult to explain the regional differences in the dependence of people on CPRs with reference to specific factors. This limitation will also apply to the regional differences in quantified benefits reported in the following discussion.

6. Large farm households used fuel for multiple purposes, e.g., cooking food and animal feed, making tea quite frequently, heating water for bath, etc. They also consumed small quantities of kerosene as well. The poor used fuel mainly for cooking food and often only once a day. In most cases the fuel requirement was higher during the rainy season, partly because of the reduced fuel use efficiency due to humidity.

7. Though varying in its extent, the practice of 'salvaging' unproductive animals was observed in practically all the study areas. Large farmers gave their unproductive animals to the poor for maintenance as it was costly to maintain them, at their own farm, using the feeding standards followed by the large farmers. When such animals became productive they were returned to the large farmer and net additions to the value of such animals (after becoming productive) was shared by the two parties. Depending on the type of animal,

necessity of seasonal migration of animals due to fodder/water scarcity, and marketability of animals, the terms and conditions governing this practice differed from region to region. In areas like Gujarat and Rajasthan such herding was an important source of income for the rural poor.

8. Income from CPR products estimated by first making an inventory of the total products collected by respondent households during different seasons and then calculating their value on the basis of the village-level prices of the products. These prices were much lower than the corresponding prices even at the taluka town level.

9. Estimation of livestock income attributable to CPR grazing is based on data on animal-husbandry practices (e.g., stall-feeding, grazing including on CPRs) and on composition of livestock income. Apportioning of animal income to CPR grazing was simple for sheep, goats, and currently unproductive animals that were almost totally maintained through CPR grazing especially by the rural poor. In the case of animals involving both stall-feeding and open grazing, only dung income was apportioned between CPR-grazing, private resource grazing and stall-feeding on the basis of animal-unit days involved. This, however, resulted in considerably underestimating animal income attributable to CPR grazing.

10. Levels and the regional pattern of CPR incomes (Table 16.4) may change if income from CPR-product processing and marketing is considered. This was indicated by rough calculations based on limited cases of processing, marketing, and handicrafts based on CPR-products in different areas. They included soap nut in Aurangabad; forest products for basket, *pattal*, and matress making in Mysore, Dharmapuri, Mandsaur and Raisen areas; sisal and other products used for making rope and other fibre in Akola, Sholapur and Mahbubnagar areas; wild fruits for making pickles and medicine in Nagaur and Raisen. These activities could add about 9–21 per cent to the already reported CPR-income in different areas.

11. A study by NABARD (1984) reported that for 10 per cent of the beneficiary households per household incremental income from IRDP in different states was up to Rs 500. For another 13 per cent it ranged between Rs 501–1,500. According to PEO (1985) study, the per household incremental income from IRDP schemes ranged from Rs 1,069–2,770. However, in several areas the incremental income from different schemes was less than or around Rs 600 per family. Kutty Krishnan (1984) reported that 39 per cent of the participants in IRDP schemes in his study village in Kerala did not have any change in their income. Another 29 per cent of the families got incremental income of less than Rs 400 per family.

12. Land reforms served as an important event to facilitate the recall of the past by the people. Moreover, the status of CPRs was greatly affected by various by-laws and side effects of land reforms (Jodha 1985a, 1985b). Hence it was quite convenient to gather details from oral history and records before this change.

13. All the village waste lands unlike other CPRs listed here do not fall under the jurisdiction of village or village panchayat. They belong to State Revenue Departments. However, since they are common access resources, for the concerned village community, they are village CPRs for all practical purposes. Historically, these commons were categorised as waste lands not on the basis of their extent of biological or economic productivity. Being uncultivable (or uncultivated in some cases), they were non-revenue generating lands. Hence, the colonial government classified them as 'waste lands'. For some implications of this categorisation, see Shiva (1986).

14. In some cases, area of CPRs also declined due to transfer of land to institutions (e.g., milk cooprátive, village school, public works department, forest department, etc.). For a brief account of causes and consequences of transfer of forests to state control, see, Singh (1986).

References

Agro-Economic Research Centre (AERC). 1985. *Minor Forest Produce in the Tribal Economy in Andhra Pradesh*', Waltair, A.P.: AERC, Andhra University.

Binswanger, H. P. and N. S. Jodha. 1978. *Manual of Instructions for Economic Investigators in ICRISAT's Village Level Studies*. Patancheru, A.P.: Economics Programme, ICRISAT.

Das Gupta, Monica. 1985. *Informal Security Systems and Population Retention in Rural India*. NCAER Working Paper No 2. New Delhi: National Council of Applied Economic Research.

George, K. M. 1984. 'Rural Development Programme: Its Strength and Weaknesses'. *Indian Journal of Agricultural Economics* 39 (3): 434–43.

Jodha, N. S. 1973. 'Special Programmes for Rural Poor: The Constraining Framework'. *Economic and Political Weekly* 8 (13); 633: 39, 31 March.

Jodha, N. S., M. Ashokan and J. G. Ryan. 1977. 'Village Study Methodology and Resource Endowment of Selected Villages'. Occasional Paper 16. Patancheru: Economics Programme, ICRISAT.

Jodha, N. S. 1985a. 'Market Forces and Erosion of Common Property Resources'. In *Agricultural Markets in the Semi-Arid Tropics*. Proceedings of the International Workshop, 24–28 October 1983, ICRISAT Centre, India, 263–77.

Jodha, N. S. 1985b. 'Population Growth and the Decline of Common Property Resources in Rajasthan, India'. *Population and Development Review* 11 (2): 247–64.

Kutty Krishnan, A. C. 1984. 'A Case Study of Integrated Rural Development Programme in a Kerala Village'. *Indian Journal of Agricultural Economics* 39 (3): 419–26.

NABARD. 1984. *Study of Implementation of Integrated Rural Development Programme*. Bombay: NABARD.

PEO. 1985. *Evaluation Report on Integrated Rural Development Programme*, New Delhi: Plan Evaluation Organisation, Planning Commission, Government of India.

Rath, Nilkantha. 1985. 'Garibi Hatao: Can IRDP Do It?'. *Economic and Political Weekly* 20 (6): 238–46, 6 February.

Shiva, Vandana. 1986. 'Coming Tragedy of the Commons', *Economic and Political Weekly* 21 (15): 613–14, 15 April.

Singh, R. P. and S. B. Singh. 1982. *Features of Traditional Farming Systems in Two Villages of Gujarat*. Progress Report 35. Patancheru, AP: Economics Programme,.

Singh, R. P., B. L. Jain and V. B. Rao. 1984. *Features of Traditional Farming Systems in Selected Villages of Madhya Pradesh*. Progress Report 61. Patancheru, AP: Economics Programme, ICRISAT.

Singh, R. and P. Chhatrapati. 1986. *Common Property and Common Poverty: India's Forests, Forest Dwellers and the Law*. Delhi: Oxford University Press.

Authors

Partap C. Aggarwal currently lives and works in an international community in Tamil Nadu. He earlier taught at Colgate University in the United States. The article in this volume is based on his doctoral fieldwork among the Meos in the Mewat, straddling Alwar and Bharatpur districts of Rajasthan and Gurgaon of Haryana.

André Béteille is Professor Emeritus, Department of Sociology, University of Delhi, and a National Research Professor. He has been a regular contributor for over 50 years to *Economic and Political Weekly*, and its predecessor, *Economic Weekly*.

Jishnu Das is a Senior Economist at the World Bank and a Visiting Fellow at the Centre for Policy Research, New Delhi. The paper in this volume was written as part of a project on Common Property Resources at the Centre for Development Economics, Delhi.

Leela Gulati is a sociologist, currently based in Thiruvananthapuram, and has worked on gender issues over many decades.

Dipankar Gupta retired as Professor from the Jawaharlal Nehru University, New Delhi after teaching there for nearly 30 years. He is currently on a fellowship with the National University of Education Planning and Administration, New Delhi.

John Harriss is Director, School for International Studies, Simon Fraser University, Canada.

Roger Jeffery is Professor of Sociology at the University of Edinburgh, Scotland. The joint paper by Patricia and Roger Jefrey and Andrew Lyon derives from their research in western Uttar Pradesh in 1982–83, when they studied the social organisation of childbearing and family building, including aspects of women's economic contributions to household wellbeing.

Patricia Jeffrey is Professor of Sociology at the University of Edinburgh, Scotland.

J. Jeyaranjan is with the Institute of Development Alternatives, Chennai. He works on issues concerning rural dynamics and labour.

N. S. Jodha has worked for many decades on the commons and has been with the International Centre for Integrated Mountain Development, Kathmandu.

Surinder S. Jodhka is Professor of Sociology and is currently Chairperson, Centre for the Study of Social Systems, School of Social Sciences, Jawaharlal Nehru University, New Delhi.

G. K. Karanth is Professor of Sociology at the Institute for Social and Economic Change, Bengaluru, and currently a Visiting Professor in the Department of Sociology, Lund University, Sweden.

G. K. Lieten is Professor in the Department of Sociology and Anthropology, University of Amsterdam.

Andrew Lyon is with International Futures Forum, Scotland.

K. Nagaraj retired as Professor from the Madras Institute of Development Studies and is currently with the Asian College of Journalism, Chennai.

Sudha Pai is Professor at the Centre for Political Studies, and Rector of Jawaharlal Nehru University, New Delhi. The essay in this volume was written together with Jagpal Singh while researching on Dalits and other disadvantaged sections in Uttar Pradesh for her book *Dalit Assertion and the Unfinished Democratic Revolution: The BSP in Uttar Pradesh* (2002).

K. L. Sharma earlier taught sociology at the Jawaharlal Nehru University, New Delhi, and is currently Vice-Chancellor of Jaipur National University. The article in this volume is based on part of his doctoral thesis.

Mukul Sharma is a Delhi-based independent scholar and journalist.

Jagpal Singh is a Professor at the School of Social Sciences, IGNOU, New Delhi.

M. N. Srinivas taught in Vadodara, Delhi and Bengaluru in a number of leading institutions. He is very well-known for his work on caste and village India. His books include *Caste in Modern India and Other Essays* (1962) and *The Remembered Village* (1976).

Anil Kumar Vaddiraju is currently Assistant Professor in the Centre for Political Institutions, Governance and Development, at the Institute for Social and Economic Change, Bengaluru. The article in this volume is part of his doctoral thesis prepared at the Department of Political Science, University of Delhi.